Cosmosophia

Cosmosophia

Cosmology, Mysticism, and the Birth of a New Myth

THEODORE RICHARDS

HIRAETH PRESS
DANVERS, MASSACHUSETTS

Hiraeth Press books may be purchased for education, business or sale promotional use. For information, please write: Special Markets, Hiraeth Press, PO Box 416, Danvers, Massachusetts 01923

First Edition 2011

Cover and text design by Jason Kirkey
Cover photograph: © iStockphoto.com / Rick Whitacre

ISBN: 978-0-9799246-8-2

Published by Hiraeth Press
P.O. Box 416
Danvers, Massachusetts
www.hiraethpress.com

To
My Daughter, Cosima Sing Teifi Richards
A cosmos of possibility for the future and of joy in the present.

Contents

Contents

Cosmosophia

Preface

Le Stelle

All truths wait in all things...
...I believe a leaf of grass is no less than the journey-work of
  the stars

—Walt Whitman[1]

A T THIS MOMENT, light is reaching me from not long after the birth of the Universe. If I look far enough into the past, I can see that this moment, this Self, is the culmination of a 13.7 billion year gestation process. And in the time it took me to write this, something new has already been born.

The first intellectual interest in my life was space. Even before I entered school, I begged my parents for a telescope, took classes at the planetarium. I dreamt of the stars. In this way, I cultivated awe as only a child can, as only an encounter with such immensity can. And at the same time, my most terrifying nightmares came not in the form of bogeymen waiting in my closet (although they occasionally did) but from this encounter with the immensity of the cosmos. Without any spiritual, cosmological framework in which to place my study of the Universe, I was terrified of the vastness of space like Blaise Pascal, who once wrote of this seemingly meaningless void, "I feel engulfed in the infinite immensity of spaces whereof I know nothing and which know nothing of me. I am terrified."[2] The science I learned in school was equally bereft of meaning, and lacked even the awe-inspiring quality of my early childhood. I turned away from science, from the cosmos, to find more meaningful fields of study, such as religion and literature.

My journey, however, was not so simple. While the notion that meaning was found in the humanities—the exclusive realm of the human mind—kept me occupied, I never quite let go of the stars. There was always, somewhere, an intuition that meaning could not merely be found in the human mind, that there was something not-quite-right about the idea that the human world of meaning and the cosmos were entirely separate realms. The idea that the human created wisdom separately from the cosmos seemed suspiciously hierarchical, dualistic. If we, like the dolphin and the mountain and the insect and the stars, emerged from the same process, did our wisdom not come from the same source?

The wisdom I have found, forming the foundation for this study, both in the great wisdom traditions of our religions and the creative insights of our artists and writers, was not ultimately rooted in some vague, intellectual realm of pure thought. Rather, it can be traced back to the earliest moments in the human story, moments that link the human story to the story of the Universe. In those days, our ancestors sat by the fire under the stars and told stories, stories that connected us to the world in which we lived, and enabled us to be compassionate to one another. The earliest humans had few defenses against the harsh world in which they found themselves. As they wandered out into the dry plains of Africa, there would have been less plentiful food than in the lush jungle; the prey they encountered would have often been bigger, faster and stronger. Many predators would have found the human an easy target. While it is undoubtedly true that humanity's greatest tool for survival was our intelligence, intelligence alone would not have sufficed. Humans required cooperation and compassion for survival. They connected to one another in loving relationship and worked together to ensure the survival of the group. They sang songs and performed rituals to give creative expression to these relationships. The clan and the ecosystem was the womb in which the first humans lived. This is wisdom. This is how we learned to be human.

At each moment in human history, we have had to ask ourselves how we can be fully human in our current situation. At each moment, we have had to figure out how to connect to our world. Today is no different. But for the first time, humans have failed to come up with meaningful new stories to replace those that no longer give us meaning. The great emptiness of the cosmos is not because the world is meaningless, but because we are failing to fulfill the central role of the human being in the world—to find meaning in the world in human terms.

Like the earliest people, we were at the edge of our world, bringing forth the connections of the past and called upon to create a meaningful future. We are poised between these depths, at the chaotic matrix of the birth canal of the cosmos. Perhaps they saw this when they painted their hand prints on the caves— among the earliest great works of art. Surely, they had seen their children's hand prints on the womb and recognized that they too were in a womb—the womb of the cosmos.

As I stared out at the sky in my youth, I had no context, no story, to connect me to the cosmos. The emptiness I believed I had found in the stars was an emptiness in my own heart, projected out onto the cosmos. At the same time, the meaning that so many have found in the wisdom of the human endeavor is a cosmic wisdom, expressed through the human. These two realms seem so oppositional according to our current worldview. Can they be reconciled?

About twenty years after my initial experience of terror, of meaningless, which came with my study of space, I had a completely different experience of emptiness. On Christmas morning, exactly 2,000 years after the birth of Christ according to our calendars, I found myself in a small village in the tribal areas of western Pakistan, waiting for the border to Iran to open so I could pass through. I was terribly sick—some bad dates I'd eaten, perhaps—and lonely. I had not expected to miss the Christmas season, but the loneliness I was feeling from months alone on the road was exacerbated by my knowledge that it was Christmas.

Christmas is rather low-key in the tribal areas of Western Pakistan.

It was dark and bitterly cold, as the desert usually is at night. The darkness, along with my sickness, contributed to my loneliness. I wandered blindly through the town to find a place to rest, and settled on a pile of burlap sacks. I lay down and looked up. Immediately I was transformed by the immensity of the stars; unlike the terror of my youth, I felt intimate with them. In a few moments, some local men, rifles slung over their shoulders, invited me to come into their home to drink tea around a fire. The isolation I had felt as an American only made this interaction feel more powerful. They saw me simply as a human being, smiling and laughing kindly when they realized that I was from America. Moments of communion are all the more powerful and transformative when creative compassion is asked of us in this way.

I write as the winter solstice and Christmas approach. The days have become short and cold. In northern California, the rains have started. Sunlight, abundant only a few months ago, is scarce. But soon, just after the solstice, the days will begin again to grow long. Many of the religious cosmologies of the West have celebrated the solstice as a return of the Sun, the birth of the divine at the darkest hour. It is, for each of us, at the darkest hour that we must be able to find our inner light. Christmas is celebrated on December 25, the mythic date of Horus' birth, not because there is any evidence that Jesus was born on that date, but because it makes sense that the divine should come to be present among humanity at the time of our greatest feelings of fear and disconnection. In the context of Cosmosophia—the new, mythic framework I am seeking to create—the winter solstice or Christmas is the perfect time to celebrate rebirth because it serves as a moment to unify the paradox of individual and the Universal. It represents both the birth of the Universe itself and the rebirth—a recognition, really—of our own divinity, our divine spark, the fullness of the cosmic wisdom we each possess and express in our own way.

The modern West, particularly America, is in a state of dismemberment. We lack a cosmological framework that provides for us an ethical foundation to guide our relationships. Increasingly, we seem to see ourselves as isolated individuals. The end product of such isolation is fear—fear of the 'other' from whom we consider ourselves separate. And out of fear, we resist authentic relationships even harder. The worldview of the West simply does not allow most of us to see our interrelatedness.

As Pierre Teilhard de Chardin points out, "coercion" results only in a "superficial unity."[3] We cannot fake it. To pretend that we are in loving, compassionate relationship to the Universe without re-imagining our fundamental worldview cannot result in true transformation or connection. We are, however, presented with an opportunity from the latest discoveries of science and from the void our dismemberment has created. The Universe creates most profoundly, most unexpectedly, at such times. As the ancients observed, the Sun is reborn at the darkest hour. Their fear was overcome through this wisdom; our fear must be overcome through the wisdom of both our interiority and our deepening relationship to the whole.

The story of the Universe is the story that ends as it began: the spark of the Big Bang is in each of us; we have, at this moment, through our creativity, the capacity to create anew the Universe, to become compassionate to the whole of creation. Chaos—and surely we live in chaotic times—is the mother of creative transformation. Even as our individual interiority emerges, our imaginative capacities allow us to return to embeddedness in the cosmic womb. This return requires more than new knowledge, but a new myth, a way of connecting us to one another, to the rest of Earth and to the cosmos. The new myth will not be created by science or philosophy, but by the collective creativity of humanity. We will need more than mere ideas; to be remade and renewed from our very roots, to become "pure and ready to climb to the stars," we need poets like Dante.[4] We are, at this moment, like my unborn daughter, putting hand prints on the edge of our world, our womb—not unlike the earliest humans did on the interior of the cave—unsure what lies beyond.

This Moment

What happens to the outer world happens to the inner world.
If the outer world is diminished in its grandeur then the
emotional, imaginative, intellectual, and spiritual life of the
human is diminished or extinguished. Without the soaring
birds, the great forests, the sounds and coloration of the insects,
the free-flowing streams, the flowering fields, the sight of the
clouds by day and the stars at night, we become impoverished
in all that makes us human.

—Thomas Berry[1]

THE WORLD WE CREATE for tomorrow has a great deal to do
with the way we interpret the world we observe today. There
are countless ways to interpret this world—no less than there are
stories the imagination can create. I begin this book with a study
of the current crisis not to advocate a pessimistic view of the
world—on the contrary, I hope that this work can contribute to
a more positive and compassionate assessment of creation than
the one we currently have—but to convey an understanding that
the world is birthing something new, unexpected and beautiful at
this moment. And this birthing may be a painful process. Neither
an unquestioning allegiance to the status quo nor a blind belief in improvement and progress is particularly helpful. The only
certainty is that change remains a constant, and the Universe is
fundamentally a process—yes, a *process*, not a place—of birthing.
This work seeks the middle path between believing the cosmos
is alien to us and beyond our control and the belief that we can
simply create our own reality. What we *can* do is participate fully
and meaningfully in the process.

Chapter One

The Great Work

THIS STUDY ATTEMPTS to get to the root of our current crisis—the disconnection, individualism, and alienation of the current Western worldview. It seeks to create a new worldview based upon wisdom that can foster meaningful and compassionate Earth communities. This, in the words of Thomas Berry, is our "Great Work."[1]

What might a worldview based on wisdom look like? No one can precisely say. For although humans have surely embodied wisdom at various eras and in various cultures, such a worldview would look different in the context of today's world. We are, as never before, a global species, more numerous and interconnected— economically and technologically, if not spiritually—than ever before. While I cannot claim to know what such a civilization would look like, I can, based on our history, suggest how we might begin to enter into the process of re-imagining our worldview.

The shape that a wisdom-based civilization would take depends on how we define wisdom. While many would say that wisdom is a trait unique to the human, or given to the human and only the human by God, I would suggest that wisdom is an attribute of the cosmos. That is, wisdom is the inherent capacity of the Universe to create meaningful relationships. It is the wisdom of the cosmos that enables the star to form through the coming together of particles; it is through wisdom that an ecosystem functions; and it is through wisdom that humanity can create meaning out of our world through culture, language and the arts. While human wisdom is expressed differently from the wisdom of the salmon dancing its way through the stream or the dynamics of the forest, all wisdom is derived from participation in the cosmos. For the human, like the maple tree and the salmon, this wisdom is an Earth wisdom, because it is the Earth that provides context for everything one experiences.

Human wisdom is expressed most comprehensively in a cosmology. A cosmology consists of the basic assumptions a culture makes about the Universe and how it operates. A cosmology provides the context for relationships and meaning in a culture. Our values and ethics are derived from our cosmology, because a cosmology tells its adherents what is most fundamentally real, and what is of value.

Often, however, the term cosmology is used to cover a wide spectrum. At times, cosmology is used to refer only to the physical Universe, with little or no overt mention of the meaning that is derived from the way it is conceptualized. Such descriptions can be referred to as "astronomical cosmologies". There is generally, however, some implicit meaning to be found in such conceptions. In the modern era, the term "scientific cosmology" has been used to describe a sub-discipline of modern astrophysics concerned with the birth and early development of the Universe.

In this study, I will use the term *cosmology* to refer to the comprehensive understanding that provides context for meaning in a culture. This definition is synonymous with worldview. There are, however, times when the term will be used to refer to conceptions of the cosmos that do not represent a worldview *per se*, but an astronomical cosmology that is only a part of a larger cosmology. A good example would be Ptolemaic Cosmology (see chapter 5) which provided a description of the physical Universe upon which the medieval worldview was based. The medieval cosmology, however, was a complete worldview, integrating Ptolemy, Greek philosophy, and Christian mythology.

Mythology plays an extremely important role in any cosmology. For it is through the myth that an individual in a culture integrates and interiorizes a cosmology. A cosmology requires a myth in order to come alive because mythology is expressed in creative or story form, connecting to the individual's imagination. A myth is a particular kind of creative expression, because it reveals what is most fundamentally real and of value.

Just as the myth engages the listener's imagination in its telling, a myth requires the teller to engage the imagination in its creation. This study is my attempt to imagine how we might go about creating a new cosmology. It is important to remember that this is only a beginning. What has been referred to as the "New Cosmology" has not happened yet. Modern science—the insights of Einstein, Heisenberg, Darwin and many others—has not been fully integrated and reflected in the values of our communities. Before we can begin this process of creation, however, it would be useful to look at where we are now.

Chapter Two

The Crisis

W HILE IT CAN unquestionably be said that each generation has faced a particular challenge or crisis, the challenge of this moment is unique in human history. The human has existed for but a geologic moment—and a fraction of that in cosmic time—and has as yet had to cope only with a limited scope of problems. Our challenges usually have had to do with the human and only the human, and generally only the human group of which we considered ourselves a part. At this moment, this cosmic moment, the human has become a planetary being. Our choices now affect the very sustenance of life on the planet. We are witnessing, for the first time, the confluence of human history and cosmic history. That a change is going to indeed happen in the way the human participates in the world is certain; how we participate in this change is yet to be decided.

Of course, human beings have always been embedded in the cosmos out of which we arise, and any separation of human history and cosmic history is artificial. But the human, possessing the capacity to communicate symbolically through language, has introduced a new element to the cosmic process. This powerful capacity allows us to choose which species lives and which dies. Strangely, however, this power has also given us the ability to behave in ways that run counter to the evolutionary processes that birthed us. The modern crisis is more than a lack of knowledge—while humanity has acquired a great deal of knowledge about how the Earth operates, we continue to act in ways that destroy it, and ourselves. This is because human action—as rational as it may seem to us—is always based upon certain core assumptions, assumptions that are usually so deeply integrated we are not even aware of them. Moreover, we must not only learn about the processes of the Earth but also re-learn how to participate meaningfully in them. Ours is a failure not of objective knowledge but of subjective participation.

In this work, I argue that the various aspects of the modern crisis share the same essential root. That is, our basic assumptions about reality (cosmology) and the story we have told about those assumptions (mythology) have led us to the brink of biological devastation and societal degradation because every decision we make is based upon those factors. No ethical choices can be made in the abstract, from a purely logical, rational perspective. Instead, every choice we make, every choice we have ever made, comes from our cosmology and our mythology. Therefore a shift in the current worldview—a shift without which we shall surely destroy ourselves and the planet—requires a radical change of perspective. While this is not an easy thing to do, such shifts have happened many times throughout human history. Often they occur due to a crisis or catastrophe. On an individual level, this kind of shift would be the work of mystics or shamans, those who can travel deep into their own psyche to return transformed. In this study, I argue that the work that is required now is nothing short of a collective mystical experience or shamanic journey for all of humanity.

THE DILEMMA

One of the central dilemmas of modernity is the dichotomy of fundamentalism and secular materialism. Our secular educational systems generally focus on the rationalist perspective, rejecting the search for meaning as well as any attempt at ethics or values. As a consequence, those who seek meaning and values in their lives often turn to fundamentalism. What fundamentalists fail to realize, however, even as they reject Modernity, is just how modern their worldview is. Only with a thoroughly modern consciousness could we interpret scripture so literally and personally. Similarly, the New Age movement, although it has attempted to move beyond this dichotomy, has remained within an entirely modern paradigm. Just as the fundamentalist seeks salvation as an isolated individual, apart from the world, many New Agers seek enlightenment as isolated individuals, apart from the cosmos. Appropriating the ancient wisdom of the mystic within a modern framework only reinforces the individualism and sense of separateness that defines the modern era.

In each of these paradigms—the secular, the fundamentalist, and the New Age—there exists a failure to fully embrace a cosmological and philosophical perspective wherein the cosmos itself is perceived as living, divine, or sacred, in which the individualism of modernity is rejected in favor of a return to experiencing the self as inseparable from the larger whole. This failure has profound ethical consequences: without the ability to experience the self as coextensive with the whole, authentic compassion for others remains elusive. And compassion, the experience of another's joy or suffering as one's own, is what the modern world truly lacks. The ever increasing injustice in the world today and the environmental crisis are not, as many in today's political world would seem to suggest, different issues at their core; they are a consequence of our isolation and fragmentation—the current Western worldview.

As the geopolitical, cultural, and ecological conditions on the planet today suggest, the Universe is not a simple process of improvement. Indeed, the language of "improvement" is rooted in the current Western worldview. For each of the gains made in the process, there are losses. I am proposing that instead of looking toward where we are "supposed" to be going, we should look at this moment, and how to find deeper relationships within the womb in which we exist now.

In this study, I attempt to begin the process of creating a new myth for the modern world, building upon the wisdom of the world's great mystical traditions. In particular, I draw on the mysticism that seeks deeper relationship and connection with the whole as opposed to leaving the cosmos altogether, for I believe that these are the practices and experiences that will foster compassion. I call my own approach *cosmosophy*, and the symbolic and metaphorical framework I have derived from the cosmosophical process I have termed *cosmosophia*.

The Crises

We are currently engaged in myriad problems that can be described in many ways. I will use three basic categories to describe them: the humanitarian crisis, the ecological crisis, and the crisis of meaning. While it is important to acknowledge the nuances and complexities that give rise to the uniqueness of various struggles, it is also important to avoid such fragmentation that we see these struggles as oppositional. As the marginalized and oppressed fight one another, the hierarchies that have led to their position in the first place are reinforced.

First, there is a humanitarian crisis. This refers to the issues of social justice that have been addressed by revolutionaries and activists throughout history. In the post-Enlightenment era, human beings have been accorded an expanding sphere of rights. While this has been a positive step for those within this sphere, we have paradoxically found ourselves in an increasingly inequitable world, a world in which billions live off of a dollar a day while the number of billionaires grows daily. One obstacle to solving some of these problems is the fact that they are approached in a fragmented way.

For example, there is a long history in the United States of enmity between those who work for the liberation of African-Americans and those who seek equality for women. Such a fragmentation is a failure of both sides to see their commonalities. An authentic feminism, one that seeks not only better jobs and entrance into country clubs, would seek the overthrow of a patriarchy that oppresses all marginalized peoples; conversely, an authentic Afro-centrism would not resort to the patriarchy adopted through colonialism but embrace its matriarchal roots. In each case, the focus on the external manifestation of the problem makes it appear more different from the other than it really is when the root cause is examined. As long as social justice issues are fought out in competing spheres of rights, they are doomed to fail.

There are various reasons for this view of rights. Largely, it can be attributed to the notion that individual rights have been based upon the radical separation of the individual from the community of life. The individual is primary in this view, giving rise to constant conflict when the rights of one individual or group seem oppositional to another's. This, as I will describe later, is rooted in the fundamental assumptions of the Western cosmology that defines what we consider to be the basic identity of the human. Although we are unaware of it because we are so immersed in it, our cosmology defines who we are and therefore what our basic rights should be. We seem to possess an intuitive sense of fairness, but repeatedly fail to meet that sense in the way we live. As our population increases and resources are reduced, the inequality only increases.

Democracy, one of the great gifts of the Enlightenment because it empowers the individual in the political process, has profound limitations for the same reason. Democracy understands the community as a collection of individuals rather than the individual as an expression of a community. In its purest form, a democracy follows the will of the (human) majority, even if that will stands in opposition to the living community. For instance, as American demographics shift from the colder and wetter northeast, the hot, dry states of the southwest will gain political power. With this power comes the ability to siphon water from the Great Lakes and dam rivers to feed a lifestyle that is clearly unsustainable: green lawns, swimming pools and air conditioning in the desert. I am not suggesting, of course, that democracy should be abandoned for the tyranny of a dictator, but that democracy, when its participants accept unquestioningly the modern belief in the primacy of the individual—and this is the only democracy we have yet tried on a large scale—has a tyranny of its own.

Second, there is an ecological crisis. It is important to note that this is not an "environmental" crisis—a word that understands the natural world as mere background for the human—but a crisis of our ecological "home" (ecology comes from the Greek *oikos*, meaning home). We have reached the brink of destroying the biosphere on the planet. For several reasons, the ecological crisis must not be considered separate from issues of social justice.

There is a pragmatic reason: This problem can never be solved as long as it is perceived as competing with the rights of the human because only the elite will care about the environment, a place for one to visit during one's leisure time, while the rest of us are concerned about the economics of feeding our families.

It is a strange paradox that economics and ecology are viewed as competing. In fact, both refer to the home and how it is managed. First, it is essential that we recognize that the economy—the way we distribute and manage the resources of our Earth home—cannot be primary; rather, it is a subset of ecology, because ecology refers to the actual cosmic wisdom of our Earth home, a home of which we are a part and in which we are embedded. Next, to make the economy primary is to abstract the human from the Earth, which is an impossibility. Finally, our economic system exacerbates the problems with democracy by allowing decisions to be made based not only on the will of the majority—in itself a problem in some cases—but on the power of the dollar. The markets, because they are abstracted from the ecological context, make decisions based on a set of assumptions that ignores sustainability issues—indeed, a set of assumptions that ignores the *real* cost of things. If we paid the real cost of gasoline, for example, including the devastation it has on the planet, the price would be far higher than what most Americans seem to think is already expensive.

The ecological crisis must be recognized as connected to other human struggles because human beings, as members of a living Earth community, cannot survive without that community. When we abuse our mother, all in the womb suffer. And it is the marginalized, at least in the beginning, who suffer the most. From Hunter's Point in San Francisco to the multitudes displaced by the dam projects in India, the poor are the first to suffer when the Earth community is abused.

Finally, we have a crisis of meaning. This is a problem that seems less significant than the other two, but in many ways envelopes them both. Even if there were not obvious practical reasons for creating a new *mythos* to guide our civilization, there would remain the fact that our psyches are becoming increasingly unhealthy in a climate of alienation from the cosmos. A great deal of our destructive—self-destructive—behavior is rooted in this psychic alienation. And even as we try to ignore the very real problems of our world, we cannot ignore the fact that our lives are less fulfilling, less meaningful.

THE CURRENT
WESTERN WORLDVIEW

While much can be said about the current Western worldview—also commonly referred to as "Modernity"—I will focus on four general, interrelated concepts: individualism, dualism, progress, and disenchantment.

The current Western worldview posits that each of us is an entirely separate and isolated individual. Theologically, this leads to the emphasis on personal salvation. Only in a fragmented, atomistic Universe could a person claim to be saved while others are damned. Individualistic theology co-arises with the individualism of our economic system, which leads both to inequality among human beings and the abuse of the Earth.

Related to individualism is dualism. Dualism can be understood in many different ways. I am defining it here as the three-fold radical discontinuity of the human from the divine, the divine from the cosmos, and the human from the cosmos. This dualism stands in stark opposition to many cosmologies that believed the human stood in delicate integration of cosmos and divine, or that the divine permeated and connected all three. It is through the dualism of the modern world that it becomes possible to abuse the Earth as we do, or to drop bombs on children in another country—in both cases, we absurdly imagine that we are wholly separate from the other.

The myth of unlimited progress is perhaps the most strikingly absurd—and the most American—myth of the West. Our economic system, largely because it is not contextualized in the ecosystem, is based upon the notion that we can continue to grow without consequences. This myth gives rise to global capitalism, the economic system that is most closely linked with the modern crisis. It has led directly to both the aforementioned increasing inequities and the ecological crisis. Global capitalism requires unlimited growth based on the exploitation of unlimited *resources*—a word that deliberately de-personalizes the Earth—as well as marginalized peoples.

Finally, the current Western worldview is a radical break from other cultures in that it sees the world as disenchanted.[1] This is perhaps the most fundamental and disturbing myth of Modernity. A world that was once seen as ensouled and alive— even divine—has come to be seen as dead and inert. Members of a living community of beings—human and non-human— are now seen as mere resources. The manifestation of all of the above myths is consumerism. It has been easy for corporations to convince us to adopt their values, because our minds have been shaped in order to receive such messages about the nature of the Universe. In the absence of the story told by the fire, the only voice we hear at night comes from the television, telling us that our lives are meaningless and will not improve unless we consume more and more of a lifeless world.

How did we get here? Of course, the West, like any other phenomenon, cannot be understood without recognizing some of the influences that gave rise to it.

In many ways, our current situation is the culmination of a long historical process. Richard Tarnas identifies our loss of enchantment, our alienation from the material world, as the central challenge at this stage of Western thought. "[T]he evolution of the Western mind has been founded on the repression of the feminine—on the repression of undifferentiated unitary consciousness, of the *participation mystique* with nature: a progressive denial of the *anima mundi*, the soul of the world, of the community of being, of the all-pervading, of mystery and ambiguity, of imagination, emotion, instinct, body, nature, woman—all of which the masculine has projectively identified as 'other.'"[2] The rise of patriarchal civilization has been well documented, occurring throughout the world, displacing the matriarchal Neolithic village with imperial civilization.[3] In the West, specifically, the seeds of our crisis can be seen in the rise of Hellenistic culture. Greek philosophy introduced a startling break from previous worldviews in that, first, with Pythagorean and Platonic philosophy, the world was perceived as a series of dualisms. This worldview was spread throughout the Near East and Mediterranean world with Alexander's conquests. While Alexander's political influence was short-lived, the influence of Greek culture was tremendous. Along with a dualistic cosmology, the Hellenistic world introduced an individualism never before seen. Because of the multicultural nature of the vast empire of Alexander, the individual became primary as opposed to one's tribe or ethnic group.

The Mysteries were the primary religious expression of this dualistic, Platonic cosmology and the notion of the individual. Cults promising personal salvation—a salvation beyond the cosmic sphere for a soul that was now understood as separate from the body—emerged throughout the Hellenistic world. In this context, Gnosticism and Christianity arose. Augustine's intensely personal theology—influenced, undoubtedly, by his Manichaean and Platonist background—would define Christianity for the next millennium.

In spite of these influences, the Western world was not entirely captivated by the spell of Modernity until much later. One could argue it was inevitable, that the seeds had been planted, but it is difficult to say. Nonetheless, the medieval world remained a deeply enchanted world, within certain parameters. Dante's *Commedia* gave poetic expression to the medieval cosmology, while hundreds of Cathedrals devoted to Mary were built. Although it is common to disparage "the dark ages"—and indeed there were many problems during that era—it was also a time of a largely unified world, an age in which the psyche felt safely at home in the cosmic womb of Mary, Queen of Heaven.

One possible break from the medieval cosmology is the onset of the Bubonic Plague.[4] As is often the case, suffering gives rise to the birth of a new worldview. Instead of the cosmic sensibility of the medieval period, the modern period is marked by a rejection of the cosmos itself. In many ways, it represents a continuation and intensification of the imperial phase of patriarchy. Indeed, one of the earliest and most striking aspects of the modern period is colonialism. Beginning with Columbus in 1492, a period of intensified and thoroughly global European colonialism allowed for the ethics of conquest, individualism, capitalism, and patriarchy to spread throughout the entire world. Many who resisted these ideals were eradicated. While colonialism had long been a feature of the patriarchal world, this new form of colonialism was spurred on by capitalism and enhanced by the emergence of the nation-state, notable particularly due to its primacy as the means of identity formation in the modern world. Human beings largely ceased to identify themselves in terms of the ethnic groups forged in communion with their bioregion in the Neolithic period, 10,000 years ago. Since the 17th century, the nation-state has largely taken over the role of religion in the modern world. This could be observed most starkly immediately after the 9-11 terrorist attacks when, curiously, the socially acceptable response to the atrocity was to conflate patriotism and religion, with the former being the primary response. At the same time, continuing what had started in the Hellenistic period, an intensified individualism emerged.

Co-arising with the political shifts of the modern nation state were shifts in worldview. Especially in the West, but also throughout the world due to the pervasiveness of Western culture, there was an increased emphasis on progress instead of the natural cycles of the Earth. This sense of progress led to, and was fed by, the scientific revolution that began in the 16th century. Great advances in technology and understanding of the Universe occurred during this period. But the alienation between the human and the natural world were also intensified, paving the way for the Enlightenment, the philosophical movement that would become the dominant paradigm in the modern West. Central to this worldview were the ideas of two thinkers, Rene Descartes and Isaac Newton. Descartes promoted the notion of the radical separation of the mind from the body and the individual psyche from the cosmos, while Newton's physics described a Universe of inert objects.

This Moment

The Newtonian-Cartesian paradigm describes our current worldview, the basic assumptions made in Modernity about reality. Just as our identity is based on the cosmic processes that have given birth to us—embodied in our DNA—it is also based on the cultural processes that have led to our current cosmology. At the same time, the stories we tell today determine the world we make for tomorrow. However, the creation of a new worldview is a complex process, one that cannot occur by simply analyzing our world and what we need.

This moment is like any other cosmic moment, in a sense. The Universe is bringing forth what is required to enable harmonious relationships to occur. At the same time, every moment is unique because new relationships are occurring. What is the role of the human at this moment? It is a question that cannot be answered simply, or figured out using the information we have. This moment requires a radical new way of relating to the cosmos.

The first words of Jesus in the oldest of the Gospels are "The *kairos* has come. The kingdom of God is upon you."[5] Usually translated as "time," *kairos* refers to more than mere chronological time (*chronos*), but a special time, a transformative time. We have reached such a moment once again.

This is no mere philosophical argument. Time and again, one hears it stated that spirituality and religion are individual and personal matters. "I can't change the world until I change myself first," is a common refrain. I am suggesting that this kind of thinking is the product of the same worldview that gives rise to many of our other problems. The individual soul is considered to be radically separate from the cosmic whole among secularists, religious traditionalists, and New Agers alike. Those who work for social justice fail to see how their interior process relates; those who follow the spiritual path fail to see how their spirituality cannot be separated from the larger processes around them. There is no easy answer to these problems: nothing short of an entirely new worldview can solve them. And to arrive at such a process requires much more than mere ideas.

Chapter Three

Toward a New Worldview

THIS CHAPTER DESCRIBES a possible way to address the crisis described in the previous chapter. It is not, of course, the final answer to all of these questions. There is, in fact, no *final* answer. We live always at the edge, dealing with whatever challenge the moment presents, ready to give birth to something new. Indeed, part of the new worldview toward which we are proceeding is to let go of the notion that we can either have a final, complete worldview, and that we even would want to. As we shall see below, the Universe is a cosmo-genesis, always giving birth to itself and to novelty, and full of surprises. At no point in the story of the Universe could the next major phase have been definitively predicted. We simply do not know what the future holds, and should embrace that uncertainty rather than fight it, for that uncertainty allows for the possibilities of the future. It inspires the imagination rather than confines us to a limited range of possibilities.

What I am suggesting, however, is that the Universe, at each of these phases, has an inherent wisdom that allows it to operate as a coherent whole. Within that whole there are microcosms that function the same way; that is, as novelties emerge with their own interiority, they possess the capacity to operate as a single whole. A human culture, for example, operates as a single whole through the wisdom of our mythologies and our cosmologies. These stories have defined the human world, and have allowed the individual to function in relationship to that world.

While the Universe cannot be anything but a single process or event, human beings have struggled to create and live by a worldview that reflects this reality. In the modern West, in particular, we have not had such a worldview.

THE IMPORTANCE OF STORY

"We are in trouble just now," writes Thomas Berry, "because we do not have a good story."[1] The "trouble" to which Berry refers is manifold: the deepening inequities of global capitalism; the oppression of women, the global south and the marginalized; the ecological crisis. We seem determined to rape the mother who birthed us, to profane the womb whence we have come. These problems cannot be solved in a fragmented way—'environmentalism' that ignores social justice, for example; or, conversely, wealth redistribution that fails to recognize that the economy is a subset of ecology—because fragmentation is part of their root cause. They have arisen because of the story we have told about ourselves and our relationship to the whole, the world, the cosmos itself, a story that leaves us isolated and separate, and the world fragmented and inert.

It is important to understand what Berry means when he says "story." We sometimes use the word story to mean something trivial, or even a lie. I once worked in a community where the children were told never to say the word lie—it was considered a "bad word"—and to replace it with "story." This says a great deal about our culture, a culture that whispers its story in our ear: *Stories are not to be trusted; what's good and real are facts that can be set into stone, ideas that exist without context.* Another word that is used disparagingly in modernity is "myth." A myth is a particular kind of story. Both refer to the way we creatively express our relationship to the world and who we are. While it is helpful if a myth is based upon the way the Earth actually operates, a myth is valid because it gives rise to a harmonious worldview—if it is *functional.* A myth is never entirely accurate because there is always something the human does not know about the Universe, making the creation of a complete story a process that is both empirical and imaginative. A myth allows us to use our imagination to complete the story that our observations begin.

"[A]ll mythology is ontophany," writes Mircea Eliade.[2] In other words, a myth is a culture's way of revealing to its members what is most real or fundamental to existence. Since the Enlightenment, and particularly since the emergence of modern psychology with Sigmund Freud, the myth has largely been studied in psychological terms.[3] While there is surely a psychological component to a mythology, the notion that a myth is real only within the isolated psyche of an individual is a failure to appreciate its full depth and power. A myth tells us what is real; and what we know to be real determines our values and our actions. The myth is the niche inhabited by the human. The question cannot be whether or not we live according to a myth, but by what myth we live. For we always live by some myth. And as Carl Jung explains in his influential essay, "The Undiscovered Self," the modern world is ready for a new myth: "We are living in what the Greeks called the *kairos*—the right moment—for a 'metamorphosis of the gods', of the fundamental principles and symbols."[4]

The myth I am attempting to engage here begins and ends with the human. This is not because the human is better or more important than any other being, but because I am human. It is from the human perspective that I write, and it is from the human that the cause and solution to the aforementioned crises may come. It is important to note also, however, that the human is simply a name we give to certain occurrences in the Universe. Fundamentally, there is not a human world and a world of everything else. The basic question I begin with, then, is "What unique contribution or expression can the human give to the Universe?" There are many answers to the question—indeed, how we answer this question defines us, tells us who we are. No individual can create this myth alone; it is created collectively and dialogically, through the communal process. I will begin with the notion that the human is the mythmaker—we create our world, the context for everything we do, through our mythology. The myth, while ostensibly about the past, has much to do with future possibilities, for we influence the future based on how we define our selves in our myths.

Barry Lopez writes, "The stories people tell have a way of taking care of them. And learn to give them away when they are needed. Sometimes a person needs a story more than food to stay alive."[5] We require stories because they speak directly to our need for meaning, a need as great as our need for food and water and air. Mythology does not merely explain or describe the cosmos; it invites us to participate in it.

The uniqueness of humans is our ability to tell a story. We can learn something and pass it on from generation to generation, allowing humanity to transform itself far faster than biological evolution allows. As a result, the fate of the Earth is, to a large extent, in our hands. For the first time, conscious choice is the primary evolutionary pressure on the planet. And so, the greatest question for the 21st century is the question of what story we will tell.

Throughout human history, cosmologies were created based on what people knew about the way the world works and the intuitions they had about what makes the world meaningful, their lives important. Myths are the means by which these cosmologies have the power to become manifest in the way we live our lives. But mythology can imprison us as much as it can empower. The myths of modernity only reinforce the schism between literal truth and myth. As the modern West has become increasingly literate, it has also become increasingly literal. Fundamentalists interpret myths literally that we know could not be literally accurate, and perhaps never were intended to be; secularists reject myth as a waste of time due to its inaccuracies. And we are all left with what Berry calls a dysfunctional cosmology.[6]

A New Cosmology

The particular characteristics of the Newtonian-Cartesian worldview made possible the ideas and discoveries that shattered it. Surely, without the scientific method, for example, Einstein and Hubble would not have allowed us to see the nature of the Universe as we know it today. Similarly, on a much vaster scale, it could be said that the human capacity to exchange information through language has allowed us to create the technologies that now threaten life on the planet. And at the same time, the human capacity for language, to creatively and symbolically orient ourselves to our world, may save us from destruction. Modernity has created many problems. But it has also given rise to the science that may become the foundation for a more compassionate and sustainable Earth community.

Modern science has several attributes that distinguish it

from the Newtonian. First, modern science describes the entire Universe as an *evolving whole*. Instead of a fragmented Universe of disconnected parts, the Universe is now understood to be a cosmo-genesis; that is, it is in a continuous process of creation. Creation was not completed in the remote past; nor is it now in a static state. Moreover, everything in the Universe was once a singularity. This brings us to the second attribute revealed by modern science, our *interrelatedness*. Both physically, because the Universe begins as a singularity, and genetically, because we all share the same, single common ancestor, we are all related. Finally, modern science overturns the Newtonian view of *space and time*. Instead of time moving through space, the space-time continuum is intimately linked and inseparable.

In addition to the great scientific minds who unveiled these discoveries, there are three Western thinkers to whom we are indebted for having produced tremendous insights as to the consequences of modern science. The Jesuit priest, mystic, and paleontologist Pierre Teilhard de Chardin was perhaps the first to recognize how a new cosmology would affect how we experience mystical communion, at least in a Christian context; cultural historian Thomas Berry first recognized how modern science could perhaps save us from ourselves and saw the need to create a new myth around it; and mathematical cosmologist and philosopher Brian Swimme, whose poetic insights about modern science have inspired me and countless others.

MYSTICISM

If the newest science can provide us with empirical evidence for a new worldview, why have we not yet embraced it? One would think that if the methods of an old worldview—the Newtonian-Cartesian worldview, in this case—undermine the assumptions of that very worldview, then it would begin to change. That would indeed be the case if mythmaking were simply based on relaying observations and ideas. On the contrary, those who know the science that tells us of our interconnections and of our peril at the present moment are often living the most disconnected and destructive lives. We in the modern West live as though under a spell—an ironic spell of *dis*enchantment.

To fully embrace a new worldview requires a radical shift that involves both the cosmic and psychic dimensions. That is to say a new cosmology emerges when we experience the world in a new way, integrate that new experience from our own subjectivity, and create a new myth to live by. This is the work of the mystic, the poet, and the artist. But there are many ways of experiencing the world in a new way, indeed, many types of mystics.

In indigenous cultures there was nothing that we might call mysticism because the consciousness of indigenous peoples recognizes the embeddedness of the human in the cosmos. There is no need for mysticism in such cases. In these cultures, the shaman serves as the precursor to the mystic. The shamanic journey functioned within a cosmology that saw humans as embedded in the natural world and inseparable from their communities. It is a journey of depth and dismemberment into the underworld—and because the cosmos is not separate from the human psyche, it is also a journey within—where the normal self is taken apart and put together again in order to return to our world re-membered as a cosmic being.

As humans increasingly relate to the world as individuals alienated from the cosmos, mysticism arose as a way to reconnect like the shaman. In this study, I will refer to mystics as those who have consciously taken on the task of creative compassion. To be compassionate requires more than mere pity—feeling *for* another; it requires us to feel *with*, to radically remove the separation between individuals and from the world. To do so is the ultimate creative act.

It should be noted that mysticism is a frequently misused term, associated frequently with the occult or to describe something vague or nebulous. Mysticism can simply be defined as the union or communion of the individual with that which is most *real or the absolute*. The most fundamental question one can ask, then, is, "What is real?" This is the basic question that a cosmology can answer. For many, this means a realm beyond the world, because this world is devalued or degraded. In this work, however, I will focus on mysticism for which the cosmos and everything in it is living and sacred; mystical union, in this case, is with the whole, with *everything*. It is my contention that living in this way—not only 'experiencing,' but *living*—can lead us to a more compassionate and sustainable way of life.

In this pursuit, the mystics have encountered a central paradox: how can we, as isolated individuals, realize the essential unity of the cosmos, experiencing, once again, the cosmos as an embryo experiences a womb? It is my contention that this paradox must now be understood in the context of modern science, which reveals a Universe that is a cosmo-genesis. Mysticism, therefore, is the creative act of the communion of our individual identity with our cosmic identity.

COSMOSOPHIA: THE COMPASSIONATE WISDOM OF THE COSMIC WOMB

In keeping with the oldest of the Wisdom Traditions—see, for example, *Job* and *Ecclesiastes*—wisdom can be understood not so much as something that comes from humanity, but is embedded in the mysterious processes of the cosmos. Cosmic wisdom is the capacity of the Universe to experience itself as a coherent and compassionate whole—a womb—even as it gives birth to novelty. As I watch my infant daughter in her crib, I can see in her eyes a yearning both to learn and grow and to regain the sense of safety and nourishment she felt in the womb. The newness of the world into which she has been born is neither better nor worse: it allows for new connections to be made—from my perspective, as her father, this is a good thing—and at the same time, there is something lost in her departure from the intimacy of the womb. For the rest of her life, she will strive—hopefully with the aid of her family and her community—to regain a felt sense of the world as her new womb. This does not mean that birth and growth and change are things to be avoided. Indeed, there is a right moment for all of these things. What we seek is not a return to the womb we have left but to embrace the metaphorical womb into which we have been born.

Cosmosophia describes a set of assumptions, metaphors or symbols upon which the pursuit of the uniquely human form of cosmic wisdom—a wisdom that allows for the Universe to give birth to itself, to give birth to new expressions of subjectivity, while always finding creative ways to connect as a whole. Cosmosophy is a discipline through which this pursuit of cosmic wisdom can be approached. The challenge of the human is that we, through our self-reflexive consciousness, have the capacity to delude ourselves into thinking we are isolated and separate. The mystic attempts to return from this sense of separation and expresses this journey through symbolic and imaginative language. This wisdom is not something we create but a mystery in which we participate.

As with mysticism, the pursuit of wisdom as articulated by the Greeks has become the dominant understanding in the West. Indeed, wisdom, for the Greeks as the first philosophers, comprised of (1) one's way of life or ethics, (2) an understanding of the cosmos, and (3) the interior life or mysticism. These three components were required to form a cohesive worldview. But the Greeks can only help us in part to find a comprehensive human wisdom. If *Homo sapiens* truly is *sapiens*, or "wise," then this pursuit is the search for nothing less than for what it truly means to be human.

The central image I will employ is that of a womb. Cosmosophy, therefore, is the art of returning to a felt sense of the cosmos as our womb, even as the Universe gives birth, even as we continuously leave behind the womb out of which we have been born. The Universe is therefore moving in two directions: it is giving birth through the process of cosmo-genesis; and it is forming creative connections to continue to experience the Universe as a womb—cosmic wisdom.

While there are many examples of mystics in various cultures who fit the above criteria, almost none of them were grounded in a cosmology that would be consistent with today's science. A proper understanding of any mystical experience, teaching, or philosophy must take into account the cosmology that provides its context, for it is that context that informs how the mystic interprets the experience. Cosmologies have changed throughout human history. Later, I will examine how mystics of various wisdom traditions found reconnection to the cosmos, a reconnection that can only be understood by understanding the particular cosmology of the mystic.

Unfortunately, religious thinkers have largely abandoned the cosmos as a part of their spirituality. Leaving the cosmos behind has become the predominant aim of most religious seekers, an aim that has done little to create a more sustainable Earth community. New Ageism, while actively seeking to undermine the current Western worldview, has largely appropriated wisdom from the past while failing to recognize the cosmology on which it was based or adapting it to modern science, replacing it instead with modern psychology.

Cosmosophia is about more than ideas, but the way we live and treat one another. As with any worldview, there is an ethics—either explicit or implicit—that comes with it. For example, the Western worldview does not recognize that we are part of a living ecological community, so we are not compelled to treat the Earth as anything but a collection of resources and commodities. This does not mean that those who run corporations that pollute are necessarily cruel people; it means that their worldview does not compel them to act differently. The Western worldview recognizes the primacy of the individual over the community. Ethical actions toward one another are seen as acts of altruism, which calls upon the individual to act for the other. *Cosmosophia*, drawing from many of the wisdom traditions, does not require us to act altruistically for the other, but to shift one's perspective to allow for an ethos of compassion by removing altogether the notion of other-ness.

In spite of what the self-help books say, none of us, as an individual, can create our own reality. The cosmosophical perspective, by showing how we are deeply connected to one another and to the world in which we live, exposes how absurd this notion really is. But we *do* create the world we live in *collectively*: the stars created our world when they exploded as supernovae, seeding our planet; the first mammals created a world when they learned how to compassionately care for their young; the first humans created our world when they made the choice to walk out onto the savannah and when they painted inside the caves; and we are creating the world for our children with the choices we make today. The human, like the star or the jellyfish or the dog, participates in this creation in its own unique way. The choices that so profoundly affect the future are made not only because of our intellect or our genes, but also because of our capacity to employ our imagination. Our stories and our poems and our songs tell us about our world, and we act accordingly. Cosmosophy, above all else, is a method for the healthy use of our imagination.

The creation of a new cosmology is nothing that can be done in a single book, or by a single individual. Such individualism is the very thing a new worldview must undermine. A new worldview is the work of scientists and philosophers, poets and mystics: scientists to understand how the Universe operates; philosophers to ponder what this means and how we should live; mystics to experience in the depths of our being a felt sense of the Universe; and finally, poets and artists, to articulate the myth by which we all live.

Even this myth is nothing that can be written by an individual. It is nothing that can be found in a single book. Our story, the shared story of humanity, used to be written every day in the songs that were sung and the stories that were told by the fire. Each time, the story was different, but the great story shared a common thread. This was how we connected to our world. Indeed, it was how we became human. Today, we must return to the fire, and remember how to become human again.

Cosmology

Salimmo suso, ei primo ed io secondo,
Tanto ch'io vidi delle cose belle
Che porta il ciel, per un pertugio tondo;
E quindi uscimmo a riveder le stelle.*

—Dante, Inferno, Canto xxxiv, 136-139[1]

THE WORD COSMOLOGY is derived from the Greek words cosmos, meaning beauty and order, and logos, which is commonly translated as "word," as in John's Gospel, but has a connotation that has to do with "meaning."[2] Logos is the word from which we also get the English word logic, and indicates a divine ordering principle, an intrinsic meaning and logic, from the divine, permeating the Universe. It should be noted that "cosmology" is, of course, an English word, derived from the Greek, and therefore thoroughly Western. Like all words, especially those referring to fundamental aspects of a culture, it cannot truly be translated. All this is to say that there is no such word, precisely, for cosmology in many parts of the world. All cultures do, however, inhabit the cosmos, whatever name they give it. What

---

* "We climbed up, he first and I second,/ so that I saw among the beautiful things/ which Heaven bears, through a round opening/ and from there we went forth, once more, to see the stars." [translation mine]

41

this means to them, however, is extremely difficult to say. Even the fact that I write in English means some of the true meaning, the felt, embodied sense of how a person relates the cosmos, is lost. So, keeping this in mind—along with the fact that even our cosmology, whatever it may be, remains elusive—we begin the important work of understanding cosmology.

Chapter Four

Why Cosmology?

THIS CHAPTER, as its title suggests, will offer an explanation for why one might want to study cosmology and how this study can have a real effect on the world, aside from being an intellectual exercise. What might we learn from studying cosmologies and what might the consequences of our current cosmology be?

Traditionally, cosmologies have provided a culture with its core assumptions about the nature of reality. That is, a cosmology provides the context for ontology, that which has "being," what is most fundamentally *real*. This has always been more than the study of a cosmos 'out there' beyond the human realm. Traditional cosmologies have served to express the connection between the human and cosmic, the interior life of the individual and the whole. A cosmology was the basic context for all of life's most important questions to be answered. To participate fully in the world, one must understand the world in which one wants to participate.

For a cosmology to be fully embodied and embedded in a culture, it cannot be something that members of that culture must think about most of the time. Usually, we simply act without thinking about the assumptions we are making about the world. In fact, we often assume that we are not acting based upon any cosmology, or, that our cosmology is based on the way things really are, while other cultures' cosmologies are wrong and based on false assumptions. "There will be some fundamental assumptions," warned the philosopher Alfred North Whitehead, "which adherents of all the variant systems within each epoch unconsciously presuppose. Such assumptions appear so obvious that people do not know what they are assuming because no other way of putting things has ever occurred to them."[1]

Modernity is different from other eras in that we have separated scientific and religious cosmologies. These are not terms that I will focus on. Instead, I will argue that any such schism is fallacious. For a cosmology to be complete, it must be integrated into the daily lives of individuals. Most in the modern world do not live our lives according to the New Cosmology, but according to the Newtonian-Cartesian cosmology. At the same time, our religious cosmologies are often inconsistent with some of what we believe to be true about the Universe based on modern science. As the review of changing cosmologies below demonstrates, it will take time for us to synthesize the New Cosmology, like all cosmologies, into a livable worldview.

The Modern Psychologizing of Religion

Before the modern era—and this will become apparent in the survey of various cosmologies in this section—religion was always implicitly or explicitly placed in a cosmological context. That is, the individual was understood to be someone insofar as that individual was able to be placed in a web of relationships—to other people, places, living beings, deities. In the modern era, however, a radical break has occurred which has reduced religion and myth to mere psychology. I say "mere" psychology not to denigrate psychology as a field, but to emphasize how much is left out when we understand myth as something that happens merely in our head, and religion to be a purely personal matter. Indeed, modern psychology—in no small part due to our capacity to isolate the psyche—has been an insightful tool. But the idea that the individual psyche is isolated and separated from the rest of the world, when applied to spirituality, has both limited our understanding of religions of the past and inhibited our capacity to apply our spirituality to modern life.

The modern study of mythology has largely suggested that myths are exclusively about aspects of the psyche or are exclusively stories to explain the phenomenal, external world. What this either-or paradigm misses, however, is that cultures other than the modern West frequently held a more fluid sense of the psyche. That is, the human psyche is not necessarily contained by the skull. If the identity of the individual were co-extensive with the whole Universe, then a myth could be both about the world and about the psyche. A myth about the phenomenal world gives meaning to both nature and the interior, because they are not rigidly separated.

Modern religion, because of the tendency toward literalism and individualism, cares little either for cosmology or mythology. It is all happening in the head, according to this paradigm. Mysticism has been deemphasized as well, and its recent resuscitation in the New Age movement has largely been devoted to its psychological aspects. There is no cosmic context.

The problem with psychologizing religion is two-fold: first, when we do not know the context—that is, the cosmology of the culture in which the myth is found—we fail to fully comprehend the religious system or how those who practiced and created it understood that system and their place in it. Second, reducing religion to psychology makes it an entirely personal matter; that is, it is not allowed to have an effect on our world. This is not, of course, the kind of effect that fundamentalists propose—theirs is an extremely modern, and therefore psychological, approach. I am suggesting that religion—though spirituality or mysticism are perhaps the better words to use—can enhance our connection to, and our compassion for, the world around us, the world of which we are a part.

Cosmology as Ground

If a cosmology is comprised of one's core beliefs about reality, it also influences how one acts and how one interprets one's experiences. While it is true, for example, that a mystical experience has a certain transcendent quality, that it goes beyond one's assumptions about the world, it is also true that one almost invariably falls back on certain assumptions when interpreting such an experience. That is to say, a cosmology provides the basic hermeneutical tools we use to discern what anything means. Hermeneutics is the term originally used to refer to scriptural interpretation. How is it that a text that is basically unchanged for thousands of years is understood in a vastly different way? Why does reading a text not yield one simple, straightforward meaning? Modern fundamentalism has claimed this is possible, largely because of a lack of cosmological awareness. As cosmologies change, so do worldviews, and so does the way we understand the very same words. A language is essentially an expression of this worldview, so a translation is built upon the foundations of a cosmology.

The definition of hermeneutics has recently been expanded

to include the interpretation that one has of anything. Any experience one has, whether it is mundane or deeply mystical, must be interpreted to give it meaning, to allow the individual to place it in the context of one's cosmology. The birth of one's child, the sunset on an empty beach, or the feeling of deep love and connection are all experiences that perhaps have a value without any story or contextualization—they allow the individual to connect to the whole, which is the core of mysticism. However, for one to begin to interpret those experiences—especially to another person, but even to one's self—requires context. This is when the cosmology is drawn upon. Who is the self that has had that experience, and what is the cosmos to which that connection has been felt?

Even if one does not have a religious or spiritual inclination, a cosmology is still drawn from. Ethics, for example, are based on a cosmology. The dualist cosmology of the Puritans was foundational to the early America culture. It was far easier to see Indians and Africans as outside of the sphere of 'the chosen' in this cosmology than it would have been had their cosmology been one that valued every member of the human community equally. Theirs was a cosmology that not only allowed for one group to devalue another; it also actually encouraged its members to exclude others, because their *own* value depended on it. This does not mean that the Puritans, or Americans in general, are unkind or unethical. They simply lack a functional cosmology for a pluralistic society. Even the most admirable members of such cultures are building from the same problematic, dysfunctional foundation. In an atomistic cosmology, ethical behavior is dependent upon *altruism*, which comes from the word *alter*, meaning other.[2] While we are considered 'good' if we behave kindly toward the other, we are still fundamentally separate. Compassion, on the other hand, is the non-dual participation in another's suffering. Later, we will see some examples of cosmologies that allow for such an ethic.

Changing Cosmologies

There are many factors that cause a culture's cosmology to shift or change completely. The common contemporary perspective on this phenomenon is that we are progressing toward an increasingly accurate understanding of the Universe. This view—in addition to its Western bias—is somewhat misleading. A cosmology is based upon the world a culture inhabits, and its validity can only be assessed based on that world. For example, if a culture is limited to a fairly small area of a particular forest, it likely has a functional cosmology for that area. Its understanding of its relationship to *that* world is not less meaningful or valid than that of the modern astrophysicist; in some ways, it is even more fully realized. James Evans explains this idea in relation to geocentric cosmologies: "Modern readers often focus on the earth-centered nature of ancient cosmologies and planetary theories. But, for accurate astronomical prediction, *it makes no difference* whether the earth goes around the sun or the sun goes around the earth. The object that is at rest merely reflects the choice of a frame of reference."[3] However, an awareness of a Universe beyond only the Earth and Sun required a new cosmology and a new physics, just as an awareness beyond that little forest would. But the emergent cosmology is not better, necessarily; it is simply more appropriate, more *functional* for a global species.

One reason for a cosmology to change is humans making new observations about our world. For example, the New Cosmology would be based primarily on observations made by scientists who were committed to the older cosmology. When Einstein's equations indicated that the Universe was expanding, he infamously—in what he would later call his greatest error—changed the equations to save the appearance of a static Universe. He simply could not yet imagine an expanding Universe. Only when Hubble observed the red-shifting of receding galaxies did Einstein and the scientific community accept this change. But observations alone do not make cosmologies change. We are still in the midst of the transition to the New Cosmology, because our culture has not yet fully accepted all the changes that science has revealed.

It is important to note that when cosmologies begin to shift due to observation or intellectual objection, there is usually a great deal of resistance. When the geocentric Universe was upended, the Church hierarchy was quick to attack those who had started this revolution. Similarly, the proponents of evolution are attacked even today. This is no philosophical or intellectual disagreement: new cosmologies transform our world, and disrupt our place in it. Such changes can be threatening and terrifying. And while it is easy to criticize the medieval church or contemporary fundamentalists for their closed-mindedness, it should be recognized that their fears are something fundamental to the human experience: we all want—*need*—to know our place in the world. To simply remove an old worldview that supplied that for a culture—even when it is necessary because that worldview is no longer functional—will produce a deeper entrenchment in a dysfunctional cosmology, the kind of entrenchment we observe today in the various fundamentalist movements.

Plato's "Allegory of the Cave" shows the resistance to seeing the world in a fresh, new way. When the prisoner, who represents us in our limited way of perceiving the world, is shown the world beyond the cave, Plato says, "on reaching the light would he not be blinded by its radiance and unable to see any of the things he was now told were real? And would he be not ready to go through anything rather than entertain these new opinions and live in this new way?"[4] While Plato correctly points out how we are often unable to perceive a new worldview when it is presented to us, his dualistic vision of the real and unreal is limited. Later, we will see how *Cosmosophia* points toward a cosmological vision that acknowledges we are always, in some ways, in the cave, and always birthing ourselves beyond it.

A more common way for a cosmology to change is for the values of that culture to change, shifting the way it relates to the Universe. In such cases, no new observations are required; a completely different story can be told about the same observation if the values of a culture are different. A prominent example can be found with the onset of patriarchy in the ancient Near East. During the matriarchal period, the popular myth told that the goddess Tiamat gave birth to the Universe. As Babylon developed into an empire and adopted patriarchal values, Tiamat changed in the myth from a beautiful birther of creation into a hideous creature who gives birth to demons. In the new myth, the male hero Marduk defeats her in battle and becomes all powerful. *He* then creates the Universe by cutting her in half: her top half is the heavens, her bottom is the Earth. But even as her power is usurped, she remains present in the myth, a memory of an old worldview.

Cosmologies can also change in response to crisis. An early example comes from the apocalyptic tradition. The uniqueness of Israelite religion—the very foundation of which was constructed in contrast to the norm in the Near Eastern world—led to a unique response to the Hellenistic revolution. The predominant religion of the Near East was centered on the worship of a combination of male and female gods, recognizing the cyclical nature of time and the seasons upon which their agriculture depended. In contrast, the Israelites, who were pastoralists in their formative stage, developed a notion of time as linear, and a notion of themselves as emerging as a part of history, rather than honoring the cycle of seasons—although there were some instances of a return to cyclical time. Unlike their Mesopotamian, Egyptian, or Assyrian counterparts, the Israelites believed that they emerged at a particular point in history. And because their connection to the divine and to immortality, was to be found in the collective identity of Israel, the end of Israel meant total annihilation. The new threat of Hellenistic culture was resisted more fiercely in Israel than elsewhere, even as the means of resistance were the product of the Hellenistic Age.

Even before Alexander, the priestly hierarchy of Israel was constantly struggling to prevent the influence of the religion of the older inhabitants of their land, the Canaanites. At the same time, the Judean priesthood sought to maintain the centrality of the Jerusalem temple.[5] When the Israelites encountered a series of crises—first all the northern tribes were conquered by the Assyrians, then the Judeans were taken into exile in Babylon— the religious response was found in the prophets, who claimed that the failure of Israel to keep YHVH's laws was to blame for these calamitous events.

In addition to the failure to keep the law, the prophet known as Isaiah admonished the Israelites for lacking compassion:

> When you stretch out your hands I turn my eyes away.
> You may multiply your prayers,
> I shall not be listening.
> Your hands are covered in blood,
> Wash, make yourselves clean.
> Take your wrong-doing out of my sight.
> Cease doing evil. Learn to do good,
>
> Search for justice, discipline the violent,
> Be just to the orphan, plead for the widow.[6]

The prophet claimed that the Assyrian conquest was due not only to the failure to keep the law, but a failure to be just and compassionate to those in need. Collectively, Isaiah and the other prophets not only upheld the efficacy of the law, they also undermined the authority of the temple hierarchy both by critiquing the emptiness of ritual without compassion and by claiming that prophetic vision, not only the Torah, could be a valid source of authority.[7] Jesus is later understood—whether it is because of his own actions or those attributed to him we cannot know—to be a part of this tradition of people who challenged the religious authorities.

Another prophet, Ezekiel, would have a profound effect on Judaism. Ezekiel's ascent to the Heavens where he encounters an angelic figure seated on a throne would become the prototype for early Jewish mysticism, called *merkabah*, or "throne-chariot" mysticism. The *merkabah* mystics were ecstatics, who, like Ezekiel, had visionary experiences in which they ascended to the heavens. While ecstasy can be viewed as a departure from the cosmos, it can also be conceived as a shamanic re-integration, a breaking down of barriers between the self and cosmos, an important distinction when applied to our current situation. Bruce Chilton has argued that Jesus was a part of this tradition.[8] For the Jesus Movement, the *merkabah* would have fit into what I.M. Lewis calls, "peripheral possession," the practice of ecstasy by women, outcastes and the politically impotent as a means of subverting the established authority.[9]

The predominant response of the Israelites to the political and cultural crises they faced during the Hellenistic period was the apocalyptic, which means "revelation," referring to that which is revealed when the mystic, undoubtedly employing the imagery of the *merkabah*, journeys to the heavens. In this way, the apocalypticist is able to gain access to divine wisdom, that which is unavailable either through the scriptures of priestly Judaism or through the intellectual inquiry of Greek philosophy. It is therefore subversive on two fronts: the internal hierarchy of Judaism, as well as the cultural hierarchy that threatened Judaism. But at the same time, the apocalyptic, while clearly attacking the foreign powers, including the Greeks, has undeniably employed the new Greek cosmology, reaching the edge of the cosmic sphere as described by Plato.

In addition, the revelations of the apocalyptic usually dealt with eschatology, that is, with the end of time. The boundary of space and time were approached as a way to leave a cosmic order that was clearly stacked against the Israelites. "The apocalypticists," writes Ithamar Gruenwald, "who lived with a deep conviction that the days of the eschatological fulfillment were close at hand, believed that whatever had been concealed from man, because of the injustice that reigned in the world, could now be released for the knowledge and benefit of the just."[10]

If there can be any single way to distinguish the prophetic and apocalyptic traditions, it is that the apocalyptic gave up on the cosmos and time, and predicted an end of time after which there would be justice.[11] The notion of the end of time was likely due to the influence of the Persians, with whom the Israelites had contact before and during the Hellenistic Age.[12] In part, this must be attributed to the nature of the Hellenistic threat. Instead of being threatened or oppressed by a specific nation whom they could hope to defeat, such as the Babylonians, the Israelites now found themselves immersed in a new world order from which there was no escape.

The nature of the apocalyptic vision, while borrowing from the prophetic by wedding *merkabah* mysticism and the Isaiah's ethics, added another innovation in the nature of the end of time. Justice would be understood cosmically; that is, eschatol-

53

ogy would be a recapitulation of cosmogony. This represents the syncretism of the prophetic Jewish tradition, Persian eschatology, and Greek cosmology.[13] The prophets had written, perhaps, with a greater sense of their own power and privilege, and had not volunteered to let it go altogether. The apocalyptics had no hope that justice could be found with anything resembling the current order, and sought to undermine it altogether. Furthermore, the apocalyptic represents an unconscious return to the cyclical in its recapitulation of the paradise of creation.

The apocalyptic provides us with a vision that addresses the deeper psychic structures that affect our situation today. Unconsciously, these visionaries realized that there was no simple answer to the threats they felt from the world as it currently existed. Their collective imagination called for, over and over again, a deep cosmological transformation. Problematic, however, was the fact that this transformation took place within a cultural context that had rejected the feminine, seemed to be running away from the Earth itself, and was unconsciously dominated by a fear of death. The apocalyptic tradition shows that when a cosmology comes to an end—in this case, the older cosmology of the Israelites was unconsciously supplanted by the Hellenistic one—there is a tendency to think that the cosmos is *ending*. The Israelites, marginalized as they were in the Hellenistic world, recast the Hellenistic cosmology from the *eschaton*—"the edge."

Much later, the Bubonic plague provides an example of a crisis that caused a similar shift in cosmology. The modern worldview emerged out of the ashes of the plague. Interestingly, the imperialism of the new age led to the destruction that yielded other shifts. While we often think of modern thinking as a blessing—and it is in many ways—several shifts in worldview brought about changes that were calamitous for others: Modern notions of "race" helped to bring about the trans-Atlantic slave trade; the misogyny of modernity, particularly the Protestant Reformation, brought rampant witch burnings; and the demonization of the Jews led to their expulsion from Spain.

After the Jews were expelled from Spain in 1492, Lurianic Kabbalah took the cosmology and mystical theology of the classical Kabbalistic tradition developed in Spain and added a more pessimistic tone. For the Lurianic Kabbalists of Safed in what is now the state of Israel, the world is broken, shattered, and the task of the mystic is to heal it.

The Middle Passage provides a stark example—one that is nearly singular in it abruptness and totality—of what can happen in the wake of a cosmology and a culture being nearly eradicated. Stolen from their homes, their land, their way of life, the African slaves were thrown into ships and taken to the Americas. Many died on the way. But those who survived the journey would find a world in which everything they understood to be true was no more. Their entire cosmology was nearly eradicated, the bioregion that had once provided its context unimaginably far away. And for generations, they, like many other Americans with histories of suffering and degradation, were required to forget.

Out of the collective death that was the Middle Passage, a new culture, a new cosmology, a *new world*, was born. The music that was to play in every café and disco in the world was born on the cotton fields. The greatest expression of American religion, of the "strange mutation"[14] of Christianity that developed in the United States, would be exclaimed from the pulpits of Black Churches, and the entire world would listen in silent admiration to Martin Luther King, Jr. as he used the Christianity that had justified slavery and colonialism for hundreds of years to humble the American Empire. King, like few others before or since, understood that the suffering of his people was a *cosmic* suffering, and that through a collective transformation all of us could find salvation.

Apocalypse Now

If one accepts the premise that we are in crisis at this moment, history indicates that a new worldview is imminent. Indeed, there is talk on all sides of apocalypse: the fundamentalist "Left Behind" series frequently tops best-seller lists, while the scientific community warns us that the Earth is near the point of death. It is certainly true that we appear to have reached many 'ends' at once. The industrial growth society has brought us to the brink of ecological disaster. Mass extinctions are bringing about the end of the Cenozoic Era, while climate change is altering the end of the Holocene interglacial period. Both Christianity and patriarchy seem at their end, as does the American empire. All of these factors make this a time of uncertainty and potential, of death and rebirth.

During the rise of Christianity, there was a similar feeling of uncertainty and a similar emphasis on the end times. The emphasis on the *eschaton* would influence Christianity profoundly. Paul appears to have believed that the end was imminent. Christian sects from Paul's time to the fundamentalists today have emphasized this eschatology. What is striking about the apocalyptic—both in Jewish and Christian-Hellenistic thought—is how wrong they were about the cosmos itself ending, and how insightful they were about theirs being an end time of sorts. An old worldview was dying; a new world order, Christianity, was born. In the gospel story, when Mary Magdalene arrives at the tomb she does not literally "see" the young man in the white robe proclaiming the risen Christ; rather, she "perceives" (Greek *"theoria"*; the same word describing other visionary experiences in the New Testament) his presence.[15] Jesus admonished his followers to realize that the Kingdom is already present; it is neither "here" nor "there," but among and within you.[16] The eschaton refers not merely to the "end" but to the arrival at an edge.[17] Jesus taught that, from the margins of society, we can live our lives in such way that we are always at that edge—the unique teaching called *realized eschatology.** At each moment, we are giving birth to the future. Later, we will explore how modern science sheds new light on the eschaton.

The Universe will continue to evolve whether or not we have the wisdom to prevent our own demise. A new world will be born from these ashes. The question is whether it is the ashes of our way of perceiving the world, or the ashes of human civilization itself, along with much of the Earth community.

---

* Generally, the eschaton refers to the end of time or the "edge" of spacetime, the end of the world as we know it. Conventionally, this is thought to occur at a particular moment in the future. Realized eschatology, however, holds that one can reach the edge of this cosmic order here and now.

Chapter Five
Cosmology in the Western World

I N THIS CHAPTER, I will briefly outline the history of Western cosmologies in order to establish a coherent picture of the current worldview. Like all worldviews, this one has a cosmology at its foundation and emerged out of a history of previous cosmologies. A cosmology is not just created from nothing, nor is it simply that we have figured out how things really are. In part, we have made certain discoveries that have made our view of the Universe more accurate. But a cosmology is always built upon the previous one. To paraphrase Paul, we see now only imperfect reflections, in a dimly lit mirror.[1] To break from both Paul and his predecessor, Plato, there is no perfect vision beyond this one. We leave one cave, only to enter another.

In each phase, I will emphasize particular aspects of Western cosmology that emerged and how they have shaped our current worldview. Contrary to what most of us believe, this worldview has more to do with how our consciousness has been shaped by our cultural heritage than by detached, rational choices. Nor is the story of Western cosmology a simple tale of progress—indeed, this is what our current worldview would have us think. While new cosmologies are often improvements in some ways, there is often wisdom that is lost as well.

It is important to acknowledge that, while this study may give the impression of a single narrative for all of Western civilization, there are actually many different stories. That what Lucia Chiavola Birnbaum calls "submerged beliefs"[2] have continued to flourish even in the face of an increasingly oppressive Western patriarchy demonstrates their power. In fact, such beliefs often live on without the conscious awareness of the people who espouse them. History is usually written by the winners; those in power have done what they can to diminish any worldview that does not serve to reinforce their power. Just as a cosmology gives an individual a sense of place in the Universe, it can also uphold certain power relationships.

Moreover, the notion that any history can be understood in a single strand should be viewed as a part of the paradigm this work seeks to overcome. If the diversity of cultural perspectives out of which various cosmologies come is ignored, humanity will be impoverished for this loss. We need multiple viewpoints to usher in a new worldview. But this chapter is primarily focused on the stream that has led to the dominant worldview in the West today, a stream that is largely responsible for the modern crisis.

The Archaic Cosmology

Before proceeding with the story of the particular cosmologies of the West, it is important to acknowledge that there was a preexisting cosmology in what would become the West that actually functioned quite well. Indeed, this cosmology, which we will call the archaic cosmology, was similar throughout the world. While I will make certain generalizations about the archaic cosmology, it should be noted that there are as many variations of these cosmologies as there are cultures—and for every generalization that is made, one can find an exception. The purpose here is to gain a sense of what some of the general patterns may have been in order to recognize some of the differences between the emergent Western worldview and the culture from which it emerged or which it overtook.

The archaic cosmology was a part of the worldview that developed in the Neolithic village. These were the earliest permanent human settlements, occurring after humans finally populated most of the world and could no longer wander and spread out. It was, in a sense, our first encounter with the fact that our planet is a sphere, and its consequent limitations. We are still, I might add, working to come to terms with this reality.

The original Neolithic village culture had several attributes that distinguish it from modern culture. We find a close link to those primordial cultures in today's indigenous peoples. Again, it must be pointed out that indigenous cultures are noted for their diversity, a diversity we risk losing, along with much of the wisdom of our species, in favor of the monoculture of globalization. The wisdom of these cultures is that of living in relationship to the particular ecosystem in which a culture arises, so they must be both more diverse and less dualistic than the modern worldview. The primordial culture was matriarchal, based on relationship rather than domination, as opposed to the patriarchy that came after it.

The archaic cosmology that arose in this context generally had three tiers. There was the mundane realm in the middle, bounded by the heavens above and the underworld below. While it is easy to refer to these realms in terms of the heaven/hell dichotomy of the Greco-Christian worldview, it would be a mistake to think of these realms dualistically. The heavens and the underworld were ultimately the realms beyond mundane experience—the sacred—and as such were linked to one another. While one could surely trace Christian or Muslim concepts of heaven and hell to the archaic cosmology, the Taoist conceptions of *yin* (Earth) and *yang* (heavens) would be better comparisons to the archaic cosmology.

The underworld is often associated with water, and wells and fountains are frequently means of linking the human realm to the sacred. In many traditions, the human world is divided into fours by intersecting rivers. The four directions remain a common means of thinking about the world. The center of the world or *axis mundi* can be represented by a tree, mountain, or temple, linking the underworld to the heavens.

Cosmology, of course, deals not only with space but also with time. Time was not always conceived of as linear, as moving in a particular direction. Like space, time for early humans was most sacred as the edges, where boundaries could be crossed. Just as sacred places were those that could connect one to the lower and higher worlds—sacred mountains and wells, for instance—the sacred times were seen as connecting one to the temporal edge. In cyclical time, each time an annual event is repeated a culture ritually participates in the first time that event occurred. This is seen in modern day New Year celebrations, or festivals like *carnival*, at which the primordial chaos is reenacted and followed by the order of creation.[3]

At the other end of cosmic time is the end, or *eschaton*. Because in the archaic cosmology time was cyclical, the end of time was not addressed until much later with the emergence of linear time. But, as we shall see below, the way that people dealt with the end of time was connected to this primordial sense of sacredness of "the edge." A boundary crossing remains a sacred event, even as cosmologies change. Indeed, the event that marks the shift in cosmologies itself can be viewed as a boundary crossing.

The Celts developed a vibrant culture across Europe with a rich cosmological tradition. Even when they were pushed to the western periphery of Europe and converted to Christianity, they continued to understand themselves as embedded in a cosmological context. We owe much of the rhythmic nature of Catholicism to the Celts. Their cosmology provides us with an example of an archaic cosmology in areas that would eventually come to be part of the West. Celtic religion, as with all pre-modern peoples, was inseparable from its cosmology. It teaches the Celts the structure of their Universe—physical, socially, and spiritually—and their place in it.

The structure of the Celtic Universe can be described with several different dimensions, beginning with the circle or wheel. The circle represents the course of the seasons and the daily pattern of the Sun. Within the circle is a cross, dividing the Universe into the four cardinal directions. Although the Church later imposed upon it Christian significance, the 'Celtic cross' was actually a pre-Christian symbol of "cosmic order and harmony."[4] Both the seasons (time) and the country of Ireland (space) are divided into fours, showing that there is not a rigid distinction between space and time in Celtic belief. The center represents the mysterious fifth direction, and the axis by which the Upperworld and Underworld are connected to the earthly realm. This axis can also be described as the *omphalos* or 'navel.' In this way, the Celtic cosmos has a circular, linear and vertical dimension.

In each dimension, the Universe is balanced by the dialectic of *samos* and *giamos*. These aspects are not dualistic; rather, they balance one another. Nothing exists without some of each. *Samos* is the *via positiva*, or, in Chinese cosmology, the *yang* aspect. In the vertical dimension, the sky or upper world represents *samos*. In the cycle of the seasons—the circular dimension or time—the summer months are *samos*. The tree of life connects the earthly realm to the sky or Upperworld, represented by the element of fire. Trees are significant in that they not only connect us to the Upperworld as their branches reach toward the sky, but also in that their roots reach downward, into the Earth, connecting the upper and lower. Trees are living beings, not abstractions. For the Celts, their presence was a constant reminder of the interaction between the upper and the lower, *samos* and *giamos*.

Giamos represents the *yin* energy or the *via negativa*. The dark half of the calendar (winter) or the day (night) is considered *giamos*. The axis or *omphalos* connects the earthly realm to the underworld through sacred waters. In this and many other ways water plays a key role in Celtic cosmology. Primarily, water represents the *giamos*, or feminine principle, as does the underworld.[5]

The dimensions of the Celtic Universe are not limited to the grandiosity of the Earth and the celestial bodies. An important feature of Celtic cosmology is the balance of the inner and outer, the microcosm and the macrocosm. Just as the year is balanced between the *samos* and the *giamos*, and among the four seasons, each day has a similar division. Similarly, as all of creation is balanced, so is the island of Ireland, each individual household, and each individual body.

Like all indigenous peoples, the Celts understood creation to be alive, and a continuously unfolding story. They recognized that they were a part of a process. The knowledge of the ancestors is passed on to us through the myths and stories that are so important in Celtic culture, allowing us to participate fully in the process.

The Earth Goddess is perhaps the best-known aspect of Celtic spirituality, popularized by neo-pagan groups. In Celtic cosmology, the Earth represents the feminine aspect of the divine, the womb whence we all have come and to which we all return. Irish kings ritually 'married' the land to validate their power. The intimate relationship between the Celts and the land was typical of the archaic cosmology. They understood that they owed their existence to the land and its fertility. This was no mere romanticizing of nature. The Goddess could also represent chaos and destruction. For the Celts, a balance between nature's destructive and life-giving attributes was essential.

As the Celtic lands were Christianized, the Earth Goddess was replaced by Mary, "the virgin mother of a celibate God," writes Michael Dames. "This was the key act in the proposed de-sexualization of the Irish landscape."[6] The loss of the Earth Goddess represents the dualism of Earth and divine. Rather than a living, breathing aspect of divinity, the Earth was understood as a lifeless rock. The exploitation of the Earth parallels the exploitation of the woman in a patriarchal society. "[V]iolence done to women is violence done to the Earth—and to the feminine within each one of us," writes Mara Freeman.[7] To the Celts, the Earth was "ensouled."[8] We shall see later that, in many ways, the New Cosmology that suggests that the Earth is alive and a part of the birth-giving, creative process of the unfolding Universe in which we all participate provides us with some similar values.

The Celtic cosmology provides a clear example of the archaic cosmology that existed in various forms throughout the world. For the most part, however, the modern worldview has displaced the Celtic vision. Many Westerners have recently become interested in the Celtic worldview in the form of neo-pagan revivalist movements. Such efforts, however well-intentioned, often fail to truly displace the Modern worldview because a complete paradigm shift requires not only changing one's mind *about* religion, but also a total shift in perspective. It is no simple process to remove one's cosmology. And, to a certain extent, the notion that we can simply appropriate indigenous or archaic worldviews as our own while we continue to inhabit the modern world is flawed—not to mention insulting to those who truly live in such a world. It would be useful, therefore, to take a rigorous look at the world we now inhabit, and the cultural heritage that has created that world. It is a world that has many positive aspects; the criticisms here should be viewed as an acknowledgement that we are at a key moment, a *kairos*, at which we are about to enter into a new phase, and we must choose how we participate in that shift.

The Hellenistic Cosmology

The cosmology of the Greeks evolved over several centuries through the cumulative efforts of various cultures and thinkers. Shamanic cultures to the north as well as the much older Egyptian civilization to the south contributed immensely to the Greek worldview. The Greeks, however, introduced several ideas that provided breaking points from the previous cosmology, ideas that would remain in Western culture until this moment. In particular, the Greeks have passed on to us a pervasive individualism and a dualism that remains a key component of the Western worldview. One might also notice that the story of Western cosmology now becomes a story of individual men. This is no accident. While Greek thinking was brilliant and innovative, it was fundamentally patriarchal and propagated the biases that patriarchy bring. At the same time, the individualism of the Greeks and their emphasis on the connection between the heavens and the human soul allows for the union of opposites, a paradigm for mysticism then and now, to enter into human consciousness.

The Presocratics represent a variety of thinkers and ideas in Greek philosophy before it became concretized. Although there eventually emerged a comprehensive Greek worldview, it did not have to turn out the way it did. In fact, many of the Presocratics had a great deal in common with the East, or the Egyptians, or the shamanic cultures to the north. The Presocratics did establish, however, a strong sense of the world as a *cosmos*—that is, an ordered, beautiful, logical whole—a sense that has remained a fundamental assumption of Western thought. The great shift that occurred with the Greeks has been described in many ways. One explanation is that it was a shift from *mythos* to *logos*, from a poetic and mythic sensibility to one of rational thought and abstraction.

The primary focus of the Presocratics was to discuss the *arche*—that which is the beginning or source of all that is—in abstract logical terms rather than through mythical participation. One such group known as the Milesians—of Ionia, or present-day Turkey—were called "hylozoists" or "those who think matter is alive."[9] Beginning with Thales, who is famous for having predicted an eclipse on May 28, 585 BCE,[10] the Milesians developed a discipline around what they called *phusis*, or the organic growth of the cosmos and the individual.[11] Anaximander, credited with establishing the first geocentric cosmology, saw the Universe as an organism which was sustained by the *pneuma*, or divine breath, which would later be referred to as the Holy Spirit of the Christian Trinity.[12] He called the *arche* "*To Apeiron*," the boundless—this represented a paradigm shift in that "the boundless" was a conceptual abstraction, not an anthropomorphic deity.

Among the best known of the Presocratics was Heraclitus, who saw the world as constantly changing or 'Becoming.' For Heraclitus, the Universe was a perpetual dance of the opposites, united through the concept of the *logos*, a view not at all unlike that of the Taoists (see chapter 6 below). The emphasis on change of Heraclitus was countered by Parmenides, for whom only the changeless was real. He called this changeless principle *ontos* or "being." Democritus and the Atomists sought to reconcile these contrasting viewpoints, positing that while the world did appear to change, there was a material substance, the atom, which could not be divided and remained unalterable and changeless. The Atomists introduced a rigid separation between spirit and matter, a split that remains with us today.

Although none of Pythagoras's writings remain, he had an immeasurable influence on Western thought. Pythagoras, whose school, like Parmenides with whom he has some philosophical affinity, came out of the Greek colonies of southern Italy, was influenced both by shamanic and Egyptian ideas, and seems to have a connection to Eastern thought. Pythagoras extended what had previously been the exclusive attribute of the shaman, the capacity to separate the soul—*psyche*—from the body. For the Pythagoreans, who were based in southern Italy, the soul is only temporarily clothed in the body, and moves into new bodies in later lifetimes. Moreover, the Pythagoreans emphasized mathematics and music. This emphasis on the harmonious and mathematical nature of reality would remain a fundamental assumption for Western philosophers and provide the foundation for the scientific endeavor.

In order to understand the Greek cosmology—and, later, to understand the emergence of Christianity—one must understand the religious movement known as the Mysteries. In various mystery cults throughout the Mediterranean, salvation was offered beyond the cosmic sphere for the soul, which was individual and separate from the body. For the Orphics and Pythagoreans, for example, the hope of immortality was based upon a complex myth concerning the nature of the human soul as a mixture of divine and earthly aspects. The purpose of life, therefore, was to subdue the earthly and elevate the spiritual aspect. This idea is based upon the dualism of body (*soma*) and soul (*psyche*); that is, death is only the death of the body, not the soul. Before the Mysteries, the *psyche* was generally thought of as something like a ghost, but the Orphics explicitly described the "light" as that which is reborn after death. The Orphico-Pythagoreans developed methods of purification, separating the pure soul from the *soma*—the body or 'tomb'—to attain immortality. For Pythagoras, philosophy was the path to apotheosis; for the Orphics, living the prescribed life and being initiated into the cult was the path to immortality and purification.

There is also evidence that the Orphico-Pythagoreans were drawing from the shamanic practices of the north, practices that would have surely involved rituals of death and rebirth. Pythagoras, a historical figure, and Orpheus, a mythic one, were often said to have come from or traveled to the north. Around this time, there is some evidence that new trade routes opened between Greece and the north. Orpheus is linked with the land of Thrace, to the north, while Pythagoras is called the Hyberborean Apollo—from the 'far north.' However, it should be noted that the Greeks had broken from the archaic cosmology, and their worldview became quite different, demonstrating how a different cosmology can lead to very different interpretations of similar practices.

Pythagoras was both a mystic and a philosopher, and it is therefore difficult to separate his 'religious' ideas from his scientific ones. While his doctrine of the soul was clearly religious, he understood it in the context of an all-pervading cosmic unity conceived through philosophical speculation. The understanding of this unity was central to the individual's purification. Above all, Pythagoras's legacy was to emphasize the concept of a unified, ordered—and thus 'beautiful'—cosmos. The abstract order of mathematics and the rhythm and structure of music—Pythagoras's cosmos was vibrating—were fundamental to this worldview.

Orphic mythology employs themes of death and rebirth found in Shamanic cultures, specifically in the form of Dionysos. The Orphic cosmogony begins with *Phanes*—"light"—bursting out of the cosmic egg. The light of *Phanes* ultimately is passed on through Zeus to the child Dionysos, who is killed by the Titans in a scene that replicates a common shamanic journey in which the shaman is dismembered and eaten. The mysteries of Isis celebrate another god, Osiris, who is killed and dismembered. Dionysos, like Osiris, is reborn. Initiation, in many cases, involves the initiate repeating "the death of the Supernatural Being, the founder of the mystery."[13]

When Zeus kills the Titans, they are turned to smoke from which humans are made. We therefore have a dual nature: we are Titanic (our impure bodies) and Dionysiac (our divine souls), because the titans have eaten Dionysos. And it is the light of Phanes, the substance of our souls, from which Dionysos derives his purity. The mysteries of Orpheus seek to purify the initiate, freeing the psyche from the body. Our rebirth, therefore, is attained in discovering our true nature.

Plato was the greatest of the Greek philosophers, at once a great synthesizer and an original thinker. His cosmology was spherical and geocentric, like Anaximander's, but his ontology was like Parmenides. For Plato, the real was the realm of 'Ideas' or 'Forms.' And like Pythagoras, Plato believed the soul to be distinct from the body. Plato's legacy was to reject the body in favor of the soul and matter in favor of the ideas and forms. His primary concern was not the structure of the Universe but the liberation of the soul, through philosophy, from its imprisonment in the body and the material world. That which endures, for Plato, is found both in the immensity of the transcendent realm beyond the heavens and in the minuteness of the individual soul—the union of opposites. Plato's emphasis was less on observation than on ideas, more on the individual soul than on the collective. For Plato, the aim of the life of the philosopher was to overcome the impermanent, the mundane. Plato's allegory of the cave beautifully articulates his belief that the real is beyond the world we normally see and perceive. What Plato failed to recognize, however, was that even as we leave the old cave behind, we are entering only into a new cave—our perception is always influenced by our context.

Plato's psyche was not limited to the individual, however. He integrated the psyche—the essence of the individual human being—with the newest cosmology. In the *Phaedo*, Plato was the first to refer unquestioningly to the spherical cosmos first posited by Anaximander. Employing Anaximander's cosmology, Plato created his own cosmogonic myth, wherein the *demiurge* ("craftsman") creates the *psyche kosmon* ("world soul"), dividing the substance of *psyche* in two to form a cosmic cross. The heavens are thus ordered with a cross made of the celestial equator and the zodiac. Our individual souls are made of the same substance, *psyche*, as the heavens. Plato began, therefore, to reconcile the paradox of the individual and the universal: it is through interiority, our deepest and most essential selves, that we can connect to the heavens, the very edge of cosmos, the immortal realm. Like Pythagoras, Plato believed that in death we gain access to the heavens. Moreover, this was a process of *remembrance* for Plato; that is, our truest selves are not the mortal bodies in which we are cloaked, but the divine souls within. Accessing the wisdom of the stars is a process of remembering our true nature.

71

Plato's genius is perhaps not so much in his originality as in his ability to fuse various ideas and present them as a cohesive system. After Plato, the idea of the individual soul became a part of the broader Hellenic world, rather than a notion only present in a collection of fringe cults. The notion of our dual nature, the human as a mixture of the divine and the earthly, was also entrenched in the Western psyche. In the *Symposium*, Plato writes that the philosopher is "midway between the wise and the senseless. The reason for this is his birth: his father is wise [*sophos*] and inventive; his mother, senseless and without resources [*en aporiai*]."[14] The West would return, in varying degrees, to this dualism, which would be played out in a chauvinism toward women, other ethnicities, and the Earth. At the same time, the possibility of connecting our inner-nature, our truest selves, to the transcendent, was made present.

Plato's most famous student was Aristotle. Although Aristotle has much in common with his teacher, he departed from Plato in some key ways. First and foremost, Aristotle had a more positive view of matter and the body. He was deeply concerned with the physical Universe in a way that Plato never was. But he retained the typical Greek dualism by separating the cosmos into two realms: the earthly, composed of four elements, and the transcendent realm, composed of ether. Whereas the lower realm was subject to change and corruption, the upper realm was incorruptible. Aristotle's cosmology was not only dualistic but, as a whole, basically unchangeable. Moreover, Aristotle was particularly interested in reinforcing the concept of a hierarchical cosmos, which he did through an extensive classification system. The notion that the Universe is structured as a hierarchy remained embedded in the Western mind throughout the Christian era and into Modernity. Because he was particularly interested in movement, Artistotle's *arche* was the "unmoved mover", which he called the *nous*, or mind—"thought thinking itself". This concept of pure, decontextualized thought would become the ideal for Western philosophy for centuries.

Whereas Plato's most famous student was another philosopher, Aristotle, Aristotle's best known pupil was an emperor, Alexander the Great. In 330 BCE, Alexander conquered the entire eastern Mediterranean and Near East, signaling the beginning of the Hellenistic age. While the Greeks lacked the organizational capacity to rule a cohesive political empire like the Romans, the cultural impact of Alexander's conquest was immeasurable.

Empires, because they are based not on ethnic ties to a particular bioregion, tend to be cosmopolitan; that is, subjects of an empire tend to identify with their individual interiority more than the land and community into which they were born. Moreover, the fact that Alexander had been taught by Aristotle, a student of Plato, provided a philosophical foundation to shift the locus of spiritual power from the *polis*, the mountain or the temple, to the interior self, from the collective to the individual. It should not be underestimated how revolutionary—and how threatening—this was. The geocentric cosmology meant that the Earth no longer had an *axis mundi* at its center. Indeed, the notion of any spatial centrality, aside from the Earth itself, was removed. Rather than atop the mountain, the gods were understood to be in the heavens, either at the edge of the cosmos or in a super-cosmic region beyond. Again, the locus of spiritual power was shifted from the social, cultural and political center to a realm to which all could have unmediated, individual access.

This shift occurred on both a micro- and a macro-cosmic level. Access to the divine was seen as occurring as a process of interiority, as well as a process of transcendence. For Plato, as it had been for the Pythagoreans, the *psyche* was the mirror of the cosmos. In the Hellenistic empire that emerged after Alexander, this would prove to be a remarkably appropriate paradigm. As Greek culture spread, individuals began to move from a collective identity to an individual one. The notion of individual immortality, salvation, or rebirth, emerged.

In many ways, the Hellenistic revolution parallels the conditions of today's world. The cultural syncretism of the Hellenistic world exists today on a global scale and a new astronomical cosmology has emerged that has not yet found a place in traditional religion. For some—the elites of Greece then and of America now—these changes have brought greater opportunity and wealth. But today, no new religious, mythic framework has emerged to fit these changes, leaving all, even the rich, with a sort of psychic schism, a mythology that is inconsistent with the New Science, and in the absence of an answer to the psychological problem of death, an existential crisis. In addition, the global economy has particularly left certain groups of people feeling increasingly isolated and alienated. Many have been pushed toward fundamentalism as a response to the economic and cultural threat of modernity.

As explained in the previous chapter, the apocalyptic was the particular response of the Israelite people to the imposition of the Hellenistic cosmology. In order to transcend the hopelessness of their situation as a marginalized people, the apocalyptics ascended through the cosmic spheres to the transcendent realm beyond. Like many a people at the margins of society, they possessed a particular wisdom that can only be attained at the edge.

The *eschaton*, therefore, was the way they experienced a world in which they no longer felt at home; at the same time, it provided hope that they might transcend their despair and hopelessness.

Interestingly, they retained the basic assumptions of the Greeks even as their approach was seen as undermining Greek hegemony. That is, the apocalyptic movement was based largely on the Greek cosmology, even as it sought to overcome Greek hegemony. The particular challenge of the marginalized is to avoid the tendency to fight their oppressors while subconsciously adhering to their oppressors' worldview. Martin Luther King, for example, attempted to reframe the paradigm in which his struggle took place, but even some of his closest supporters have been unable to comprehend the full depth of his teachings.*

The Hellenistic cosmology introduced many new innovations and discoveries about the Universe. Its legacy, however, is not in its accuracy but in the way it provided the foundations for the Western worldview. All who were heavily influenced by the Greeks would henceforth place a greater influence on the individual soul, a soul that was linked not to the impermanent human body or nature, but the transcendent realm beyond. It is difficult to say what prompted such a shift in the ancient Mediterranean world, but it would be clear what the next major shift would be.

---

* King was a harsh critic of the injustices of capitalism and imperialism and believed that the plight of his own people was tied to the economic hardships of, for instance, Appalachian Whites, and to the suffering of the Vietnamese people. Andrew Young, however, who was King's chief supporter during the movement, later worked for Wal-Mart. When criticized for working for a corporation that uses quasi-slave-labor overseas and decimates locally owned businesses in the U.S., Young responded, "I think [small businesses] have ripped off our communities enough. First it was Jews, then it was Koreans, now its Arabs. Very few Black people own these stores."

The abstractions of the Greeks could not capture the imagination of the masses. A new *mythos* was needed. The radical teachings of a poor outcast from the backwater province of Galilee in Palestine would precipitate such a revolution. At the same time, the emergence of Christianity can best be understood in the context of the Mysteries and of the Apocalyptic. Paul's cosmology was thoroughly Greek, and his mysticism, as we shall see later, can best be properly understood in that context.

THE MEDIEVAL COSMOLOGY

With the fall of the Western Roman Empire and the advent of Christianity as the dominant religious force in the West, a new era was ushered in. It was based not on any new observations about the Universe, but on a synthesis of Greek ideas with the *mythos* of the Israelites. The story of the Universe and the story of the soul were inextricable during the Middle Ages. Whereas the Hellenistic Age that preceded it was marked by the incredible diversity of views and myriad innovations, the Christian era was notable in its cohesiveness and singularity.* New ideas always bring with them a certain amount of anxiety. Perhaps, there was a collective need to return to a more cohesive worldview after the tumultuous Hellenistic Age. Whatever the case, the energy that the Greek world had put toward new ideas was channeled by the Christian world into contextualizing those ideas into a single story.

When Christianity established itself as the dominant reli-

---

* It should be noted, however, that there remained a strong presence in Medieval Christiandom of pagans, Jews, Muslims, and others. Much of what we consider to be orthodox Christian beliefs and ideas come from these non-Christian influences.

gious force in the West, the Hellenistic cosmology had already been solidified. The Greco-Egyptian Astronomer Ptolemy (c. 90 CE – 168 CE) represented the culmination of the Hellenistic cosmology. His worldview was essentially Aristotelian, and he systematized Aristotle's physics into a coherent view of the Universe. Ptolemy's Universe was a geocentric model in which there was no empty space. He adopted Aristotle's theory of the elements, as well as his theory of natural motions. Like the Greek thinkers before him, his primary purpose was to explain in theoretical terms the motions of the planets in keeping with certain preconceived notions about the order of the Universe. He adopted the Pythagorean tradition of "Harmonics," and he adhered to the notion that celestial bodies must move in circles. The Earth lies motionless in the center of Ptolemy's Universe. These ideas, outlined in Ptolemy's *Almagest*, would form the basis for medieval cosmology and would not fully be overturned until the scientific revolution.

At the same time, as Christianity became the religion of the empire, the primary concern became the Platonic salvation of the soul. Augustine was the dominant theologian of Christianity until Aquinas. Augustine's was an intensely personal theology, focused far less on the cosmos than on the individual soul. Before he became a Christian, in fact, Augustine had been a Platonist and a Manichaean, and like Plato and Mani, he had a fairly pessimistic view of the material world. Augustine wrote during difficult times, as the Roman Empire was falling, as the secular order that had stood for centuries was passing away. His concern, building on the foundation established in the Hellenistic world and adapting it to the morality and mythology of the Israelites, was to save the individual soul from the corrupted and fallen world. Original Sin, after Augustine, would be a dominant theological concept and a primary means of defining the role of the human in the cosmos.

Christian Europe retained little of the writings of classical Greece, even though many of the core assumptions they held had been introduced by the Greeks. Plato's *Timaeus* was the only text available for much of this period, and the Middle Ages were dominated then by efforts to fit it into Christian context.

But in the 12th century CE, Christian Europe was introduced to the writings of Aristotle by Muslims, who had preserved many of the classical texts and translated them into Arabic. The era called the High Middle Ages brought about a subtle shift in emphasis with Aristotelian physics, with a newfound interest in creation and the cosmos. This effort was again largely undertaken in theological terms, as Christian theology began to attempt to understand not only how the soul can leave the world but how the divine participates in the world.

The Incarnation stands out as the prototype for divine participation in the cosmos in the Christian epoch. The Hellenistic cosmology of the ancient world at the advent of Christianity promoted a strict dualism between the cosmic sphere of matter and the spiritual, transcendent realm. Christ represented the entrance of the divine into the human, in the world, bridging the gap between Creator and creation. The relationship of the first two "persons" of the Trinity was mediated by the third, the Holy Spirit—the Christian version of Anaximader's *pneuma*.

The Trinitarian theology of the orthodox Church was the answer to the more dualistic theology of the Gnostics. Although the Gnostics were thoroughly repressed, dualistic theology remained a powerful force in Christianity, particularly due to the influence of Augustine. During the high Middle Ages, however, there was a renascence of both the feminine and of the notion of creation as revelatory, thanks in part to the powerful mind of Thomas Aquinas (1225-1274).

In the twelfth and thirteenth centuries, 500 churches dedicated to the Virgin Mary were built,[15] while mystics such as Hildegard of Bingen (1098-1179) and Francis of Assisi (1181-1226) brought a creation-centered and cosmological sensibility to the Church. Aquinas, in response to these cultural forces, forged a new approach to learning, Scholasticism, which emphasized the Socratic Method, Aristotelian physics and the belief that nature, not only scripture and the words of the church fathers, was revelatory.[16] In Aquinas, Christendom had an alternative to the world-denying dualism of Augustine. Moreover, he turned away from Augustine's individualism, finding the value in the individual through participation in the ordered whole. He writes in *The Summa Contra Gentiles*: "To take away order from created beings is to take away what is best in them; the individual things are good in themselves, yet all of them together are best because of the order of the Universe. For the whole is always better than the parts, and is indeed the end to which they tend."[17]

Aquinas's influence on the West is immeasurable. Not only did he provide a way to intellectually and systematically frame the notion of divine immanence, he also set the stage for the scientific revolution. "Aquinas's insistence on the immanence of God in creation," writes Bede Griffiths, "as he understood it, in the light of Aristotle's philosophy, actually led to his condemnation after his death by the orthodox theologians of his day. But today it can be seen as a vindication of the method of modern science in the attempt to explore the mystery of the created universe."[18] His eventual condemnation is a testament to how threatening to those in power it was—and continues to be—to find God in the world, accessible to all.

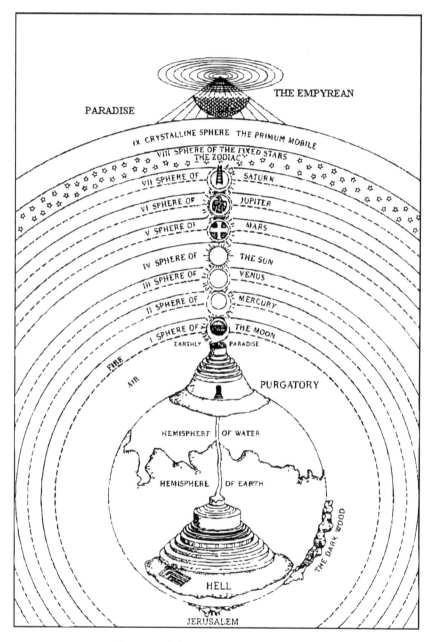

Figure 1: The Cosmology of Dante

While Aquinas provided the theological expression of the synthesis of Aristotelian physics and Christianity, another Italian, Dante Alighieri, would give this worldview its complete poetic expression in his *Commedia*. One of the first great literary works written in the vernacular since the spread of the Roman Empire, this poem describes the poet's mystical journey through the three tiers of creation, *Inferno*, *Purgatorio*, and *Paradiso*. From the Ptolemaic foundation of the cosmic spheres, Dante would synthesize Aquinas's Aristotelian approach with neo-Platonic concepts, particularly those found in the *Timaeus*. His cosmos, like those before him, consisted of series of spheres moving around a static and central Earth [see Figure 1]. These spheres had included, for medieval Europe, the seven planets and the stellar sphere or firmament. Beyond the stars is the Empyrean or divine realm. Arab astronomers added the ninth sphere, the "Primum Mobile", to account for the precession of equinoxes.[19]

From Plato, Dante inherited the notion of an ensouled cosmos in which the interiority of the soul was connected to the transcendent divine of the Empyrean. From Aristotle, Dante adopted the idea of a hierarchical order in which a divine intelligence permeates the Universe, from the divine, through the planets, and throughout creation. The Christian, Islamic and Jewish traditions of angelology were adapted to this hierarchy, with the nine orders of angels corresponding to what was now nine cosmic spheres. He parted with Augustine, who advocated a more direct link between the soul and the divine, and agreed with Muslims like Avicenna and Ibn 'Arabi in positing that we connect to the divine through an angelic cosmos, not by surpassing the Universe. Dante's was a living cosmos, and one in which every aspect, even hell, was a part of the divine hierarchy. The angels and planets move according to the divine will; the human, with free will, must make moral choices not to leave this cosmic order, but to allow for humanity to be, as a whole, more in line with the divine will.

Like other thinkers in the High Middle Ages, Dante placed a particular emphasis on the divine feminine. For Dante, divine wisdom was personified through Beatrice, a woman with whom he had been in love as a young man. Unlike many male versions of the divine feminine, this was not an abstract, disembodied deity, but a living, breathing woman.

Each aspect of Dante's journey ends with *le stelle*, the stars (see quotes at the beginning of the sections "Cosmology," "Mysticism," and "A New Myth"). His journey is one of return to the primordial unity, the unity of the divine, while embracing the multiplicity of creation. At the end of the *Commedia*, when Dante reaches the Empyrean, the hierarchy is inverted. The material periphery of the Universe is the spiritual center; the vastness of the stars is condensed into a single point of light, the divine consciousness. Later, it will become apparent how this notion of inversion can be significant in the New Cosmology.

More than a poet, Dante was a mythmaker. He was, in many ways, the last mythmaker in the West who understood that the task of the poet is to give a culture a sense of how it relates to the world. While he reinforced the established cosmologies in many ways, Dante also showed that, as a mystic and poet, he could create a world of meaning that would transform politics and theology.

The medieval world had many problems—problems that have been well documented elsewhere—but it also provides for us a model of a holistic worldview. Individuals were aware of where they fit in the cosmos. The predominant symbol for the cosmos was the womb of Mary, Queen of Heaven. Indeed, there was a feminine sensibility to this period in spite of the lack of rights for women. Matters of the soul and of the cosmos were not considered entirely separate matters. In short, a person was a part of a cohesive whole—Mary's womb—and was connected to the whole through the cosmic symbolism of the Church. The sacraments, the Church calendar, the daily rituals of the monastic life all were connected to the great cosmic harmony.

No single event can explain the shift that occurred with end of the Middle Ages. Generally, as the Middle Ages are usually assessed negatively by historians, the focus has been on the improvements in knowledge and scholarship that followed. However, there was also a more problematic aspect of this shift. The Bubonic Plague that ravished Europe shortly after Dante's great work had a devastating affect on its collective psyche. The result was a far more pessimistic view of the world, the results of which were complex. Europe eventually began to break out of its womb. But as it did, it exploited and terrorized the rest of the world. At home in Europe, the already precarious position of women and Jews worsened.[21] Europeans had to come to terms with a world that was bigger than Europe, bigger than the Church. A new cosmology was needed. This time, a new method, the scientific method, would be the conduit for this new cosmology.

THE SCIENTIFIC REVOLUTION

The scientific revolution was a particular aspect of the broad shift in worldview that occurred in the West giving rise to the current Western worldview, sometimes referred to as "Modernity." Interestingly, it was a period that began by returning to the past—the Renaissance was largely brought about by a return to the humanistic traditions of classical Greece and Rome—but it was an age that would come to be known through relentless progress. A series of "revolutions" marked this transition.

Following the Renaissance was the Protestant Reformation, which began in 1517 with Martin Luther posting his Ninety-

Five Theses criticizing the Vatican. Luther was an Augustinian monk, and his brand of Christianity, while removing some of the abuses of the institutional Church, also eliminated much of its cosmic and feminine symbolism. The Church and Mary's womb no longer provided the primary context for the community. It would be the individual, henceforth, that would be the context for emerging Protestantism in the West. "The peculiar paradox of the Reformation was its essentially ambiguous character," writes Tarnas, "for it was at once a conservative religious reaction and a radically libertarian revolution."[22]

The Protestant Reformation, in its emphasis on the literalistic reading of the Bible hastened the schism between the Church and science. The cosmology of divine immanence promoted by Scholasticism was often overshadowed by an individualistic, atomistic, and dualistic worldview that opened the door for capitalism.[23] At the same time, the political revolutions that brought about secular democracy arose in this context. So, while greater freedoms were afforded to many in the modern period, the relentless acquisitiveness and conquests of capitalism and colonialism caused increased inequities. Today's industrial civilization could not exist without capitalism or the industrial revolution which followed. While the human footprint had always impacted the Earth, industrialism allowed for exponential growth of human ecological exploitation. The industrial revolution was the way in which the new economic system applied the knowledge brought forth by the scientific revolution.

Copernicus is generally credited with the beginnings of modern scientific cosmology. His cosmology, however, was essentially Ptolemaic, with one major exception: For Copernicus, the Sun, not the Earth, lay at the center of the Universe. His heliocentric model did away with Ptolemy's epicycles, and explained the retrograde motions of the planets through the Earth's movement, undermining centuries of the Aristotelian belief that the Earth lay motionless at the center of the cosmos. But Copernicus retained many of the assumptions of Aristotelian physics, and, in fact, sought not to dismantle but to reconcile Aristotle and Ptolemy with his heliocentric model. As is so often the case, however, his system led to a series of new ideas that would ultimately go much farther than he likely imagined.

Galileo would attempt an entirely new physics that completely undermined Aristotelian physics. In spite of the common emphasis on the role of the Inquisition in his suppression, Galileo's first and primary opponents were philosophers, not the Church.[24] Perhaps his most enduring contribution was to establish a scientific method in which "objective" and quantitative measurement were the basis for any analysis. While highly effective in terms of scientific progress, the notion of objective analysis would prove to be far more than a pragmatic tool, for it would henceforth define reality in the modern cosmology.

But even as Galileo ushered in a modern physics in breaking with Aristotle, he retained the Ptolemaic spheres. Johannes Kepler, largely using Tycho Brahe's observations, introduced the idea of the elliptical orbit. This innovation allowed for a far more coherent and accurate understanding of the solar system, but also called into question the core assumptions of the West about how a harmonious Universe looks. No longer was the Earth at the center; no longer was the predominant idea of the perfect shape, the sphere, the shape of the Universe. Increasingly, the individual psyche became the locus of meaning—a development for which both Protestantism and capitalism were particularly well-suited. As Europeans began to colonize the entire globe, a cosmopolitanism that was similar to that of the Alexandrian revolution was intensified—except that, this time, it was a cosmopolitanism that rejected the cosmos.

The schism between science and Christianity was nearly complete. While Catholics were increasingly suspicious of science, Protestants generally saw the cosmos as bereft of meaning and the soul cut off, separate from the cosmos. Protestant Churches were not generally concerned with what was going on beyond the personal, the individual. In either tradition, even those who believed strongly in what would later be called the social gospel or who loved the natural world of creation would have great difficulty articulating why one should be concerned with one's neighbor, one's community, one's world, other than the philosophically dissatisfying notion that it would allow the individual soul to leave that world behind. The Protestant paradigm was largely adapted to Catholicism in the counter-reformation, leaving a highly individualistic and acosmic theology throughout the Christian West. Because science was beyond the sphere of influence of ethics, scientists were not expected to do anything other than observe the dead Universe and create as efficient and fast-growing economy as possible. Indeed, the modern human, because of the emerging cosmology, was seen primarily as an *economic* being, a consumer of a world made up not of living beings but of products. Finally, the scientific revolution was based upon objective knowledge. Paradoxically, this, along with many other factors, came with a sense of detachment and estrangement from the cosmos that has led to the modern crisis, but gave rise to the knowledge of modern science—and the potential for the wisdom of participation as opposed to objective knowledge.

The Newtonian-Cartesian Worldview

The Greek project finally found its full expression in the philosophy of Plato and the Ptolemaic/Aristotelian Cosmology. The Medieval worldview found its full expression in the theological synthesis of the Greeks with Christianity and in Dante's poetic expression of that synthesis. The exponents of new cosmologies live at the margins. The cultural world they inhabit seldom resembles the worldviews they birth. Often, it takes great lengths of time before a new paradigm can be fully woven into the fabric of a culture. It is important to recall that those with the most revolutionary ideas often still lived largely according to the old worldview. Modernity—the paradigm according to which we are currently living, for the most part—is no different. There is always a tipping point, a moment at which new ideas give birth to a new culture. The Newtonian-Cartesian worldview represents the fullness of the modern era, the expression of the modern cosmology that became more than thoughts thought by scientists and philosophers, but assumptions lived out by peasants and people on the streets.

In addition to the various revolutions mentioned above, the philosophical revolution synthesized these shifts into ideas that would define modernity. Central to this movement was the French philosopher Rene Descartes. Descartes understood the Universe not as an organism, but as a machine. God's relationship to creation was therefore one of an architect or—perhaps more appropriate now—an engineer. A strict dualism emerged in the West at this point, to an extreme never before recorded. Individual human self-awareness—expressed in Descartes famous dictum, "*Cogito, ergo sum*"—was the primary basis for all knowledge. He separated *res cogitans*—that which the human perceives within—as entirely separate from *res extensa*—the phenomenal world. In the West after Descartes, the human mind was seen as separate from the world.

Isaac Newton managed to synthesize the mechanistic philosophy of Descartes with Kepler and Galileo's laws.[25] While his own spiritual inclinations led him to see his work as undermining Cartesian relativism, Newton drew extensively from a Cartesian foundation. It was easier now to create a worldview that entirely separated religious belief from science. Newton was far from an atheist, but his mind, like all truly modern minds, had begun to separate matters of the spirit and matters of the cosmos. While he saw the presence of God in his cosmology, it was a God that was moving further and further from the chaotic world of nature. The divine had set the Universe in motion and watched as it unfolded according to a rigid set of laws.

Newton's Universe was outlined in the *Principia*, first published in 1687.[26] He described a Universe that was infinite and governed by mechanistic laws. His theological leaning toward the Arian heresy—which denied the Trinity—tended toward a rationalist, deist worldview shared by many of the "founding fathers" of the United States. The philosophical movement known as the Enlightenment, which ascribes to the Newtonian-Cartesian worldview, was the tradition out of which many of those "founding fathers" emerged. This was a wholly individualistic worldview, giving rise to modern capitalism, the idea of 'race,' and the myth of progress referred to in the first chapter.

As with any cosmology, the implications of the current Western worldview go far beyond the realm of science. The modern human being—regardless of one's knowledge of Descartes, Newton, or the Enlightenment—fully accepts the notion of an atomistic Universe in which particles are governed by mechanistic laws. Humans too are considered atomistically, in keeping with the extreme individualism of Protestantism. Human consciousness is alone and isolated in the Universe, our souls the realm of personal religious pursuits if not utter meaninglessness. The phenomenal world has little to do with spirit. Indeed, by the time the United States was born, the disenchantment was nearly complete. The West was ready to conquer a world of dead resources and strange races. However, as is so often the case, the very knowledge that gave rise to this destruction would open the door for the possibility for an entirely new—and at the same time very old—wisdom.

MODERN SCIENCE

While much has been made of the modern schism between religion and science, the schism between psyche and cosmos perhaps describes modernity more clearly. With Freud, systematic language was employed to understand the workings of the psyche. Even the soul did not require religious language, allowing for a comprehensive secularism. But regardless of where the modern person stands in regard to the science/religion debate, the basic assumptions of the isolated psyche, posited by Descartes and developed by Freud, are retained. That is to say, neither religion nor science generally includes the psyche in discussions of the cosmos. We have, thanks largely to Freud's brilliance, a far greater capacity to understand the way the human psyche works; but at the same time, we are no better at relieving its despair. For modern psychology has been built upon a dualistic foundation, an assumption that the human is separate from the cosmos and fundamentally alone. But from the ashes of Modernity has come the possibility of a new cosmology, leading us, potentially, to rediscover our place in a more interconnected and—if we are able to make it so—more meaningful world.

Although the story I have relayed so far has been primarily one of those who looked out at the stars or deeply into the soul, a cosmology, as all indigenous peoples know, is incomplete without addressing the living community. Most Western thinkers, however, have historically ignored the community of life in assessing the place of the human in the cosmos. With Darwin's *The Origin of Species*, first published in 1859, this all changed.[27] Just as Freud's work was made possible by the Cartesian framework, Darwin's work was largely possible due to the Newtonian cosmology. The notion that there were natural laws that were obeyed invariably was applied to living beings, whereas before the fundamental assumptions about plants and animals had been that they were created by God in a hierarchical manner. Moreover, the emphasis on evolution in terms of human history advocated by Vico, Hegel, and Marx opened the philosophical door for such thinking.

The implications of Darwinian evolution are immense, and cannot be left out of any modern cosmology. In the modern discourse—both religious fundamentalists and scientists are guilty here—it has been assumed that because random muta-tion is a part of the process, evolution is therefore meaningless. It is possible, however, that simply because evolution does not promise the *same* meaning as traditional religion does not make it meaningless. It is our task to ascertain what it means; no side in the debate has done very well so far in this pursuit because few have really tried.[28]

While it is in fact true that random mutation plays a role in evolution, it is also true that natural selection is just as important. Without the choices made by the participants in the process, evolution could not occur; without the chaotic nature of random mutation, life would be far more static, less interesting. Moreover, evolution coupled with genetics has shown us that we all have a common ancestor. There is no hierarchy with neo-Darwinism; rather, life evolves and diversifies as a single whole in which each species is equally evolved. We are connected through a shared past. This filial connection can be extended to all of life. Every living being on the planet shares some genetic link. While this is easy enough to understand intellectually, it is a difficult leap to embody it in a lived cosmology. Finally, evolution undermines Cartesian dualism in showing that the human mind emerges in the natural process. While many have felt threatened by the notion of consciousness as an emergent property, this is due to the extent to which they have failed to recognize evolutionary processes as sacred in themselves. Human consciousness is an expression of a wisdom that is inherent in the processes of the Earth, rather than deposited into the human from beyond. We are sacred because of our kinship to all life.

Darwin's work, while it shook the world tremendously, still took place in the context of a Newtonian cosmology, whereas the work of Albert Einstein would radically extend Newtonian science. Like Copernicus, Einstein can be properly placed at the end of the old worldview more than the beginning of the next. Einstein's greatest contributions were two ideas that would usher in the new era in astrophysics: the connection between matter and energy and between space and time. Einstein's famous equation $e=mc^2$ describes the relationship between matter and energy. Previously considered distinct entities, Einstein showed that small amounts of matter were equivalent to tremendous amounts of energy. Whereas in the Newtonian cosmos time was separate from space, Einstein linked space and time in what is known as the space-time continuum. That is, the Universe can only be properly understood in terms of space and time together, unlike the Newtonian Universe wherein time becomes an abstraction, moving through static space. The Universe, therefore, is not created *in* space, but is an event, a process in which time and space emerge together. Nothing has a simple spatial location in such a Universe, nothing is truly static. When one looks out at the stars, one is looking into the past, at light that has been traveling for ages.

For all his genius, what Einstein could not see, however—because he was still largely living in a Newtonian world—was that the implications of some of his work showed that we are living in an expanding Universe. Einstein even famously adjusted his equation—adding something he called the "cosmological constant"—to retain the appearance of a static Universe even when the mathematics seemed to show this expansion. The astronomer Edwin Hubble's observation of "red-shifting" galaxies—that is, light waves that had shifted to show that they were receding—finally convinced Einstein, and the world, the Universe was indeed expanding. Observations have further shown that, just as life has evolved from a single ancestor, all the Universe has emerged from a single point.

Although Einstein ultimately came around to reject the static Newtonian Universe, he never could come to terms with the implications of quantum physics. Indeed, few of us have. While anything close to a comprehensive explanation of quantum physics is beyond the scope of this work, I will highlight some of the key aspects as they relate to the emergent worldview. Whereas Einstein's laws of relativity reflect the large scale behavior of the Universe, quantum theory relates to the extremely small. In fact, evidence points to the notion that there are a different set of laws determining the small scale behavior of the Universe. Quantum theory describes a world not of fixed particles, but one that, at its most fundamental level, consists of probability waves. Moreover, the Universe appears to be, at the quantum level, non-local, which has presented a "serious problem to Einstein's theory of relativity, thus shaking the foundation of modern physics."[29] While quantum theory seems not to change the behavior of the Universe either at large scales or at the human scale, it seems likely to have had a far greater impact on the early Universe, when the entire Universe was small enough to act according to quantum theory. The large-scale structure of the Universe today, therefore, has arisen due to quantum fluctuations of the early Universe.

All of these discoveries and theories have led modern science to arrive at vision of the cosmos quite different from that on which the Newtonian-Cartesian was based. It is a vision of the Universe that is a single whole, creating itself moment by moment. This notion of cosmo-genesis, that creation did not occur in the remote past but is happening constantly, repeatedly, presents us with a new way of looking at our selves. We do not look at creation from the outside, nor does the divine look at us from the outside, but as a seamless whole in which all participate. It is impossible, therefore, to entirely separate the observer and the observed, because we—even those who study the Universe— are of the Universe.

There is, however, no myth in our culture of these discoveries, no worldview based upon these ideas. Knowing a set of facts about the world is far different from living one's life according to that information. While scientists, because the nature of the scientific method has been to accept that which is verifiable through observation, have recognized these insights, our cultural institutions have not. Because of the very nature of the worldview upon which it has been founded—that of the alienated individual Cartesian ego in static and meaningless space—the West has continued to adhere to the Newtonian-Cartesian assumptions about reality even as our science dismantles them.

So, what is the worldview in which we are living today? Clearly, most of us have not adopted and internalized the New Cosmology. Our religious institutions certainly have not. But why is this important? Why should they? The New Cosmology, like any other cosmology, is surely imperfect. Many of the assumptions it holds will one day be extended by more rigorous, profound, and comprehensive knowledge. What matters in the development of a worldview, however, is not simply accuracy but coherence and functionality. We are living according to a worldview that does not facilitate a coherent relationship between the individuals of our society and the cosmos as a whole. Our worldview is not problematic due only to its inaccuracy, but because it is incomplete. We have failed to turn the discoveries of modern science into a functional cosmology because we have not lived it embodied it, and given creative expression to it. Since Dante, we have been waiting for a song of the cosmos to help us rediscover our place in the world. This is not an issue of understanding facts, but of participation in a new myth. It is a problem of *mythos*, not *logos*.

Our current worldview has little to do with the modern science. Because of the fragmentation of the Newtonian-Cartesian worldview, it has endured even in the face of scientific evidence— evidence discovered through a method entirely embedded in that very worldview—that refutes many of its assumptions. Because we have built up such a strong sense of the ego's isolation, it continues to reify, even when evidence points to a self that is far less static than we had once thought.

There is surely a great deal of wisdom in the Western traditions. This study seeks not to reject the West, but to derive what wisdom we can from these traditions and to see what we improve upon. From the Celts to modernity, there is indeed much wisdom to be derived. Each phase of the story gave us brilliant insights as well as unfortunate losses: the Greeks gave us the insight into the great mystery of the soul and the stars—the union of opposites—while at the same time advocating an extremely dualistic and individualistic approach; the Middle Ages provided the best example of a coherent worldview in the West, but remained mired in a dualistic and judgmental theology; the modern period allowed for unparalleled individual rights while injustices and exploitation continued to occur throughout the world, and the individual became isolated and alienated as never before. The Western tradition ought not to be rejected completely nor embraced unquestioningly; rather, what is most important, especially for those of us mired in it—of course, in the wake of colonialism and globalization, who is not?—is to understand it. It is possible, however, that the challenges of this moment are too vast to be answered within the narrow parameters of the West.

Chapter Six
Cosmology in the Wisdom Traditions

THE WEST IS NO LONGER simply the West. From where I write, I can hear languages from all around the Pacific Rim and Spanish dialects from various countries and cultures through my window. There are Buddhist Temples, Taoist Centers, Tongan Churches, Mosques, Spanish Catholic churches, and African American Protestant churches all within walking distance. The story of the West is no longer the story shared by a huge number of the inhabitants of Western nations, particularly in America. *And what a gift this is.* The colonialism—both militaristic and economic—that has marked the modern era has opened the door for the birth of a worldview that draws from the wisdom of many different cultural traditions. But this is a challenge as well. Every culture brings a variety of assumptions about reality, assumptions that are so deeply held that there are usually unspoken. If we are to understand one another, learning a new language is only a start and learning about a religion only an intellectual exercise. We must learn to inhabit a new cosmos.

One often gets the impression that the formation of the Western worldview was a process of improvement. While it is certainly true that we have a more accurate vision of some aspects of our Universe, it is not true that the worldview of the West is an improvement in every way. Newtonian physics was quite accurate when we were concerned only with our own Solar System. The primordial cosmology was accurate in terms of the ecosystem in which the Neolithic people were embedded. We have not improved, but have sought to understand a larger Universe. In this process, the West has improved by some standards and regressed by others. Moreover, the purpose of a cosmology, it must be remembered, is meaning, not accuracy.

To re-imagine our worldview requires not only a critical look at Western cosmology, but also a look at the cosmologies that form the foundation of the world's wisdom traditions. This chapter will review the cosmologies of many of those traditions—aside from Christianity, which developed in the context of the previous chapter's cosmologies—in order to serve two purposes: first, such an exploration can give us an idea of how other cultures understand the world in order to challenge some of our current assumptions; and, second, if we hope to understand how the mystics of the wisdom traditions actually understood their participation in the Universe, it is essential that we also understand their cosmologies. With this knowledge, we will possess the capacity to both challenge the modern cosmology and to approach the mystics to learn how we might create a new worldview.

Submerged Cosmologies

In chapter 5, I mentioned "submerged beliefs" or "heresies," the remnants of earlier worldviews that remain alive among the marginalized of any society. Along with these beliefs are aspects of earlier cosmologies. The West has not completely eradicated older cosmologies; rather, those cosmologies have been co-opted and adapted to fit the dominant paradigm. The cosmologies of the oppressed remain particularly vibrant at the margins of a society. Indeed, there is a particular wisdom—a wisdom that has a special place in the New Cosmology—at the margins, among the oppressed, women, and "dark others."[1]

As most of the world has embraced the patriarchal paradigm, women have been marginalized in most societies. Indeed, the history of the West has been dominated by the progressive marginalization of the feminine. This process has not only led to oppression of women, but also to the 'othering' of the darker skinned peoples of the world and to the current ecological crisis. As Tarnas suggests, the feminine has been marginalized both in societies and within the psyche of the individual.[2] This process can be understood through the theological and cosmological assumptions held in modernity and can be traced through the beginnings of those beliefs with the advent of patriarchy. It is an unfortunate consequence of mental colonization that, often, liberation movements have failed to challenge the dominant worldview, opposing their oppressors but failing to undermine the core assumptions of their society.[3]

The notion that the Universe is a living, chaotic process has been extremely threatening to those in power. Part of what has characterized the study of cosmology in the West has been a way of giving a hierarchy, an order, a structure to the Universe so it can be controlled. There is an unspoken fear of the feminine power of generativity, and the uncontrollable and unpredictable aspects of the Universe. We have paved over much of the world trying to control it, and the results have been disastrous.

It should be noted here that none of these ideas is 'mine' or completely new; they have existed in the divine wisdom of the cosmos and have continued to live through matriarchal societies and the subaltern cultures within patriarchy. I encounter them not only through research, but also through the memories I encounter in myself. "All humans," writes Lucia Birnbaum, "carry the memory (often unconscious) of the dark mother and her values."[4] For Birnbaum, this describes the primordial wisdom tradition of the dark mother goddess in Africa. My work is at once a process of remembrance and creativity—creative because the perspective I bring to the issue is unique. So, while my ideas are not new, I present them from a unique perspective in a unique way.

Any discussion of a return to a feminine theology must include cosmology because a feminine theology is one of immanence, of the divine not merely intervening but being embedded in the cosmos. Such a principle can help us overcome the dualism of spirit and matter that has dominated the West and has decimated the planet.

Primary examples are found in the ruins of Isis temples throughout the Mediterranean and the Black Madonnas all over Europe, which represent the continued presence of the dark mother in an oppressive, patriarchal context. Isis provided the alternative to the imperial religion of Rome that required the worship of the emperor;[5] the Black Madonna allows the dark mother to be worshipped in what was predominantly a world of white Jesuses.

While Europe's Christianization required it to veil the old gods—including the gods of Celts mentioned in the previous chapter—in a Christian guise, the Africans upon whom Christianity was forced saw immediately that the Christian saints and liturgical calendar was not fundamentally different from their own African beliefs. Particularly in Catholic countries, African slaves continued their forbidden religious practices by associating Catholic saints with the *Orishas* of the West African Yoruba tradition. Traditions such as Haitian *Vodoun*, Brazilian *Candomble*, and Cuban *Santeria* kept much of the wisdom of Africa alive in the New World. When I was in Salvador da Bahia, Brazil, at the festival of the *Lavagem do Bonfim*, I watched Catholic priests and Yoruba priestesses march through the streets together. Most Brazilians in that region, as is typical of a matriarchal or pagan perspective, practice a combination of Catholicism and Yoruba religion. The syncretism of *Candomble*, *Vodoun* and *Santeria* were not merely acts of creative genius on the part of the African slaves. Surely they were. But they also saw something that the Europeans could not: in spite of the centuries of suppression, the immanent, feminine divinity remained present in European religion, hidden and submerged.

African Cosmology

The Yoruba religion is typical of African beliefs in that there is a transcendent supreme being, *Olodumare*, and a pantheon of beings who are the primary loci of worship and praxis. The *Orishas*, although often translated as "gods," are more accurately described as forces of nature. The divine, present throughout the natural world, expresses itself in various forms in creation. This is closer to Dante's Angelogy, in which the heavenly spheres mediate between the human and the divine, than to the Augustinian theology in which the soul and the divine are directly linked and exclude the natural world. For this reason, Yoruba religion was more easily adapted to Catholicism than to Protestantism, which tends to be more Augustinian. These divine presences, of course, can also be found in the human psyche which is not entirely distinct from nature.

Interestingly, quintessentially African beliefs are more common in Salvador da Bahia than in many parts of Africa. While

I worked for a development aid organization in Zimbabwe, the 'liberal' foreign aid workers frequently spoke disparagingly of the indigenous Shona beliefs. They were understood as an obstacle to development. As one African scholar puts it, Western attitudes about non-Western communities have colored the very concept of development in Africa:

> Underlying jaundiced perceptions are clashing world-views that are informing the definition of development. Western economic perspectives define development in aggregative terms—gross national product, gross domestic product, and the like. Continuing colonial ideas, these perspectives purport to measure socio-economic progress. Modernization theory has merely articulated more precisely the old idea of progress through successive stages of economic growth. These views separate economic growth from religion. Indeed, *it was hoped that religion and ethnicity would disappear.* [Italics mine][6]

The reader will recognize many of the core myths and cosmological assumptions in Western attitudes toward Africa. The notion of progress has a particularly poignant significance in relation to Africa, for Western paleontologists now acknowledge universally that our common roots are in Africa. The desire for progress, therefore, requires us to consider African worldviews inferior. It should be pointed out that this attitude is the same on both ends of the political spectrum.

The African worldview is a far more holistic one than in the modern West. As a consequence, the primacy of an abstract economy, separate from ecology and spirituality, is foreign. As with religion, traditional African economics are communal, because the human is understood primarily in the context of the community, not as a radically isolated individual. This is described by the proverb *umuntu ngumuntu ngabantu*—"a person is a person through persons."[7] The Akan people of Ghana consider the individual to be made up of three elements: the *okra*, which is the innermost self, and connected to the supreme being—notice the link between interiority and immensity; the *sunsum*, which is something like the shared spirit of humanity—our identity as community; and the *homam*, or physical body, which is linked to, not isolated from, the others. For the Akan, the divine relates organically to humanity as a parent.[8] Leopold Senghor's philosophy of Negritude describes the individual as being part of a universal living force that renders the cosmos at once infinitely small and infinitely large.[9]

Traditional African notions of time differ dramatically from the modern West. Most striking to the Western traveler in rural Africa is the lack of abstract time. The aid organization for which I worked, which was run by northern Europeans, attempted to schedule literacy lessons according to a strict schedule in spite of the fact that no one in the area had a clock or a watch. Time and events were not separated, so the notion of being late to a meeting made no sense. A "1:00" meeting, something that is planned to occur in the abstract future, simply does not exist until it actually happens. An event happens when we make it happen—in this case, when the women in our classes had cared for their children, fetched the water, cooked the food, and tended their fields. In many African cultures, the same word is used for both space and time.[10] The only clocks that existed in the area of the bush I lived in were brought by Westerners. It was not, as many frustrated aid workers believed, that the culture encouraged laziness or an inability to comprehend, but that the abstract future of plans and appointments was simply not a part of the cosmology.

The influential African scholar, philosopher, theologian John S. Mbiti refers to the two kinds of time in African cultures with the Swahili words *Sasa* and *Zamani*.[11] The latter is derived from the word used in Islamic cosmology for time, *Zaman*,[12] and refers to macro- or deep-time, whereas *Sasa* is normal time, or micro-time. Although it appears to refer primarily to the past, especially the distant past of the ancestors, *Zamani* time contains within it a past, present and future. When events have been actualized in *Sasa* time, they move into *Zamani* time. In most African cosmologies, the unfixed future is of little significance. Worldviews that place the apocalyptic moment at a fixed point in the future are extremely difficult to reconcile with such a perspective.

African wisdom lies in a place of particular importance for *Homo sapiens* because it is the place of the human's emergence. We all come from Africa; our species has been shaped by the particular conditions we encountered there and any wisdom that the human can express is, at least in part, shaped by the African context. Modernity's rejection of African wisdom is a reflection of our desire to forget our roots, our failure to remember who we are. Moreover, we shall see later that African cosmology is in many ways more closely related to the New Cosmology than the modern worldview.

CHINESE COSMOLOGY:
THE TAOIST/CONFUCIAN WORLDVIEW

The term "Far East" describes a cultural reality as much as it does a geographic one. Of the world's great civilizations, none is more different—I speak entirely from my own subjective experience here—from the West than that of China. Many of the challenges to the Western traveler in China are superficial, such as the surprise with which one is confronted at being a foreigner, but more radical are the fundamental assumptions made by that culture about the world.

Unlike in the West, the Chinese have traditionally not chosen a single religion while excluding all others. The lines between the wisdom traditions tend to be blurry. Most Chinese have traditionally adhered to some combination of Taoism, Confucianism and Buddhism. Buddhism was brought to China from the Indian subcontinent, and therefore was adapted to the Chinese worldview, just as Maoism was the particular Chinese adaptation of Marxist dialectical materialism. Taoism and Confucianism, however, are indigenous to China and form the basis for Chinese cosmology. Like many of the world's wisdom traditions, these arose during the axial period as an extension of the indigenous traditions of China.

The differences between Chinese and Western cosmologies are glaring. While Western observers of the stars from the Greeks onward have had specific expectations about how their observations should conform to certain abstract ideas, the Chinese have had fewer fixed, preconceived notions about the Universe. An infinite Universe was posited very early on in China, whereas Giordano Bruno was burned at the stake in part for such a suggestion in 1600 of the Common Era. The flexibility of Chinese cosmology enabled early Chinese astronomers to observe supernovae—most notably in 1054 CE—that were virtually ignored in the West where Aristotelian cosmology did not allow for such changes. In China, change and flux was considered the normal state.

The Tao is the most fundamental of all concepts in Chinese cosmology. The Universe is permeated with the Tao. The reader will recognize clearly the similarity between the *logos* and "becoming" of Heraclitus and Taoist cosmology. Tao literally means "way" but is more accurately described as the "inexpressible ultimate principle"[13] of the Universe, the identity at the core of both the human and of the world. One of many descriptions by Lao Tzu, from Chapter twenty-five:

> There was something formed in chaos;
> It existed before heaven and earth.
> Still and solitary,
> It alone stands without change.
> It is all-pervasive without being exhausted.
> It may be the mother of the world.
> I do not know its name, but name it the Way.[14]

The Tao is at once pre-existent to creation and permeating everything in the world. Because its very nature is change, it is paradoxically constant in spite of the fluctuating and changing of yin and yang and the elements. The Tao, therefore, is present in each of us in the form of potentiality. Each moment, in this view, is a chaotic matrix of creation and possibility.

The central framework for Chinese cosmology is what Confucian scholar Tu Weiming calls "the anthropocosmic vision."[15] In the Chinese view, the human forms part of an organic triad consisting of Heaven, Earth and Humanity. The human lies at the center of Heaven and Earth and is, by definition, a spiritual being.[16] It is noteworthy that the triad through which, for the Confucian, the human is spiritual mirrors the three-fold radical discontinuity of modernity. By isolating the human from Heaven (or the divine) and Earth (or the cosmos) Western spirituality is diminished. In the Chinese view, human spirituality means responsibility for cosmic harmony, both through interior processes and external action. Chou Tun-I (1017-1073 CE) describes this through his synthesis of the Taoist *t'ai-chi* diagram [see Figure 2, overleaf]—commonly called the 'yin-yang' diagram in the West, the *t'ai-chi* literally means "Great Ultimate"[17] and refers to the integration of yin and yang—and Confucian cosmology:

> When the reality of the Ultimate of Non-being and the essence of yin, yang, and the Five Phases come into mysterious union, integration ensues. *Ch'ien* (Heaven) constitutes the male element, and *k'un* (Earth) constitutes the female element. The interaction of these two vital forces engenders and transforms the myriad things. The myriad things produce and reproduce, resulting in unending transformation.[18]

In Chinese cosmology, the human is defined in terms of relationship and constant flux, rather than the radically isolated individual. Indeed, for the Chinese, the human does not even have a single soul. The notion that the body is somehow separate from the soul is foreign to Chinese cosmology. Moreover, the body is viewed as a microcosm: The conditions and fluctuations of the cosmos as a whole are found in the individual body; the cosmos, like the body, is viewed as a single organism. "The great man [sic] regards Heaven, Earth and the Myriad things as one body," writes Wang Yang-ming (1472-1529 CE).[19] These concepts are fundamental to Taoist mystical practice.

Chinese cosmogony begins with *Wu-chi*, primordial emptiness, and moves into the undifferentiated state of the *t'ai chi*. The process of creation arises out of differentiated—but never completely separate—yin and yang, Earth and Heaven energy. Any understanding of Chinese religion and cosmology requires a thorough understanding of the concepts of yin and yang. They are both cosmic—Earth and Heaven—and interior. The balance of these principles within the human is seen to parallel the harmony of nature. The relationship between yin and yang is non-dual rather than oppositional. Taoist philosophy here gives one of the most eloquent examples of the coincidence of opposites. We live in a Universe in constant flux. Although we often attempt to grasp at absolutes, the true reality in the Chinese worldview is the constantly changing interplay of yin and yang, and the unity in the diversity of creation. The universal energy through which this interplay occurs is called *ch'i*. At once spiritual and physical, *ch'i* permeates everything, so there is no void.

In the *I Ching*, "The Book of Change," the principles of yin and yang are represented by lines—solid lines for yang and broken lines for yin—which are combined in threes to form the *bagua*, or "eight trigrams" [see Figure 2]. These symbols are somewhat less abstract, representing natural forces. The *I Ching* then consists of sixty-four hexagrams which make up the various "patterns of the...universe...according to their specific laws of change in an organic whole."[20]

Figure 2: The Bagua and the Tai Chi Diagram

While the Tao is far less gendered than notions of God tend to be, it also has a decidedly feminine flavor. The emptiness of the primordial *Wu-Chi* is rediscovered in each of us with the cessation of egoistic attachment in what is sometimes referred to as the "Mysterious Female."[22] This is our internal center, our womb of potentiality and becoming—less a spacial center than the deepest aspect of the self. At this center—our womb—there is unlimited space and time. It is the center of both the Self and the cosmos. Taoist practice, which will be addressed in further detail in chapter 9, places a great deal of emphasis on the notion of reversal and return. It is to this primordial state of emptiness to which we return.

In the Confucian view, as in most worldviews, ethics and morality are integral to cosmology. Just as all the cosmos is connected through *ch'i*, everything is also connected through the principle of filial piety or *ko*. While this notion is generally understood to apply primarily to one's relationships to other humans, it can be extended to the whole of the cosmos. Japanese neo-Confucian Kaibara Ekken explains: "All [people] may be said to owe their birth to their parents but a further inquiry into their origins reveals that [people] came into being because of nature's law of life. Thus all [people] in the world are children born of heaven and earth, and heaven and earth are parents of us all."[23] For Ekken, the *tai ch'i* was the spark of all life, and human beings and nature all arose through it. The principle of *jen*, or "humaneness," could therefore be extended to all people and all of nature because we are all connected through a filial relationship. The ethics and morality of the neo-Confucian worldview, therefore, give rise to the compassion one has for one's kin extending to all.

I have excluded Buddhist influences on Chinese cosmologies because Buddhism comes from the Indian Subcontinent, and its view of the Universe comes from an Indian foundation. However, it should be noted that Mahayana Buddhism is largely a synthesis of Buddhist practice and Chinese cosmology. Later, when the discussion shifts to mysticism, we will approach Buddhism from a Far Eastern perspective. For now, it is important to establish the core cosmologies of the cultures in which these great traditions arose.

SOUTH ASIAN COSMOLOGY:
THE FOUNDATIONS OF BUDDHIST AND HINDU WISDOM

Any traveler to India will immediately notice the lack of rigid boundaries in South Asian culture by simply walking the streets. The smell of cow dung and incense and curry and garbage assaults one's sense of smell. People bathe and defecate in the streets; rich and poor are found in close proximity and with unparalleled extremes. It is a place where people bathe and urinate in the River Ganga; the same river where, in Varanasi, dead bodies are placed to ensure their liberation; the same river where little candles are placed in Haridwar to represent people's wishes. I was told by a Sadhu in Rishikesh that "God is everywhere, God is Ganga"—he then asked me for money for medicine because he was sick from drinking from the river.

Two central ideas permeate all the South Asian traditions. First, in the South Asian worldview, the natural and moral order are connected and expressed through the concept of *karma*. Literally meaning "action," *karma* refers to the way that the cosmos is created and re-created through actions. Furthermore, our moral choices have an effect; that is, what we do gives rise to a corresponding consequence. Although there are many theistic South Asian traditions, this notion lends itself to a sense of an internal ordering principle rather than the theistic notion of design, particularly with Buddhism.

Second, the South Asian worldview emphasizes the primacy of consciousness. Whereas modern science generally reduces consciousness to something emergent in the human, South Asian cosmology has always emphasizes that, ontologically, the Universe consists primarily of consciousness. This concept will become important as the discussion shifts to cosmosophy, for, although the English word "consciousness" presents some problems in that it is used in many different ways, the South Asian worldview is informative in the way it conceives of an already-present *wisdom* in the cosmos. Indeed, my use of the word wisdom would be a far better translation of the Sanskrit *chit*, the word generally translated as "consciousness."

The cosmology of South Asia gave rise to two major wisdom traditions, Buddhism and Hinduism, and several other smaller traditions. This cosmology begins with a vision of the Universe not too different from the archaic cosmology. *Mt. Meru* or *Sumeru* is the center of the world, connecting upper and lower worlds. The world itself originally consisted of four elements in some South Asian systems, while a fifth element, *akasa*, similar to Aristotle's ether, representing space, was added later.

The Indian notion of time differs markedly from the West. There are two terms for time in Indian thought: *mahakala*, which refers to absolute time; *vyavaharika*, or relative time. There is an enduring sense of the vastness of time in these traditions. And while it is true that they have a cyclic element in the various *yugas*, or epochs, the Universe is not strictly conceived as a repeating cycle. There are elements of novelty even in the repetition. In general, there is a pattern of descent from a golden age in the past to the corrupt present in which we await a return.

Of the many philosophical traditions in South Asia, *Samhkya* philosophy, because of its later influence on the *Bhagavad Gita* and its contrast to the non-dual (*advaita*) traditions, bears mentioning. *Samhkya* philosophy understands the Universe dualistically, through the constant interplay of *purusha*, the timeless, the unchanging; and *prakriti*, the constant flux of nature. Later,

111

the *Gita*, written during the first five centuries preceding the common era, will attempt to reconcile the duality of *Samkhya* philosophy with the non-dual traditions, and the *purusha* will be understood internally.

Seldom do religions come to us at a specific moment in a neat little package. This is particularly true of Hinduism. What we now refer to as "Hinduism" is actually a modern term describing the fusion of the beliefs of the indigenous peoples of the Indian subcontinent and the Aryan peoples who came to India from central Asia, and the subsequent transformation and diversification of those beliefs over several millennia.

The earliest expression of this syncretism is found in the *Vedas*, the oldest of the Sanskrit texts, probably coming from an oral tradition, describing the ritual praxis of the Aryan dominated culture that emerged on the Indian subcontinent. While this culture clearly established a hierarchy in which the patriarchal Aryan worldview was dominant, it also integrated many of the more feminine and Earth-based perspectives of indigenous Indians. The Vedic period focused primarily on ritual as a means to restoring cosmic harmony. The idea of *rta*, or "order" was primary in the *Vedas*.

In one cosmogonical story from the *Rig Veda*, the origin of the Universe is described as the ritual dismemberment—sacrifice—of the *Purusha*. This is undoubtedly related to the common shamanic motif of ritual dismemberment. There is a similar story in Egypt, for example, describing the dismemberment of Osiris. Sacrifice, therefore, in the Vedic context, is an act of remembering. That is, remembering that we are not the fragmented, separate beings we believe ourselves to be, but are actually a part of the cosmic whole. To sacrifice, as in many other cultures, is a means of restoring cosmic harmony.

The Vedic chant of the seven cosmic spheres exemplifies this process. In this practice, there are seven sounds corresponding to seven spheres, beginning with the Earth (*bhur*) and culminating with the transcendent realm of Truth and Being (*satyam*). Like contemporary Western cosmologists, the ancients intuitively recognized that to look deep into the heavens was to see our common, divine heritage. At the same time, such a chant was not a rejection of the Earth, but a balancing of the Earth and the heavens.

Later, chants were developed that focused on the *chakras*, the seven spheres within the human. This was also not necessarily a rejection of the world, but the recognition that each individual is a microcosm. The external *tapas* of the Vedic fire sacrifice was transformed into the internal *tapas* of yoga. This was made possible primarily by the shift in consciousness that occurred in the *Upanisads*, the Vedantic period that followed the Vedic. A further discussion of the mystical yogic traditions will be found in chapter 9.

Buddhist cosmology, which also comes out of the Vedic context of India, quickly took a somewhat divergent path. In Buddhist philosophy, the Universe consists of *loka-dhatu* (the physical Universe) and *damma-dhatu* (that which arises in the mind). Both come into existence through *karma*. Buddhist cosmogony begins with the notion of "primal purity". There is an inherent value in existence in this understanding. The foundation of the Universe is "Being" (Tibetan *gzhi*), a term similar to the German *"grund"* used by later Christian theologians, meaning the ground of being, reason, or cause of everything else. Being is reality—everything else is not necessarily illusory, but it *is* derivative. And because all is derived from Being, we are all intimately linked. There is no ontological dualism, no distinction between various aspects of the cosmos, because everything has co-arisen.

In Buddhist terms, the evolutionary process occurs through *paticca samuppada*, or "dependent co-arising."[24] The illness and the cure give birth to one another. That is, cosmic processes are such that for every problem there is a corresponding solution. Moreover, matter and consciousness are interconnected in this view, not hierarchically arranged. "The doctrine of dependent co-arising permits no polarization of consciousness and nature," writes Joanna Macy. "Matter, seen as co-emergent with mind, is neither temptress nor trap."[25] Buddhism, therefore, teaches that the world is not something to escape, but something to transform.[26] In this view, it is the human's task to engage the world with compassion—to "suffer with"—because we are intimately interconnected.

Consequently, the ethos of compassion is central to Buddhism. Compassion is less about how we feel about others than how we identify our selves. An unlimited, expansive self is *naturally* compassionate, whereas the altruism of the Cartesian self requires a great deal of work. But there is a middle path between the annihilation of the self and its concretization. Unlike in the dominant understanding of "mind" in the West the Buddhist concept of *citta* is inseparable from cosmos. In fact, the cosmos itself could be viewed as arising and evolving due to *citta*. This is quite different from the "create your own reality" view, which takes Cartesian notion of the isolated and ontologically alienated mind as primary and therefore sees the phenomenal world as mere projection. In Buddhism, one must awaken to the notion that such dualities are ultimately illusory, and provide the foundation for *duhkkha*, which is commonly translated as "suffering" but, in a cosmological sense, connotes a constriction of space, a limitation of time.

The Buddhist traditions point to the tendency to think of the self as fixed and immutable. Around this notion, while apparently liberating for those who fear the idea of constant change and flux, is the constriction and limitation of the self. *Anatman*—"no self"—does not mean that we don't exist; rather, we are a constantly changing and transforming aspect of the cosmic whole. In part, our avoidance of pain is based on our sense of limitation. Suffering is impermanent according to the Buddhist view. Its very nature is temporal. But our fear is that we will somehow run out of time, that our reified self will somehow cease to exist, or that we won't have enough, causing us to run from pain and suffering. The ethical value of presence to pain is central to Buddhism because it allows us to remove the barriers between another's experience and our own. Indeed, it allows us to cease to think of experiences as "ours" at all.

The self, in its having the attribute of *shunyata* or "emptiness," is no different from any other aspect of the Universe. If we attempt to pin down the core identity of any thing in the cosmos, we are forced to realize that it has no isolated identity. The being of each is shared with everything else. It is like searching through the dictionary, seeking a precise meaning. Each definition takes us to other definitions, until we ultimately return to the word with which we start and realize that no word has any intrinsic meaning without the others. *Shunyata* does not mean that the world is meaningless, or that it does not really exist, but that existence and meaning are fundamentally shared. *Shunyata* means that we live in a world full of surprises, that as soon as we think we understood what something is, it can change.

The interconnectedness of existence is visualized in *mandala* practice, a method to envision the self as the cosmos, and the cosmos as the self. These involve cosmic images, showing the interconnection between the individual and the whole, the cosmos and the self. The human being is recognized as a microcosm, and we are birthed by the processes of the Universe as a whole. A well known example is the *kalachakra mandala*, which shows the six realms in which one could find oneself. While good karma can lead one to a better realm—the human realm, for example, instead of the "hungry ghost" realm—each realm has its negative side. The *Purushakara Yantra* demonstrates clearly the micro/macro symbolism by depicting the cosmos as the *Purusha*, the cosmic person.[27] (See chapter 9 below)

The earliest ideas of liberation, or *moksha*, in Buddhist practice, involved leaving the cycle of birth and death altogether. This notion is changed, however, with Mahayana Buddhism, which developed in the context of Chinese cosmology. It was with this form of Buddhism that the various "buddha-realms" took precedence over Mt. *Sumeru*-centered cosmos.[29] The Bodhisattva, the enlightened being who chooses to be compassionately reborn until all beings are enlightened, is the paradigmatic figure in Mahayana Buddhism. It also introduces the notions of both the Buddha and *moksa*, or "liberation," as cosmic. "In Mahayana Buddhism," writes Akira Sadakata, "the Buddha is the universe itself, and there is no distinction at all between the universe and the Buddha."[30] The concept of the Universe as an organic whole is applied to Buddhism in the form of the Universe as the Buddha's body. And because we are all part of that Universe, we are inherently awakened. Indeed, "Buddha" means awakened one. We only have to realize it. All beings, in this understanding, have an inherent Buddha Nature.

The *Tantric* traditions, especially in Tibet, have a particularly cosmic sensibility and are the most esoteric of all the forms of

Buddhism. In these traditions, the cosmos is viewed as a radical continuity of being. From an ethical standpoint, this means recognizing that all beings are already enlightened. In *Tantric* practice, the energy of *duhkkha* helps to awaken us:

> For as long as infinite space and sentient beings exist,
> The compassion of the victorious ones and the actions
>   of sentient beings continue without end.
> Those to be guided and enlightened guides
> Manifest through inconceivable interconnections.
> When the characters and dispositions of those to be
>   guided are activated,
> [The compassion of] the guides [arises], and the con
>   figurations of the realms and the dimensions of
>   awakening appear;
> The miraculous methods of guiding others manifest
>   beyond all bounds.
> The sphere of reality never changes into something else;
> Yet blessings, vows, actions, and natural laws
> Cause oceans of realms to appear.[31]

The very nature of the cosmos is such that the sickness and cure co-arise. This does not mean, however, that life does not also bring suffering with it, too. The Buddhist holds the truth and reality of suffering along with the truth and reality that, in an infinite Universe, this suffering can be transformed into *Sukkha*, the unlimited time and space of the Pureland.

Finally, a note should be made about Japanese Buddhism. While most of Japanese Buddhism came through China and can be categorized as a variant of a Chinese tradition, Japanese Buddhism has its own unique flavor. Just as Chinese Buddhism was adapted to the rich Taoist-Confucian worldview already present in China, the Japanese interpreted Buddhism through the prism of Shinto religion. This tradition, like many other indigenous traditions, emphasizes the aliveness of the natural world. Not only are plants and animals living and ensouled, but rocks, waterfalls and mountains all have a spiritual nature as well.

The Shingon tradition of Japan emphasizes interrelatedness. "Infinitely interrelated like the meshes of Indra's net," writes Kukai, who brought this tradition to Japan from China in the ninth century, "are those we call existences."[32] "Indra's Net" is a common metaphor used to demonstrate the Buddhist notion of existence. Each jewel in the net reflects all the others; one underlying reality underlies each unique aspect of existence.[33] Dogen (1200-1253), who also comes from the Shingon tradition, shares much in common with Kukai's thought. He describes the cosmos as a "*sutra*"—a word relate to the English word "suture," indicating a connecting thread, and also sacred Buddhist scriptures:

> What we mean by sutras is the entire cosmos itself... the words and letters of beasts... or those of hundreds of grasses and trees....The sutras are the entire universe... they are the self and others, taking meals and wearing clothes, confusion and dignity.[34]

Most fundamental to the Japanese worldview, and to Buddhist cosmology in general, is the notion that we are living in an organic, interconnected whole in which the self, our truest and most fundamental identity, is coextensive with every other aspect of that whole.

The non-dual traditions are never far from slipping into a subtle dualism in their assertion that the world we see before us is illusory, or *maya*, as is sometimes the case in *advaita vedanta*. Whereas early Buddhism is somewhat dualistic in its emphasis on freeing oneself from the cycle of death and rebirth, later Mahayana and Vajrayana (Tantric) traditions tended to be more grounded in cosmic process and therefore far less dualistic. As always, the Western appropriation of Buddhism is a post-Cartesian, post-Freudian approach that emphasizes the radically separate psyche and largely ignores the cosmological context for these traditions. This is not to suggest that Buddhist practice has no use for anyone with a background in Western psychology; the synthesis of modern psychology and Buddhist practice is indeed useful. However, it is extremely important to recognize that the human psyche, for the Buddhist, is not fundamentally separate from the cosmos.

ISLAMIC COSMOLOGY:
THE SYNTHESIS OF WESTERN *FALSAFAH* AND EASTERN *HIKMAH*

The Islamic world, stretching from North Africa, through the Mediterranean, and across Asia, straddles East and West. As an Abrahamic faith, Islam has much in common with Judaism and Christianity and shares with those faiths a great deal of influence from the Hellenistic cosmology. Indeed, Greek philosophy was kept alive in the Islamic world while it was largely forgotten in the West until Aquinas. But the Muslims did more than translate Plato and Aristotle—one of the great intellectual and spiritual achievements of Islamic civilization was the synthesis of Western philosophy and Eastern wisdom that lead to the formation of a unique and robust cosmology.

Perhaps one reason why Islam is so poorly understood in the West is that it has been, from its very inception, a civilization-building tradition. As such, it finds some of its most eloquent and beautiful expression in the rhythm of Islamic society. For the Muslim, every aspect of culture is an expression of faith that places the Muslim in relationship to the divine and the cosmos, from the prayers to the buildings to greeting one's neighbor. The traditional Islamic village is a microcosm and is understood in its ecological context,[35] while the traditional Islamic city serves a similar cosmological purpose in that it is designed "to create a human ambience in which religion, commerce, education, and daily living were all combined and integrated into a whole in which unity dominated over multiplicity."[36] One cannot help but be caught up in the rhythm of the Islamic world. I can recall vividly, traveling across the Middle East during Ramadan, the call to prayer each morning, the sound of my neighbors cooking their morning meal before sunrise, and the beginning of the daily fast. It is especially important for Westerners to gain a felt sense of this worldview in light of the current geopolitical situation. Facile definitions of *Sunni* and *Shia* cannot help us to understand such a rich and longstanding civilization.

Like all cosmologies, Islamic cosmology gives the individual a sense of relationship to the whole, and to the real. In Islam, the world *al-haqq* is used to indicate that which is "real." To understand what Islamic cosmology means by "real," one must understand what is probably the central tenet of Islam: *Tawhid*, or the unity of *Allah*. The first half of the testimony of faith, the *Shahadah*—"there is no God but God"—declares this concept as fundamental to the Islamic worldview. From a more mystical viewpoint, this declaration can be understood to imply that there is no *thing* but God—that is, *Being* is attributable only to *Allah*, and therefore things are real, or have the attribute of *al-haqq*, insofar as they participate in the divine reality. *Tawhid* is not only the seed of all creation, but also the interior spark that each individual possesses, imagination and human possibility, attributes that are central to the cosmologies of many Muslim thinkers.

The modern worldview is antithetical to such holistic thinking in its dualistic objectification and fragmentation of the world. In the traditional Muslim view, the fragmentation of modernity—and this includes both fundamentalism and secular materialism—is *shirk*, denying the unity of God. The subtleties of the Islamic worldview require one to recognize that, just as each of us participates in God's reality, we are each real and divine; but at the same time, none of us, in terms of our limited identities, is God. We are at once God and not-God.[37]

In spite of the differences, the Islamic Universe has a great deal in common with the West in its hierarchical structure and the dualism of "visible" and "invisible" worlds.[38] The beginning and end of this hierarchy, in the form of the Godhead on one end and the human soul on the other, is divine. The two-fold division is similar to Plato's dualism, and tends to place less value on nature and the body. The invisible is perceived to be closer to the divine and therefore more "real."

Islamic cosmology gives a central role to the human and, like all traditional cosmologies, this role is an integral part of the cosmos. Human interiority or *nafs* is central to both the spiritual psychology of Islam and its cosmology. The *nafs* is not separate from the cosmos, but a unique expression of the whole, a microcosm sharing in *Allah's* divinity.

The paradox of our divinity and our remoteness from the divine is a common theme in Islamic cosmology. The human lies poised in between divinity and corporeality, and our experience is colored by this in-between-ness. Creation is understood to be both a "centrifugal movement away from the Source"—the diversification and uniqueness of the individual—and a "centripetal movement toward the Source"—our increased subjectivity and rediscovery of the divine in our own *nafs*. This is commonly referred to as *al-mabda'wa'l-ma'ad*, "the Origin and the Return."[39]

The risk in this process is that we can become alienated in the centrifugal movement; at the same time, deeper connections are possible through our enhanced individuality and imaginative capacities.

True human nature, or *fitra*, is not assessed negatively as with Original Sin. The primordial Adam—a cosmic being—was taught all the names of God. Humanity's task, in the Islamic worldview, is to *remember* our true selves. We are in a state of forgetfulness, not of sinfulness, and must only remember who we really are. The central practice of the Sufi, therefore, is the *dhikr*, or remembrance.

No complete understanding of Islamic mystical cosmology can exclude the work of Ibn 'Arabi, the mystic and philosopher born in Spain in 1165. His major work, *al-Futuhat al-makkiyya*, "The Meccan Openings," is an extraordinarily complex text that combines mysticism and cosmology, myth and reason. For Ibn 'Arabi, rational and mythic consciousness must co-exist harmoniously.[40] Too much reason or rational thought leads to the divine being perceived as purely transcendent. This can be seen clearly in Christian theology after the Enlightenment when there was an increasing tendency toward deism. Ibn 'Arabi's theology, like that of most of the mystics I make reference to here, is panentheistic. The divine is both immanent and transcendent, present in the world and beyond anything in the world.

The problem with abstract deism, according to the Islamic worldview, is that it removes the divine from participation in the human world. While it is understandable why rationalistic theologians have resisted overly literalistic anthropomorphizing of the divine, anthropomorphism is only a problem when we have failed to divinize the human. William Chittick explains: "[T]he Islamic God is anthropomorphic, because the Islamic human is theomorphic."[41] That is, anthropomorphic visions of the divine are a problem because of a limited notion of who the human is. The fundamentalist, for example, who refers to God as a 'man in the sky,' does so with the modern consciousness that has limited the human to either mechanistic processes or the ego, failing to see the Self as co-extensive with the Universe.

Traditionally, revelation occurs in Islam in three ways: nature, human interiority, and the *Qur'an*. The *nafs*, the true Self, is unlimited. Each moment is a unique disclosure of the divine to the individual. According to Ibn 'Arabi, "we are endlessly changing and forever new."[42] Again, the "real" is not our fixed identities, but constant change. As for the Taoist, this change is often conceptualized through the masculine and feminine. In both the mystical and intellectual Islamic tradition—in stark contrast to the way in which "orthodox" Islam is presented today—sees a strong feminine counterpart to the masculine divinity. Rumi, for example, described mothers as "everywhere" in the creative, birth-giving processes of the Universe.[43] Many of the divine names used for *Allah* in Sufi practice have a feminine component. *Ar-Rahman*, for example, "the compassionate," shares a root with the Semitic word for womb.[44] The world comes into being, according to some Sufi traditions, through the *nafas al rahman*, or "breath of compassion."[45] Creation is continuous as the Universe pulsates into being through this divine inhalation and exhalation.

This leads to the question that contemporary Western cosmology seeks so strenuously to avoid: *Why is there Creation if the only purpose is to return to the Source?* Ibn 'Arabi frequently quotes the well known *hadith*, "I was a Hidden Treasure but unrecognized. I longed to be recognized, so I created the creatures and I made myself recognized to them, so they recognized me."[46] For Ibn 'Arabi, one answer is *love*. Our separation allows us to yearn for reconnection. Moreover, our capacity to reconnect has to do with the *imagination*. "[I]magination is one of the wombs within which forms appear," he writes.[47] For Ibn 'Arabi, the process of creation occurs through the formation of new wombs in which novelty is created. For many Sufis, this leads to the notion of creation as a continuous process.[48] The cosmos was a process of constant renewal and creation, giving birth to itself at every moment. The school known as the *Ikhwan al Safa*—a *Shia* group originating around 1000 BCE in what is now Iraq who heavily influenced Islamic mystical cosmology—refers to the "Hidden Treasure" as an "embryo."[49] The continuous process of creation—*creatio continua*—is both process of divine self-revelation and return, where the human attains, through the imagination, the capacity to create as well.

The Islamic cosmological traditions offer a special insight into both pre-modern cosmology and the emergent worldview. Poised between East and West, Islamic cosmology is, in many ways, a synthesis of other cosmological systems. At the same time, Islamic cosmology provides unique insights. Particularly important for the purposes of this study are the imagination and the metaphor of the womb. These two ideas allow for the individual to engage actively and creatively, through the imagination, in the birth giving process of a Universe that we experience as our womb.

Kabbalistic Cosmology

In the Christian-centered West, familiarity with Judaism often serves as the greatest obstacle to truly understanding it. Because Greek-influenced Christian theology has colored Christian understanding of the Hebrew Bible, a much more dualistic interpretation is often offered than is merited. While it is true that certain forms of Judaism have had dualistic aspects, the Jewish tradition has generally been far more creation-centered than later

Christian commentary would suggest. The original "Wisdom Tradition" of the ancient Mediterranean world was not Greek philosophy, but texts like *Song of Solomon*, *Job*, and *Ecclesiastes* which placed wisdom in the natural processes of the cosmos that were beyond human understanding. The 139th Psalm is an excellent example of the non-dual presence of the divine in creation:

> Where shall I go to escape your spirit?
> Where shall I flee from your presence?
> If I scale the heavens you are there,
> if I lie flat in Sheol, there you are.
>
> If I speed away on the wings of the dawn,
> if I dwell beyond the ocean,
> even there your hand will be guiding me,
> your right hand holding me fast.
>
> I will say, "Let the darkness cover me,
> And the night wrap itself around me,"
> Even darkness to you is not dark,
> And the night as clear as the day.
>
> You created the my inmost self,
> knit me together in my mother's womb.
> for so many marvels I thank you;
> a wonder am I, and all your works wonders.
>
> You knew me through and through,
> my being held no secrets from you,
> when I was being formed in secret,
> textured in the depths of the earth.[50]

The divine is present at each dimension of the early Jewish cosmology: the heavens and the underworld (*Sheol*), the rising Sun and the setting. The opposites of light and dark, above and below are reconciled.

The cosmogony of the Israelites is best understood in the context of the awe and wonder that is clearly present in the words of the Psalmist, not later Christian notions of Original Sin. Ultimately, a creation myth becomes a part of the ritual cycle of a people. In Judaism, for example, *Rosh Ha-Shona*, the Jewish New Year, is also a recapitulation of creation. The Jewish people enter into sacred time to return to the moment of creation each year. This return, called *teshuva*, is a key aspect of Jewish mysticism. *Yom Kippur*, the "Day of Atonement," comes along with *Rosh Ha-Shona*; it is a time for people to take account of their lives, to repent, and to return to harmony with the divine. Similarly, weddings can be understood as a reintegration of the primordial split between the masculine and feminine, the beginning of differentiation. "[T]he bride has ritualistically bonded with the groom on a cosmic level," explains Eliahu Klein. "She has re-enacted the process of creation. This empowers the wedding ceremony and ensures its success."[51]

Whereas early Jewish mysticism had dualistic components that were connected to the apocalyptic—this was called *Merkabah* mysticism, based on the book of Ezekiel—the focus of this work will be the cosmology that developed with the Kabbalistic tradition, beginning in medieval Spain and Provence. Kabbalistic cosmogony is expressed through the ten Sephirot, commonly referred to as the "tree of life" [see Figure 3]. It is a both a map of the human soul and the cosmos, beginning at the moment of creation and at the depths the soul, where human and divine consciousness meet. Science cannot tell us much about the first moments of creation other than that is was devoid of

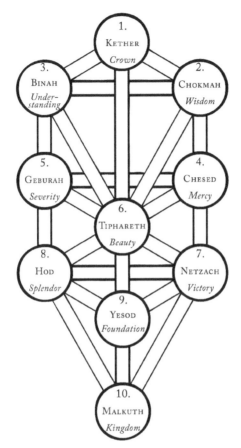

Figure 3: The Ten Sephirot

matter, but teeming with potentiality. The Universe begins with singularity, according to scientists, infinitely small and in perfect equilibrium. For Kabbalists, this state is described as the *Ayn Sof*, or the infinite, a state beyond space and time, without beginning or end. "A blinding spark flashed within the concealed of the concealed," states the Zohar, "from the mystery of the infinite."[52] The infinite must contain its opposite—*Ayn Sof* gives rise to the first *sephirah*, *Keter*, which is also described as *Ayin*, emptiness.

From emptiness and infinity—this is still in a state of non-differentiation and timelessness—singularity arises. This is the second *sephirah*, *Hokhmah*, or "divine wisdom." "This primordial point is identified with the wisdom of God, *Hokhmah*," writes Gershom Scholem of the *Zohar*'s cosmogony. "[T]he mystical seed which is sown into Creation, the point of comparison apparently being not only the subtlety of both but also the fact that in either the possibilities of further being are potentially, though as yet invisibly, existent."[54] In emptiness, infinity, and singularity, the Kabbalist has described the pre-cosmic state. As we shall see, because this state is beyond space-time it continues to exist at all times and all places. Singularity, or *Hokhmah*, remains the closest human beings can get to divine consciousness and remain human. The emptiness of *Keter* or the infinity of *Ayn Sof* is beyond human perception. Indeed, even *Hokhmah* is considered to be beyond rational perception.

The first Sephirah of differentiation and plurality is *Binah*. It is here that we begin to enter the realm in which science can make a tenuous attempt at an explanation. An important point is that in order for time to have a direction and for space to differentiate, perfect balance must be disrupted. A continued state of perfect equilibrium would have left the cosmos perpetually in *Hokhmah*. The Universe, however, evolves through a harmonious balance between balance and imbalance. The name for the divine associated with *Binah* is *Elohim*, which literally means "the gods" although it is general translated in the Bible as "God." *Binah* represents the divine pluralizing itself. "With Beginning [*Hokhmah*]," states the *Zohar*, "the unknown concealed one created the palace [*Binah*], a palace called God [*Elohim*]."[55] Creation is not, in the Kabbalistic view, a way to understand the Universe being created *by* God—it is God expressing itself in plural form, *as* the Universe.

Isaac Luria's cosmology is based upon the *Zohar*, but with an added dimension. Luria lived not long after the expulsion of the Jews from Spain in 1492. That event, like many in the history of the Jewish people, shattered many Jews' sense of meaning and connection with the world. It was, in this sense, a cosmic event—the expulsion required a cosmology that sought to repair a people's sense of alienation and despair. Luria explains that creation occurred with God's contraction, or *tsimtsum*, to allow for space in which to differentiate. Although different from the New Science that describes an expanding Universe, the consequence is similar: space allows for differentiation.

The divine, in Luria's cosmology, then began to pour divine light into the ten vessels, or *sephirot*. But the vessels were not strong enough to contain the divine light and shattered. The Universe was fractured, filled with divine sparks. It is humanity's task to heal the broken world—a process called *tikkun*. While Luria's cosmology is more dualistic than the Zohar and his divinity is more theistic, it recognizes in its creation myth the degree to which humanity is engaging in the on-going process of creation. For Luria, humans have a special role in creation. The destructive forces of the Universe are seen, in Lurianic Kabbalah, as providing potentially sacred work—*tikkun*. Eliahu Klein compares Luria's shattering of the vessels to supernovas.[56] When stars explode, they not only cause destruction, but also scatter the elements of life—of which we are made—throughout the cosmos (see chapter 12). This destruction allows for more life.

The *sephirot* represent a triad of realities: the divine, the cosmos, and the self. Each of these ideas represents a way to know the divine: transcendence, immanence, and interiority. To properly understand the Kabbalistic notion of divinity, it is essential to understand that the Tree of Life is a map of the divine, the cosmos, and the soul.

The transition from Merkabah mysticism to classical, medieval Kabbalah was a cosmic shift in consciousness. A dualistic conception of the divine as found in the heavens was transformed into the notion of the entire cosmos as God. Gershom Scholem explains, as with the transition in South Asia from the Vedic to the Vedantic, Kabbalah interiorized the cosmos:

> [T]he new Kabbalistic Gnosis or cognition of God, which in Hekhaloth tracts is not even mentioned, is related to a deeper level of mystical reality, an 'inner Merkabah', as it were, which can be visualized only in a symbolic way, if at all. Briefly, this gnosis concerns God himself [sic]. Where previously the vision could go no farther than to the perception of the glory of his [sic] presence on the throne, it is now a question, if the expression be permitted, of the inside of this glory.[57]

While Scholem perhaps overemphasizes the Gnostic connection—the dualism of the Gnostic movement, while similarly emphasizing this interior access to God, was, in fact, antithetical to Kabbalistic panentheism—he describes one aspect of the new vision of God in Kabbalistic thought—interiority.

What the Gnostics miss is the sense of embeddedness in the cosmos, central to Kabbalistic cosmology. Kabbalistic pantheism is rooted in a cosmology that describes the common source of all matter. Because everyone has evolved—this includes both living and non-living matter—from the initial point of singularity, each is fundamentally the same. For the Kabbalist, the point of singularity is divine—*Hokhmah*, which comes from both the pregnant nothingness of *Ayin* and the *Ayn Sof*—so all is divine. The sixteenth century Kabbalist Moses Cordovero explains: "The essence of divinity is found in every single thing—nothing but It exists. Since It causes everything to be, no thing can live by anything else. It enlivens them. *Ein Sof* exists in each existent.

Do not say, 'This is a stone and not God.' God forbid! Rather, all existence is God, and the stone is a thing pervaded by divinity."[58] The *sephirot* are not merely sequential, or descriptive of events in the past. They continue to be present in each individual and in the cosmic whole. *Ayn Sof*, for example, is the presence of God in all—how could it be infinite if it were not? Human beings, therefore, are divine in that we are embedded in the cosmos. We have access to the divine not by looking beyond, but by looking within.

At the bottom of the Tree of Life—which is really the top*— the tenth *sephirah*, *Malkhut*, known as the *Shekhinah*, is found. The *Shekhinah* is the divine feminine, present in the phenomenal world. The divine is present not only inside of us, but among us. From the perspective of cosmic evolution, the immanent divine presence represents the womb-like, compassionate quality of the cosmos. Although compassion, *rachamim*, is associated with the male *sephirah* of *Tipheret*, it shares the same root as the Hebrew and Arabic word for womb. The womb can be understood as a microcosm. We are embedded in the cosmos as the embryo is embedded in the womb. Differentiation allows for each aspect of the Universe to manifest this cosmic compassion individually. But the evolutionary process can also lead to alienation and isolation from the whole. The *Shekhinah* connects us. Isaac Luria describes rebirth as re-entering the Divine Mother's womb.[59] The sages speak of accessing divine (feminine) wisdom through "sucking," that is, by nursing at the breast of the divine. Luria

---

* The 'roots' of the tree are the Ayn Sof, so the common depiction is actually inverted. My own observation is that the Zoharic cosmogony describes emanation from a single point in all directions, not a top to bottom structure, which is surely an unconscious retention of the archaic cosmology as found in Merkabah mysticism. – T.R.

connects this to the divine name *El Shaddai*—both *El Shaddai* and *Elohim* are translated as "God" in the Bible—related to the Hebrew word for breasts:

> When the mother is nursing her children,
> she becomes the embodiment of the Divine Name—
> El Shaddai,
> through the nursing breasts.[60]

The cosmic wisdom of the *Shekhinah* can only be accessed through the consciousness of an embryo in a womb.

As with its neighbor and cousin, Islam, the Kabbalistic cosmology places a particular emphasis on the experience of the cosmos as a womb. Even if one looks at it as a metaphor, it should be noted that it is an organic, living metaphor, not an abstraction. The world is lived by human beings, at every level, through metaphors. The pre-modern world recognized this. The notion of *mere* myth or *mere* metaphor arises in the literalistic modern period. Modernity had a huge effect on the practice and understanding of the Jewish tradition. Most Reform and Conservative synagogues are modeled after the Protestant Churches of northern Europe and North America. Consequently, much of the cosmic sensibility and mysticism has been deemphasized. There has been, however, somewhat of a resurgence in Kabbalah recently, and we will return to how the Kabbalist participates mystically in this cosmos in chapter 9.

For every generalization one can make about the cosmologies of the great wisdom traditions, exceptions are easily found. The purpose of this overview of these traditions has not been to provide a comprehensive survey, but to focus on the particular aspects of the wisdom of the world's traditional cosmologies that are relevant in this study. These are offered so that the reader can gain a general feeling for what the Universe may be like in these traditions. In this pursuit, a few general observations can be made:

First, each of these cosmologies understands the cosmos as an organic whole, alive, divine, or sacred. This changes completely the way one understands one's world. Rather than a collection of disparate parts, the world's wisdom traditions see every aspect of the Universe as interconnected; and because everything is, at least in part, sacred, everything has an inherent value.

This view allows for the individual to relate to the whole not as a separate being, and even more than as a mere part, but as a full expression of the whole, a microcosm. In many of these traditions, the human is understood in terms of a cosmic being, or *anthropos teleios*—the Universal human who is both beginning and end of the world. The Cosmic Christ, Adam Kadmon, al-Insan al-Kamil, and the Purusha will be examples of the primordial cosmic person that will arise later in the study of mysticism. This notion of the person as cosmic will be crucial in how we actually experience the cosmos, an experience that will be undertaken in that section as well.

Finally, the cosmologies described here are not only attained through observation, but also in the synthesis of observation, art, and philosophy. There is no schism between science and religion in these traditions. The notion, therefore, that science can "discover" a cosmology is misleading. A cosmology—if it truly includes all of the cosmos, including the human—must be a holistic worldview.

The actual experience of these factors is something far different from having a conceptual understanding. These cosmologies could be described as "mystical cosmologies" because they provide the context for a mystical experience of the interconnection and embeddedness in the cosmos—a living, divine Universe. Each of these worldviews is complete and without the need for correction in its particular context. That is, just as each human being is a full human being, each tree a full and complete tree, every worldview—insofar as it is functional—is true and complete. So I do not attempt to correct them. However, it is important that—if we are to honestly attempt to create a culture in which full participation, awe, and love for the Universe is possible—that our cosmology be consistent. The Newtonian-Cartesian worldview, according to which modern, Western civilization is based, is vastly different from any of these worldviews. Modern Science describes a cosmogenesis that is somewhat different—although not without significant similarities—from any traditional cosmology. To understand what we mean by mysticism, or mystical participation, we will now explore various mystical traditions in the context of the cosmologies that gave rise to them.

Mysticism

Io ritornai da la santissim'onda
Rifatto sì come piante novelle
Rinovellate di novella fronda
*Puro e disposto a salire a le stelle.**
—Dante, *Purgatorio*, Canto xxxiii, 142-145[1]

I F A COSMOLOGY is a worldview, mysticism is a way to experience and embody that vision, or to break through into a new worldview. It can allow one either to create a new cosmology or to experience a cosmology more fully. The mystic interiorizes the mythology and cosmology of a culture, allowing for new and deeper creative expressions; at the same time, the mystic can travel to the edge of the cosmos and the periphery of a culture, re-imagining and recreating its myths and cosmologies. Mysticism is often unknown and unnecessary when a cosmology is functional, but when we have become alienated from the cosmos—that is, if a cosmology is dysfunctional as in modernity—we require a mystical transformation, to cross the border into a new way of perceiving. This can be a perilous journey, however, narrow as a razor's edge. Often, mysticism becomes a practice of pure transcendence, of leaving the world behind. This section is an exploration of functional mysticisms—those that lead to deeper connection and communion and, ultimately, greater compassion.

---

* "I returned from the holiest wave/ remade, like new trees/ renewed of new foliage,/ pure and ready to climb to the stars." [Translation mine]

135

Chapter Seven
Indigenous Wisdom and Shamanism

S TUDIES OF MYSTICISM seldom look at its origins and why human beings need or want to become mystics in the first place. When mysticism's roots *are* discussed, there is often an implicit assumption that mysticism—like philosophy or science—represents an improvement from the past, a way of knowing that our inferior ancestors lacked.* There are indeed ways in which mysticism represents the human reaching the fullness of its creativity, spirituality and wisdom, but this study does not assume that the mystic's way of knowing is an improvement on the past. Instead, mysticism represents human beings' capacity to participate meaningfully in the Universe even after they have become alienated and lost from it, even after they have lost their sense of embeddedness in the cosmos.

---

* Among the most common examples of the traditional Western academic approach to mysticism are Evelyn Underhill, *Mysticism: A Study in the Nature and Development of Spiritual Consciousness* (Mineola: Dover Publications, 2002) and William James, *The Varieties of Religious Experience: A Study in Human Nature* (New York: Longmans, Green and Co., 1928).

Neolithic Wisdom Emerges

With the emergence of the human—an animal with self-reflexive consciousness and language—there also emerged a new way of connecting to the world. This is what we call culture, and it is expressed through art, mythology and cosmology in the context of what we now refer to as indigenous culture. This wisdom was at once unimaginably ancient—as old as the Universe itself—and completely new, for the human gave unique expression to it, understood this wisdom in a particularly human way. The same can later be said for the mystic, who comprehends this wisdom as an individual, returning from a state of alienation to find connection. The mystic's wisdom, it is important to recognize, arises out of an already present wisdom. To understand mysticism, therefore, one must also understand the way the precursors of mystics found and articulated this connection to the Universe.

Every human being on the planet can trace his or her roots to a relatively small group of Africans. For millions of years, our hominid ancestors lived in Africa, and for over half of the 200,000 years that modern *Homo sapiens* has been around, humans did not leave Africa. Interestingly, it likely was an ecological crisis that pushed our ancestors into the first great human migration.* This walk into the vast expanses and new ecosystems of the Earth remains deeply embedded in the human psyche. Our tendency now, at this moment of ecological crisis, is to dream again of leaving these problems behind. But it took very little time—in geologic or cosmic terms—for humanity to fill nearly every

---

* According to the National Academy of Sciences, climate change during this time period caused severe droughts which may have forced our ancestors to leave Africa in search of food and water. See http://www.pubmedcentral.nih.gov/articlerender.fcgi?tool=pubmedid=17785420

biome on the planet. We soon had nowhere else to wander without encountering more people with whom we had to compete for resources. While we tend to like to think of settled, horticultural life as preferable to the nomadic, farming is in fact much more difficult than the hunter-gatherer lifestyle. We had no choice but to learn to live in harmony with one another and with the ecological community in which we settled. Farming emerged not because we thought it would be nice to stop moving around, but because when we finally did stop moving around, we affected the ecosystem in ways that led to its emergence.[1]

As horticulture emerged, the indigenous cultures of the Neolithic village were born. Many of the indigenous peoples remained hunter-gatherers, but they, like those who settled into villages, began to develop cultures both limited and inspired by their specific ecology. While these cultures had many general similarities, there was also an astounding diversity. The cave paintings were created during the Magedelenian period, just before the Neolithic and during this period of wandering (16,000 to 10,000 BCE). These celebrated the relationship between the predator and prey, and, in the handprints found on the walls of the cave, the sense of embeddedness in the cosmic womb felt by the early human cultures.

There was far more democracy and far less hierarchy in Neolithic cultures. Often described as matriarchal or gylanic—meaning a balance of masculine and feminine—the Neolithic village emphasized internal cooperation and relationship, rather than power and domination.[2] The early humans had no choice but to cooperate in order to survive. Since the time, 70,000 years ago—and probably earlier—when ecological crisis reduced the human population in Africa to a mere 2,000 people there had been an evolutionary imperative for compassion. As mammals we loved our young, but as humans we used symbolic language to express love for our communities. We told stories that bound us to the group upon whom we depended for survival. At the same time, these stories, these myths, did not necessarily link us to human beings beyond our particular group. There is evidence that violence between tribal and ethnic groups was commonplace.

The mythology of the indigenous peoples of the world provides a framework of meaning and understanding the relationship of the human to the natural world. Just as farming emerged not as a product of conscious decision but as an extension of an already-present relationship, the stories we told reflected a pattern of connection to the cosmos that emerged out of pre-existing ecological patterns. The archaic cosmology, described in some detail in chapter 5, was an early form of human wisdom. Just as the mammal expresses cosmic wisdom and compassion in its own unique way—in the way it cares for its young—the human expresses compassion through culture. This was largely done collectively. The myth arises in community, and is passed on and shared in the spirit of the interactive, oral tradition.[3] The following creation story from the Huichol people of Mexico exemplifies how the myth is a story not only of ancestry, but also of present identity:

> Grandfather Fire is the original light, the original wisdom, the universe's own memory. In the beginning he took the raw energy of creation and transformed it into a vision by creating colors and images and into sound by singing. In this way he gave us human knowledge, and we are forever grateful. Grandfather Fire is alive in every flame and spark, and fire is to be treated as an honored being.[4]

This myth reveals not only this people's beliefs about its origins but also who they are and what they value. The Universe is alive and sacred, not merely a collection of resources to be exploited.

The ecosystem—recall that *eco* comes from the Greek *oikos*, meaning home—was our first home. In many ways, the early cosmologies were reflections of both the womb and of the tents in which our ancestors lived. The central axis is both "navel" and the pole which upheld the tent.[5] The earliest cosmologies were often represented in terms of the three levels—heavens, Earth, and underworld—described earlier. Later, the ecology of the seven cosmic spheres emerged in many indigenous societies, based on the seven observable planets.[6]

More important than the details of this cosmology was what it told us about our relationship to the cosmos. The diversity of the indigenous peoples is so significant because their culture arises in relationship to the ecosystem. In the modern industrial world, where we celebrate Christmas with Evergreens and fake snow even if we live in a desert, and we awaken at the same time every day of the year regardless of when the Sun appears, globalization has largely glossed over this connection to place that has always been so fundamental, not only to humans, but also to each living species on the planet. The reader will recall the difficulties I encountered in Africa when my N.G.O. attempted to force a Western, abstract sense of time upon the rural people with whom we worked. In addition to compassion, therefore, the key concept in the archaic cosmology was embeddedness. The cosmologies developed by our ancestors did not create this connection to place, but were mythic expressions of the human's embeddedness in the ecosystem.

The Shaman

It is in the context of the emergence of the first human cultures—the human expression of wisdom—that the shaman emerged. While one aspect of the shaman is the personal power that is accessed, this capacity is always grounded in the collective worldview of the community.[7] The cosmology of the specific group to which the shaman belongs is fundamental to the shaman's work. Mircea Eliade describes shamans as those who do "not create the cosmology, the mythology, and the theology of their respective tribes; they… interiorized it, 'experienced' it, and used it as the itinerary for their ecstatic journeys."[8] The shaman experiences the specific cosmology in a deeper way.

In addition, the shaman is defined by the capacity to engage in the ecstatic journey, in which the soul leaves the body and travels to the edge of the cosmos. The shaman, according to Eliade, is one who passes "from one cosmic region to another."[9] A breakthrough occurs, allowing the shaman to access a type of knowing that is inaccessible to the other members of the community. It is important to remember here that the indigenous sense of self is more fluid, less rigid than the modern. While later readers have generally assumed that shamanic journeys necessarily involve a certain dualism between body and soul, individual and cosmos, a less individualistic reading of the shamanic journey would understand the journey of depth and the journey to the edge of the cosmos to be one and the same. The breakthrough occurs in both the psyche, transforming the shaman, and the cosmos in which the shaman is embedded, changing the world.

There are many problems with Eliade's work, notably his tendency to think of shaman-*ism* as something somewhat fixed both in terms of its content and in terms of its place in an evolution of humanity.[10] For Eliade, as for many other scholars, there is an implicit assumption that shamanism is necessarily inferior to classical religion. If there is any reason humans tend to move from shamanism to other forms of religion, it is that the religions of empire generally tend to crush indigenous societies, not because one is objectively better than the other.[11] We may, in fact, be headed toward an increasingly shamanic worldview, at which point we will look back at the Christianity as "primitive." We simply do not know.

Nonetheless, Eliade's work is extremely valuable, particularly in his insight into the shaman's capacity to break through cosmic barriers—an archetypal human pattern found in initiation rites as well as in the mystical traditions. This capacity is extremely important in moments of transition and crisis. The ability of the shaman to perceive that to which a cosmology has made us otherwise blind allows us to overcome our prejudices, our limitations, our inflexibility in the midst of change. The shaman occupies the place of the artist—indeed, the paintings in the caves are the product of the shamanic insights. The creativity of the shaman is expressed through mythic language. But it is important to remember that all human language is symbolic. In shamanic culture, the mythic and the literal are not rigidly segregated.[12]

I.M. Lewis offers an alternative emphasis to Eliade's ecstasy, in that he focuses on the role of enstasy or enthusiasm—"peripheral possession"—in the capacity of the shaman, particularly women, to be subversive. He argues that the shaman frequently plays the role of empowering the powerless in a society.[13] The shaman not only leaves for another cosmic realm but also brings power to this one. By nature, Lewis argues, the shamanic is more unpredictable, more democratic than other aspects of a religion or culture.

To conclude, Piers Vitebsky offers four attributes of the shaman that can summarize the role of the shaman for this work.[14] First, the shaman is focused on the specific, *local* ecosystem in which the culture is embedded and of which that culture's mythology is a reflection. Second, shamanic work is *holistic*. Although other groups are often not considered in this worldview, the shamanic journey represents a participation in the cosmos as a whole. Third, this work is in constant flux. The shamanic worldview is *eristic* in that it acknowledges the risk and difficulty of intervening in a cosmos in crisis. Finally, Vitebsky argues that the shaman is often a *dissident*. Even within indigenous cultures, the shaman often works against the status quo of the elders or non-ecstatic priesthood. This emphasis only increases in times of the oppression of an outside group. One will notice the similarity between this category—and possibly the other three—and the founders of many of the wisdom traditions. As mystics, Jesus, Gautama, and Muhammad, to name a few, found themselves on the periphery of their culture, ushering in cosmic shifts in consciousness.

Shamanism and Mysticism

While Eliade's generalizations about shamanism do present some problems, he is probably correct in his assertion that, due to their position at the periphery of a community, the uniqueness of their vision, and their capacity to internally experience the culture's mythology, cosmology and theology, "it would be more correct to place shamanism among the mysticisms than with what is commonly called a religion."[15] Of course, to separate mysticism or shamanism from religion is difficult, considering the degree to which they inform one another. Nonetheless, one can place shamanism correctly as the precursor to mysticism. As such, however, they are not exactly the same because shamanism is local by definition. Shamanism assumes embeddedness in that particular, local cosmology, whereas mysticism generally arises from an alienation from a cosmology and loss of embeddedness. Consequently, mysticism allows for a universality that shamanism generally does not. This is not to say that mysticism is an improvement on shamanism; rather, it is the appropriate response to particular conditions—especially the conditions of globalization and empire.

As a result of the loss of the particular context that gives rise to shamanic wisdom, there are a great many problems with understanding shamanism in modernity. Whereas shamanism is inseparable from the cultural forms the shaman embodies, the "Protestant notion that true religion is an interior disposition towards 'spirituality' or committed assent to belief" has made understanding the specific cultural forms of the shaman difficult.[16] The New Age, in its tendency to psychologize, makes this understanding even harder. "The New Age may be cosmopolitan," writes Vitebsky, "but at the same time, it moves away from cosmology by dissolving the realm of the religious."[17] We should be careful, therefore, of appropriating shamanism from our modern worldview. The embeddedness of shamanic and indigenous worldviews is that to which we must aspire at our moment of greatest alienation. What better way to remember our connection to the Earth than to reconnect to the ecosystem in which we live? But we also must not delude ourselves into thinking we are less deluded than we are.

While the shaman does not necessarily give rise to the mystic, mysticism could not exist without the wisdom of the shaman and of indigenous cultures. Furthermore, indigenous cultures find their wisdom in the context of the ecosystem in which they are embedded. It is easy for modern humans to forget that they are a part of the Earth and the cosmos and to think of wisdom as something that comes exclusively from the psyche or the transcendent. The shaman reminds us of our ecological context and the cosmic roots of wisdom. It is the task of the mystic, however, to return from alienation.

Chapter Eight
The Union of Opposites

A s STATED AT THE OUTSET of this study, mysticism is one of the most frequently misused and misunderstood terms in the English language. Often conflated with the merely 'mysterious' or the occult, mysticism has become a popular subject in the New Age section at bookstores. Even more condescendingly, but no less inaccurately, mysticism is used to imply that something is irrational or backward in many circles, including secular, scientific atheism, as well as the religious in the post-Enlightenment era. "The words 'mysticism' and 'mystical' are often used as terms of mere reproach," writes William James, "to throw at any opinion which we regard as vague and vast and sentimental, and without a base in either facts or logic."[1] Even a more robust academic treatment of the word will yield various, occasionally conflicting, definitions. With such confusion, it is important to clarify what is meant by the term mysticism in this study.

Literally, mysticism comes from the Greek "*mysteria*," meaning "closed-mouth festival," referring to the "Mysteries" at

Eleusis, the earliest of the extant Greek Mystery Cults where all participants were forbidden to describe what went on during the initiation ceremony. The Mysteries, at Eleusis and throughout the ancient world, were places where the soul of the initiate found union with the divine, the ultimate reality. It is out of this context that the term mysticism came to be used to refer to a particular type of spirituality, that in which the individual experiences union with the ultimate, the real. Rather than something that was forbidden to be spoken of, the mystery became a paradox that could not be explained through discursive reason.

What one means by the ultimate, of course, is defined by one's theological and cosmological assumptions—this will be clear in the following chapter, as some of the mystical traditions of the various wisdom traditions are placed in the context of their cosmological traditions. For the initiates at Eleusis, although little detail is available about the content of those rituals, one can logically surmise that the mystery had some consistency with the cosmology of its time: the innermost depths of the individual and permanent soul, one could find union with the transcendent realm beyond the cosmic sphere. Plato would later articulate this notion in his philosophy, preserving it in Western thought.

In the Eleusinian mysteries, as in all the mystery cults of the ancient world, there was an opportunity for the reconciliation of the polarities of individuality and the cosmic whole. Mysticism, therefore, is a way in which humans deal with alienation; and alienation is one of the central dilemmas of humanity. We have the gift of depth, of interiority. We are universes of wisdom, each of us, within. But we can become isolated, alienated, cut off from the rest of the cosmos. What we seek is the paradoxical capacity to be unique and creative, but at the same time to be able to connect to the rest of the cosmos. This connection is the work of the mystic; it is the uniquely human form of cosmic wisdom. Just as the shaman helped the human community to find its place in the cosmos, extending the wisdom of the ecosystem to the form of cultural expression, the mystic extends indigenous wisdom to the individual. Neither has improved on the earlier form of wisdom, but each has found an appropriate expression for the moment. It is important to recognize that mysticism and shamanism are not the same, as is sometimes suggested, for mysticism presupposes a sense of separation that that shamanism does not. It matters little if this separation is illusory. What is important is that the culture of the mystic is one in which humans are raised to experience themselves as separate from one another and from the cosmos. For this reason, mystics are generally understood to be *exceptional*.

It should also be noted however, that in the cultures in which mysticism flowers there remains the possibility of reconnection and the valuing of participating in the Universe this way. While the mystic does not come from a completely embedded, indigenous culture, mystics are far more prevalent in cultures in which there is a cosmic sensibility allowing for reconnection to occur—this is perhaps one reason why there are many more mystics in the Catholic tradition than the Protestant.

Today, there is a multitude of ways mysticism is understood. Although originally applied in a Western context, mysticism is used to refer to the union of the individual with the ultimate reality in a variety of religious traditions. Because of its Western, and therefore Christian roots, the term does present some problems when applied to other faiths. However, as long as the cosmological context in which it is applied is properly understood, mysticism is a term that can be applied to all of humanity's wisdom traditions, for the experience of alienation is neither specific to the West nor to Christianity.

The study of mysticism, like shamanism, presents a particular set of problems in the modern world. Many of the cultural shifts

149

discussed earlier have led to the marginalization of mysticism as a valid way of knowing. For example, the Protestant Reformation removed much of Christianity's mysticism. Mainline Protestantism has become a highly rationalistic form of religion. Later, the Enlightenment would usher in an era in which mysticism was shunned in favor of scientific knowledge. The point here is not to oppose scientific knowledge to mystical experience—this is what is done in the modern crisis—but to suggest that wisdom is realized when one can participate mystically with the insights science gives us. Indeed, to be a scientist is to participate meaningfully in creation. Another major problem, particularly for the New Age, is that mysticism cannot properly be understood—especially if we are thinking of mysticism as a deeper way of participating in the cosmos—if we fail to recognize its cosmic context. Too often, the Cartesian ego, not the cosmos, is the context for mysticism, reducing it to personal or psychological experience.

The Roots of Mysticism in the West

A more thorough overview of the Christian mystical tradition can be found in the next chapter. This section, however, will explore the roots of Western mysticism in order to establish what is meant by the term. Mysticism is particularly important in the West because, to begin with, the term originally refers to a particular aspect of Western spirituality.

In the West, mysticism must begin with the philosophy of the Greeks. As Pierre Hadot has demonstrated, Greek philosophy was not, as philosophy in the modern university tends to be, a purely intellectual endeavor, but a holistic transformation of the individual.[2] The philosopher was required not merely to learn ideas, but to change his (unfortunately, this was an exclusively male endeavor) lifestyle. Ultimately, philosophy in this context was a pursuit of an interior transformation allowing the individual to transcend the limitations of the ego. This involved not only the ideas with which we associate philosophy today, but also practices and changes in lifestyle, as well as ethics. *Theoria*, which we now think of as mere theoretical or 'heady' knowledge, was a means of attaining mystical, intuitive knowledge for the philosopher, knowledge that—as for the Gnostics later, but without the changes in behavior and intellectual discipline of the philosophers—was already present in the individual. *Theoria* was also used in the Bible for the kind of perception which allowed Mary Magdalene to "see" the figure in a white robe telling her of Jesus's resurrection.[3] For the Platonist or Neo-Platonist, philosophy aimed toward an ever-elusive union with the transcendent—the individual soul, separate from the body, uniting with the ultimate reality, beyond the cosmos. Generally, philosophy differs from cosmosophy in that it did not see wisdom as an inherent aspect of the unfolding cosmos but as something exclusively from the transcendent.

When the Greek philosophical schools came in contact with the mythology of the Near East during the Hellenistic Age, the Mysteries were born. The reader will recall the apocalyptic, emerging among the Israelites (chapter 4), and the Hellenistic Cosmology (chapter 5) that provided the context for the Mysteries. The Mystery Cults of the ancient world allowed for the individual to have an initiation, to cross a boundary. Like the shaman, the initiate crossed a cosmic boundary, allowing the soul of the individual to connect to the world soul. In this way, the mystic is living at the edge, close to the abyss.

The mysticism of the early Christian Church has its roots in the Mystery cults and philosophical schools of antiquity.[4] Paul, the Church's first theologian and in many ways the creator of the Christian religion, understood the Christian faith in terms of the

Hellenistic cosmology. Pauline mysticism, however, introduced the notion that the world was permeated with the presence of the Cosmic Christ and the Holy Spirit. In addition to the ecstatic ascent through the cosmic spheres,[5] the early Christian mystic was able to find communion through the enthusiasm of the Holy Spirit entering the human and of the presence of the mind of Christ—*nous*—in each of us.

The story of mysticism in the West has vacillated between this recognition that the divine permeates creation and the more dualistic and individualistic strains. Christianity is, after all, a synthesis of Near Eastern *mythos* and Western *logos*. With the onset of the scientific revolution, however, Western mysticism lost much of its cosmology, as the cosmos became the exclusive realm of science. Both due to Cartesian dualism and Kant's assertion that spiritual gnosis is unattainable, mysticism has become an exclusively personal issue, one that is shunned in most Protestant denominations and viewed with suspicion by most Catholics. The obvious exceptions are the fundamentalist, Evangelical churches—employing superficial, quasi-mystical practices such as speaking in tongues which are borrowed from scripture literally without an understanding of the cosmology of the Bible's authors—whose mysticism is a combination of Biblical literalism and Cartesian dualism. Indeed, since Calvin first suggested that the human was "nothing but mud and filth both inside and outside,"[6] mysticism in the Western Christian Church—especially American Protestant Christianity—has been dualistic and world-denying.

General Attributes of Mysticism

An important question in today's world—a world in which many of us come in close contact not only with Christianity, but with a variety of the world's religions—a world in which the parochial perspective of Christianity is often insufficient—is, "What value does mysticism have beyond the West?" To answer this question, one must discern what the attributes of mysticism are that are not specific to Christian and Western thought.

The broadest and most general definition of mysticism has to do with *union*. Evelyn Underhill's classic study of the subject describes "the Unitive Life [as]... the life in which man's [sic] will is united with God."[7] While Underhill acknowledges the inadequacy of this description, her answer is to describe mysticism in terms of the subjective consciousness of the individual, ignoring the cosmological context of the tradition of the mystic. Furthermore, the term "God" can mean many things, and, for some traditions, is not at all applicable.

What, then, are we finding union with? And if we have attained union, how can we be said to have an interiority that is "ours"? One common way of talking about union without necessarily becoming fixed on a dualistic theology or the Cartesian ego is to use the term "non-dual." This simply means that, while the world consists of contrasting or oppositional pairs, the ultimate nature of everything is ultimately the same. In a mystical epistemology, therefore, the knower and the known are not separate. In Patanjali's *Yoga Sutras*, this state is described in yoga practice:

(I-40) Gradually one's mastery in concentration extends from the primal atom to the greatest magnitude. (I-41) Just as the naturally pure crystal assumes shapes and colors of objects placed near it, so the Yogi's mind, with its totally weakened modifications, becomes clear and balanced and attains the state devoid of differentiation between knower, knowable and knowledge. This culmination of meditation is *samadhi*.[8]

153

"The eye with which I see God," writes Meister Eckhart, "is the same eye with which God sees me."[9] This has been shown on both macro and micro levels in the New Cosmology. In quantum physics, for example, the observer has been shown to have an effect on the observed. And when one is observing light from the birth of the Universe—"Cosmic Background Radiation"—it is one's own birth that is observed.

The non-dual character of mystical knowledge leads to the ineffability of mystical knowledge in general. It is often said that one cannot put words to such deep mysteries, giving the notion of *mysteria*—"closed mouth"—a different connotation. But while it is true that many mystics are hesitant to speak or write about their experiences, and some are even silent altogether, there is a huge body of material by mystics of all kinds attempting to use words to describe the mystery. Rather than silence, the language of mysticism is often symbol and metaphor, poetry and myth. The mystic is closely linked with the artist, because it is art, not discursive reasoning, that best conveys the non-dual.

Traditional academic studies of mysticism, such as William James and Evelyn Underhill, have largely focused on the shift in consciousness that occurs for the mystic. While they both correctly note that there are many similarities in that state of consciousness across cultures, they largely ignore the subtle differences in the cosmological contexts for mystics of different traditions. This is not to say that mystics of different faiths are entirely oppositional. To the contrary, only in understanding their context can we discern the deeper unity that lies at the heart of these traditions.

In many fields, the internet, the government—understood through the Hobbesian "social contract"—or the economic forces of globalization are seen as bringing forth a new unity in the human species. But this unity is largely superficial, and assumes that the human is primarily individual; that is, the assumption made when we understand government as arising due to individuals making conscious decisions to live and govern in community is that the human starts as an individual without community. It is far more consistent with history and anthropology to say that the human is primarily a communal being. We are primarily social, and isolation is a disturbance of our normal state. The mystic extends the already-present communal nature of the human to include not only one's social, ethnic or national group, but all of humanity and all of the cosmos. As the previous chapter described, indigenous cultures are internally compassionate, but often fail to extend this compassion beyond their group. The ethical dimension of mysticism, therefore, lies in expanding the unity we all possess, of which we have intimations expressed in our communities and in our families. The mystic, by breaking through the boundaries of caste, ethnicity and culture, expands this feeling for our kin to include the entire living, ensouled Universe.

In academic discourse (as well as New Age bookstores) mystical union has largely been described as an "experience"—that is, the subjective interiority has an experience of connection to the objective Godhead. This understanding is due to what we think is most real, and has its roots in the Protestant Reformation, the Enlightenment, and even as far back as Parmenides: What is real is that which is *changeless*. But if we live in a cosmology in which everything is in flux, or in which a dynamic tension exists between the equally important categories of "being" and "becoming," the real is not necessarily *fixed*. When we ascribe real value to the world, to nature, to our bodies, we are not seeking to leave those things behind, but to participate more fully in them. Mysticism is no longer adequately described as experience, but as *participation*; it is at once always different and universally the same.[10]

Various Mysticisms

Paradoxically, even as mysticism seems to unify people of disparate faiths and cultures, there are as many types of mysticisms as there are mystics, because no two people can experience the ultimate reality in the same way. It would also be a mistake to assume that mysticism is exactly the same across different wisdom traditions. Each views the cosmos in a unique way, and the experience of how we connect to the divine and the cosmic is framed differently in each. This section will attempt to outline three broad categories into which many, but not all, mystical traditions can be placed. In doing so, we can establish a criteria to look at the world's great mystical traditions to see how they can be applied to this study.

First, there is transcendent mysticism, in which the individual seeks to leave the cosmos altogether. This form of mysticism is found among cosmologies in which the ontological status of the phenomenal world is considered to be unreal, or if the phenomenal or material world is considered corrupt or evil. The Gnostics, who arose in the context of the Hellenistic cosmology, are the paradigmatic example of this type of mysticism. Hans Jonas describes the problem, both ethically and metaphysically, with the Gnostic worldview: "Where there is ultimate otherness of origin, there can be kinship neither with the whole nor with any part of the Universe. The self is kindred only to other human selves living in the world—and to the transmundane God, with whom the non-mundane center of the self can enter into communication. This God must be acosmic, because the cosmos has become the realm of that which is alien to the self."[11] For the Gnostics, the natural world was considered corrupt and degraded, something to escape. A heightened sense of the individual is present in such examples, for it requires one to seek personal salvation that leaves behind other people, other beings, and the natural world.

Transcendent mysticism is not the form of mysticism emphasized in this study because it fails to fully embrace and value the world of which we are all a part. As the study of cosmology teaches us, that which we consider most real is that to which we ascribe the most value. If we believe this world to be unreal—and this includes not only trees, rivers, and animals, but other human beings—we devalue it. However, the transcendent mystic does have much to teach us. It is in this type of mysticism that the depth of interiority of the human comes into its full flowering. The capacity of the individual to connect to the divine is something we surely need in the modern world. Our challenge, however, is to embrace both the individual and the world in which we are embedded. The modern appropriation of mysticism, because of our Cartesian individualism, tends toward this form.

The next form of mysticism, generally associated—perhaps too simplistically—with the East, eviscerates the individual ego altogether. This type of mysticism, of which *Advaita Vedanta* is a primary example, could be said to offer the opposite emphasis of modern psychological approach to mysticism. That is, one's personal salvation or enlightenment is de-emphasized. Because the ultimate reality is singular, the mystical experience of that reality necessarily eliminates the illusory identities and distinctions of the phenomenal world. While such traditions are generally called "non-dual" they risk slipping into a subtle dualism in which the natural world is less valued because it is considered illusory.

Last form unites, paradoxically, the depth of interiority with the cosmos, neither eliminating individual nor the cosmic. Various forms of nature mysticism, such as Walt Whitman's, are primary examples of this type:

All truths wait in all things . . .
I believe a leaf of grass is no less than the journey-work of
  the stars[12]

This study will show that, although it is less commonly discussed in popular discourse—perhaps this is due to the fact that
it is nuanced and difficult for modern people to grasp concep-
tually—there is a strong tradition of this type of mysticism in
all the great wisdom traditions. In this type of mysticism, the
mystical journey of depth and interiority connects one to a very
different type of transcendence—the realization that each of us is
a unique expression of the cosmic whole.

Panentheistic theology forms the foundation of this form.
Everyone and everything is considered valued as living and divine.
Rather than rejecting the body, it is honored and engaged in this
mystical approach as a part of the world of creation. Again, the
poet and the artist give this mysticism its voice. It is primarily
this type of mysticism that will be employed in cosmosophy.

COSMOSOPHICAL MYSTICISM

Why do we need mysticism today? After all, is it not an anti-
quated, superstitious way of looking at the world, inconsistent
with today's science? If mysticism is the particular way in which
humans respond to the crisis of alienation, then we have never
needed it more. From the cosmosophical perspective, mysticism
is the human expression of a tendency of the Universe to find
connections and unities even as it expands and unfolds. The central task of the human is to express this unity creatively, and to
participate in cosmic processes in ways that are meaningful to
human beings. Exactly how this should be done is never exactly

the same, because the Universe—of which human culture is a part—continues to change and unfold. So, this is not a criticism of other kinds of mysticism, but a suggestion as to what kind of mystical participation might be appropriate at this moment.

To begin, cosmosophical mysticism is interfaith. Today's world is no longer one in which we can segregate our religious traditions. We encounter one another as never before. This requires looking back at our religious traditions to understand them fully and accurately, as well as looking forward to the new wisdom that is coming from the insights of modern science. While I have been careful not to suggest that all mysticisms are the same, it is also true that mysticism is a way to discover that many of those traditions have certain commonalities, and those commonalities find their greatest expressions through the mystics.[13]

The mystic, like the shaman, is at the edge. A particularly important concept in cosmosophy, as we shall see in chapter 11, is to live at the edge, poised between repose in the womb and giving birth to novelty. A dynamic tension exists for the mystic between the cosmic womb and the birthing Universe. The mystic both participates more deeply a culture's cosmology or mythology and has the capacity to see things in an entirely new way. And in being at the edge, at the periphery of a culture, the mystic is especially well-suited to teach a society through poetry, myth and symbol.

Because mystics can break through cultural boundaries, and because they often position themselves at the margins of a society, they can have a subversive element. The cosmosophical mystic draws upon the wisdom of the margins, undermining hierarchies and upsetting the status quo. Moreover, there is an ethical aspect to this kind of mysticism. The barriers that limit compassion to one's family or one's group are broken when the mystic breaks through these cultural barriers. Compassion is extended

159

to include the entire community of life. In this way, the interior, emotional quality of love connects the whole in a very real way.

Cosmosophical mysticism is most fundamentally the union or integration of opposites. This union is played out in many of the world's wisdom traditions. This can include the body and the soul, the human and nature, or the individual and the cosmic. This final category—the individual and the cosmic—is the primary emphasis of cosmosophy. The mystic is one who is able to discover that the deepest identity—like Hegel's "identity of identity and difference," at once unique and universal—is not one of isolation and loneliness, but of *cosmic interiority*.

The central task of humanity is the reconciliation of these opposites to discover our own unique expression of this cosmic interiority. If mysticism is indeed participatory, and not merely personal or psychological, then it is essential to understand the cosmology in which we are grounded. In today's world, we must ask ourselves how we can participate fully in the New Cosmology. But cosmosophy it not wedded to any specific cosmology. The next chapter will explore how the mysticism of the wisdom traditions can inform cosmosophy, our approach to developing a new worldview.

Chapter Nine
Mysticism in the Wisdom Traditions

As ALLUDED TO in the previous chapter, it has been suggested that the world's wisdom traditions, in their most profound expressions, are fundamentally the same. This view, commonly called the Perennial Philosophy, holds that there is an enduring truth, accessible from many different spiritual paths. Cosmosophy does not entirely reject that view, but attempts to find a nuanced 'middle path' between the notion that all religions are basically the same and the rejection altogether of the Perennialist perspective. From the viewpoint of cosmosophy, the world's wisdom traditions do share a certain commonality. However, this common ground is not necessarily something that is fixed or in any way 'the same.' The world's wisdom traditions can give us access to truths that are unfolding, evolving, and changing, just as the beholder of these truths is ever-changing. This is not to say that there is nothing enduring in the cosmos, but to suggest that that which evolves and changes is equally true and valuable.

In order to understand and appreciate the true beauty of our mystical traditions—and, perhaps even more importantly, how they might be applied to our lives today—it is essential that we understand both their similarities and the uniqueness of their visions. The world's wisdom traditions have tremendous internal diversity. This work does not attempt to give an exhaustive account of their mystical traditions, but to focus on the aspects of these traditions that relate specifically to cosmosophical mysticism as described in the previous chapter. In each example, it is important to keep in mind the cosmology upon which these mysticisms are based as described in chapter 6, for mysticism is fundamentally a means of participating more deeply in the cosmic whole. Our understanding of the cosmos unfolds, just as the cosmos itself unfolds. It is hoped that an exploration of how these traditions approach mystical participation—and the union of cosmic interiority and the cosmic whole—may give us an intimation of what enduring principles might be applied in the context of the New Cosmology. Of course, these truths must always be approached tentatively, and are better expressed not systematically or literally, but through the language of myth, art and metaphor.

CHRISTIANITY

The internal diversity of Christianity, like all of the faith traditions discussed here, makes generalizations difficult. While both the Greek influence on Christianity and the emergence of Protestantism as a modern religious movement have pushed Christian mysticism toward dualism, there is also a strong creation-centered Christian tradition.[1] This type of Christian mysticism has drawn both on the teachings of the historical Jesus and the tradition of the Cosmic Christ to engage in a mystical communion that involves a deepening of the connection between the human and the natural world. While this study largely focuses on the Western

Church because of its geopolitical and demographic dominance, it should be pointed out that the Eastern Orthodox Church has perhaps the strongest tradition of mysticism in Christianity.

Ironically, considering the way the Christian Right has distorted its message today, the Christian story is fundamentally revolutionary and subversive. In the first words attributed to him in the earliest of the Gospels, Jesus begins his ministry with a proclamation of the *kairos*: "The [*kairos*] is fulfilled, and the kingdom of God is close at hand."[2] The "kingdom," or *basileia* in Greek, is the same word used for the Roman Empire. The *kairos*, usually translated as "time", means something other than normal time (Gr. *Chronos*), a unique time in which a shift is occurring. The *kairos* is the moment at which the Universe is giving birth to something new. The message that Jesus brings undermines the order of his time, which was the dominated by the Hellenistic worldview and the Roman imperial cult.

After his announcement of the *kairos*, Jesus admonishes his followers to "repent." While this word in the Western tradition— that is, in its Latin and subsequent English translations—has a guilt-laden connotation, the original Greek text refers not so much to repentance but to a "*metanoia*"—an interior transformation of the *nous*, or mind. Moreover, the Aramaic translation of *nous* does not refer to the rational mind but to the heart. In a foundational statement of Christianity, Jesus calls for an interior transformation of the heart in the context of a cosmic shift, the ushering in of a new era.

Jesus, as he is portrayed in the synoptic gospels, can be considered part of the apocalyptic tradition. What is less easy to discern from these texts, however, is what is historical and what is not. One approach is to look at what seems unique in the gospels, what could not possibly have been inserted to fit within an established tradition. A unique attribute, albeit an inconsistent one, is *realized eschatology*, the notion that the revelation describes not a future moment but something that exists already, among us, if we are only able to perceive it. Christopher Rowland describes this as the "vertical rather than the horizontal way of thinking on early Christian doctrine."[3] That is, there was an ability on the part of the mystic—like the shaman—to access spiritual power and knowledge here and now.

While the Romans did not have the cultural effect on the Near Eastern world that the Greeks did, they were the dominant political force of the time of Jesus, and therefore provided the sociopolitical context for early Christianity. As the dominant earthly power, the Roman Empire was seen as the greatest threat to Israelite national identity. Unlike the Greeks, who added some cultural innovation to the Israelite worldview, the Roman influence was largely political. Caesar Augustus, while ushering in an era of peace and prosperity in the Roman world, also instituted various reforms seeking to promote 'family values' and the imperial cult.[4] It was mandatory that Caesar be worshipped as the 'son of god.'[5] This was not unlike the elites of the American empire seeking to gain support for their agenda from the lower classes by defining American identity in terms of 'family values.' In both cases, this allows the frustration of the lower classes to be redirected from those in power to ethnic minorities, those who do not adhere to the norm of the dominant culture. As is the case today in the modern American Empire, the Romans understood that the maintenance of a diverse empire required a shift of belief. In the absence of a cohesive cultural identity or mythology—that is, in the context of a trans-cultural empire—the United States also has had to create a mythic identity, based on the notion of America as chosen, of progress as our birthright, and of the peoplehood of disparate European groups as Americans to the exclusion of others. This myth is largely based upon Israelite beliefs—a non-autochthonous people, emerging in history, chosen by God—but applies them from the vantage point of the imperial power. This has proven to be a dangerous combination for the Earth.

The Israelites resisted the imposition of the imperial cult with a greater zeal than any other group. In part, this was due to the economic conditions of Roman Palestine. Increasing debt to their Roman overlords left many peasants destitute.[6] The wordplay of sin/debt—the same word in Aramaic—makes evident that this was on the minds of the early Christian community.[7] For both economic and religious issues, sin/debt was seen by the Israelites as something owed through no ethical fault of their own. To release one from this debt, as Jesus frequently offered to do, was to undermine the structure of the society. The situation is partly mirrored in the developing world today as globalization has made it increasingly difficult for peasants to get a fair wage. Like the peasants of first century Palestine, the poor of today's developing world are often trapped in a cycle of debt and hunger.

Jesus would undoubtedly have known this situation well. His own status was that of an artisan, commonly translated as a "carpenter," but more accurately described as a landless day laborer.[8] Perhaps the best modern equivalent for such a person would be the undocumented immigrants who find work as day laborers in all of the major cities of America. Like Jesus, they are not citizens and have little recourse if they are treated unfairly.

John Dominic Crossan paints a picture of first century Palestine dominated by "patronal relationships."[9] Roman society was structured in such a way that access to power could be reached only through a patron, that is, an individual with a higher social status. For Jews in first century Palestine, a series of irreversible, hierarchical relationships would have frustrated any attempts at rectifying one's situation.

Any understanding of the historical Jesus and the origins of

Christianity should begin with the Jewish context in which he lived. Although he undoubtedly was influenced by other cultural and political forces, Jesus was interpreting those forces from a Jewish perspective. It is certain that his primary teaching focus was other Jews, and likely they were his sole focus. In this context, the fact that Jesus was a Galilean is inarguable—surely it would have been easier to invent a messiah coming from Judea. Coming from the north, Jesus seems to have an antipathy for the temple hierarchy, exemplified in his disagreements with the Sadducees and his minor rebellion with the moneychangers at the temple. This would have been consistent with a long history of the imposition of the supremacy of the Jerusalem temple on the rest of Israel. For Jesus, the temple authority is undermined through his table fellowship, in which he invites all, the clean and unclean alike, to share in the "sacrifice."[10] Whether the notion of the meal as sacrifice is present in the teachings of the historical Jesus is unclear, but even if it is a later Christian construction, it represents an unconscious recognition that the table fellowship represents a new form of sacrifice, unmediated by the priests of the Jerusalem temple. In a unique way, Jesus has democratized sacrifice, making it trans-imperial and allowing for anyone to partake. In allowing the individual to make this unmediated connection to the cosmos, as sacrifice always does, mysticism undermines social hierarchy.

While I have said that the language of the mystic tends to be poetry, myth, and metaphor, there is no evidence that the historical Jesus ever wrote anything during his short life. There are some whose lives are lived with such depth that life itself becomes their poem. Of course, he was known as a storyteller, weaving his lessons into the lives of his poor and illiterate followers with his parables. The historical Jesus was a mystic whose life became myth. No teacher that existed so far on the periphery of the Temple cult,

Roman power, and Greek culture could have made claims to such knowledge without engaging in a mystical practice to gain such access to divine wisdom. Furthermore, his journey into the desert after his baptism can readily be seen as a sort of shamanic journey.[11] His return from the desert, like his return from Egypt, represents a return to the phenomenal world, and engagement in the world rather than a departure. Jesus, like other apocalypticists, has accessed spiritual power which, whatever his intention was, undermined the earthly power of the temporal and religious authorities. But the uniqueness of the mysticism of Jesus is found in his realized eschatology. The Kingdom, for Jesus, is not found in the *basileia* of the Romans, nor in the priestly hierarchy in Jerusalem, nor in the zealots who seek to overthrow the Romans. For Jesus, the Kingdom of God is already present within each of us, at each moment. "The Kingdom of God does not come with your careful observation, nor will people say, 'Here it is,' or 'There it is,' because the Kingdom of God is within [among] you."[12]

Some scholars refer to the period of the ministry of the historical Jesus as the 'Jesus Movement.'[13] During this time, it remained exclusively Jewish, and, although it was influenced by the overwhelming cultural dominance of the Hellenistic worldview, the movement generally can be placed in the context of the Near Eastern Jewish tradition. Several decades after the death of Jesus, however, the ministry of Paul would bring this movement from the margins into the broader Greco-Roman culture. Scholars refer to this second phase of Christianity that spread throughout the Roman Empire among both Jews and Gentiles as the 'Christ Cult.' Many consider it to be one of the Mystery Cults that proliferated at this time. It is in this phase that Christianity becomes Hellenized, thanks largely to Paul. Paul's mysticism has a great deal in common with the Mysteries because it is based on the Hellenistic cosmology. The Christian mysticism of this period involves both ascents into the heavens[14] and the Pentecost, the descent of the Holy Spirit into the Earth.[15] As mentioned in chapter 5, the divine becomes present in the flesh with Jesus, breaking through the cosmic barrier, erected by Aristotle, between the heavens and the Earth. Paul links the capacity of the human to participate in Christ's divinity to our interiority, the *nous* of Christ we all possess.[16] Finally, Pauline mysticism is based on his notion of the Cosmic Christ. His writings say little about the teachings of the historical Jesus. Instead, Paul's emphasis is on the mystical resurrection through Christ. What kind of rebirth is perhaps the central question of early Christian mysticism.

While the early Christians were Jewish, the Greek notion of a soul (*psyche*) distinct from the body, as that which is 'reborn' after death, had begun to integrate with some Jewish systems of belief. The Apocryphal *Wisdom of Solomon* states: "But God created man [sic] for immortality, and made him an image of his own eternal self; it was the devil's spite than brought death into the world, and the experience of it is reserved for those who take his side. But the souls of the just are in God's hand, and torment shall not touch them."[17] The Hellenized Jews who wrote the Apocrypha adopted the doctrine of the resurrection of "the souls of the just" found in the ancient mystery cults of the era and in Plato.

The Book of Daniel speaks of astral rebirth, a notion that developed in the Hellenistic Age. While the astrology of the period comes from Near Eastern cultures, Babylonia in particular, it did not emerge as a part of individual salvation until the Hellenistic period.[18] The Greek idea of a detachable soul, coupled with the new need for connection in the cosmopolitan empire, led to the emergence of the soul's ascent to the heavens upon the death of the body. Daniel, like Jesus later, combined the notion of personal salvation so common in the Hellenistic world with the prophetic notion of a radical transformation in the world, an inversion of the injustices of imperial society.

Jesus is clearly not referring to bodily resurrection in the gospels, nor is he adopting the Platonic dualism of body and soul. Instead, we will be "like angels in heaven"[19]; that is, while we will still have bodily form, we will undergo a transformation from material to spiritual entities. Paul uses Aristotelian language to put this doctrine in a form that his Greek audience will understand:

> But, you may ask, how are the dead raised? In what kind of body? How foolish! The seed you sow does not come to life unless it has first died; and what you sow is not the body that shall be, but a naked grain, perhaps of wheat, or of some other kind; and God clothes it with the body of his choice, each seed with its own particular body. All flesh is not the same flesh: there is flesh of men, flesh of beasts, of birds, and of fishes—all different. There are heavenly and earthly bodies; and the heavenly splendour of the heavenly bodies is one thing, the splendour of the earthly, another ... So it is with the resurrection of the dead. What is sown in the earth as a perishable thing is raised imperishable. Sown in humiliation, it is raised in glory; sown in weakness, it is raised in power; sown as an animal [psychic] body, it is raised as a spiritual body.[20]

Here, the natural cycle of the planting of a seed and the growth of the plant is compared to the death and rebirth of the human. In antiquity, it was believed that the seed *died* when it

169

was planted. In shamanic cultures, the shaman typically enters the underworld, and 'dies' in order to gain access to the divine realm, or the heavens.[21] Paul repeats this pattern, suggesting that it is neither the body nor the psyche that is reborn, but the pneumatic or spiritual body. It is through the *nous* of Christ that we are capable of this rebirth. When we attain it, we are part of the cosmic body of Christ, in intimate knowledge of God and of others who are aware of their divinity.

Perhaps even more than Paul, the paradigmatic early Christian mystic is Augustine. Augustine was heavily influenced both by Gnostic ideas and neo-Platonic philosophy, and provided a dualistic theological framework for institutional Christianity. However, there were several movements which have rejected this trend. In the Medieval period there was a flowering of Christian mysticism, beginning with the Celts, who built upon the Celtic cosmology described in chapter 5 to create a form of Christianity that rejected the Manichaean tendencies of Augustinian Christianity.

Because Ireland managed to avoid much of the cultural decay of the post-Roman world, the Celts had a huge influence on Medieval Christianity in general, particularly the mystics of Germany.[22] Meister Eckhart's (1260-1329) mysticism was perhaps the closest of the Christian mystics to the non-dual traditions of the East. His was largely an apophatic vision of God: "[B]e silent and do not flap your gums about God."[23] Eckhart further prays that God will "rid us of 'God.'"[24] He rejects the Fall/Redemption view of salvation common in Western Christianity. "Salvation," according to Eckhart, "[is] when we marvel at the beauty of created things and praise the beautiful providence of their Creator."[25] We are not saved by someone outside of our selves because of our sinful nature; we are saved in recognizing what Hildegard of Bingen calls our 'original wisdom.' This wisdom is alive in each of us, according to Eckhart, because we have a spaciousness,[26] an entire cosmos,[27] within.

Perhaps due to his deep connection to the Beguines, a women's spiritual movement of his time, Eckhart employed feminine imagery in his mysticism. For Eckhart, the "spark of the soul"—the depth where the entire cosmos is present—is where *birth* takes place.[28] For Eckhart, we are not merely saved by Christ, but we, like Mary, are giving birth to Christ in ourselves.

Hildegard of Bingen, a religious leader who clashed with the male hierarchy, as well as an accomplished writer, artist and composer, was another German mystic of this period. Like Dante, she conceived of the Universe holistically:

The Earth is to the sun,
as the soul is to God.
The Earth,
at any point,
can be located by its relationship to the sun.
The Earth has a scaffold of stones and trees. In the same way
    is a person formed:
        flesh is the earth,
        the bones are the trees and stones.
The soul is the firmament of the organism, then.
In the manner in which the soul permeates the body with its
    energy, it causes and consummates all human action.
This is how a person becomes a flowering orchard.
The person that does good works is indeed this orchard
    bearing good fruit. And this is just like the earth with its
    ornamentation of stone and blossoming trees.[29]

171

For Hildegard, the human is the microcosm of the world. And the world—reflected in her artwork, largely cosmic visions not unlike Eastern *mandalas*—is an organic whole, sacred in every aspect.

The medieval worldview provided a holistic vision for the individual to participate in the cosmos. Each individual was considered a microcosm, the cosmos itself the womb of Mary, and the (Christian) world united through the cosmic Christ. For mystics like Dante, Eckhart, and Hildegard, communion with the ultimate reality was made clear by this organic vision. The Great Chain of Being, the hierarchy that placed all of creation in relationship to the divine—limiting as it was to science and progressive politics—provided a means to reconcile the opposites of our interior life and the cosmos as a whole.

Unsurprisingly, the modern era marked a turning away from the mystical traditions of Christianity, especially of those seeking communion with the cosmos and nature. The schism between science and the Church left the soul to the mystic, but the cosmos ceased to be sacred. The beginnings of the New Cosmology, however, brought one of the great truly modern mystics, Pierre Teilhard de Chardin. A Jesuit priest and Paleontologist—either appropriately or ironically, the Jesuits are perhaps the most modern of the Catholic orders—Teilhard was essentially a Pauline and Johannine mystic who recognized that Christians had long based their mysticism on the static cosmology of the Greeks. He sought to articulate a mysticism for Christianity that made sense in terms of an evolving cosmos by understanding the Cosmic Christ not in terms of Heaven above, but as the "omega point" in the future. That is, transcendence, for Teilhard, is not in the heavens, and is not something that the individual soul can aspire to; rather, humanity—indeed, creation as a whole—is evolving together toward mystical communion with the Christ.

Influenced heavily by Teilhard and by the medieval mystics, the Creation Spirituality tradition as articulated by former Catholic priest Matthew Fox is perhaps the best contemporary example of a Western mystical tradition that fits the cosmosophical criteria. It is worth noting that Fox, in an openly hostile atmosphere at the Vatican toward feminism, homosexuality, and liberation theology, was removed from the Church. His work, in the prophetic tradition of Jesus Christ, has been highly critical of the Vatican in its failure to take the side of the marginalized on social justice issues. But it is far different from most modern proponents of the social gospel in his emphasis on both cosmology and mysticism.

While Christian mysticism traditionally speaks of the three-fold path (Illumation, Purgation, and Union) of ascent based upon the neo-Platonic tradition, Fox breaks with most Western mystics and scholars of mysticism in that he teaches a fourfold mystical path which, consistent with the New Cosmology, is non-hierarchical. Like Teilhard, he realizes that speaking of "ascent" is appropriate for Paul, but not with today's cosmology. Fox's first path, the *Via Positiva*, is the way of celebrating the beauty and blessing that is creation. Creation Spirituality rejects the emphasis on Augustinian dualism and Original Sin. The theology of the *Via Positiva* is cataphatic, affirming that God is found in all things. In general, Fox, like Ibn 'Arabi and others, emphasizes panentheism. The *Via Negativa* is the way of silence and mystery. This is found in Eckhart's admonition to "be silent" about God. The *Via Creativa* is the way of creativity. In Creation Spirituality, we are all considered artists and co-creators of the Universe. Finally, the *Via Transformativa* is the way of change, spiritual activism and transformation. As we are all artists, we are also all prophets, called upon to work for justice in the tradition of Jesus. Above all, the Creation Spirituality tradition teaches that each of us—not merely a few people off in a monastery somewhere—is a mystic, and has the capacity to connect to the divine.

While it is generally true that mysticism in the Protestant Church has been suppressed except in the extreme dualism of fundamentalist churches like the Pentecostals, there is one major exception. The Black Church in America has integrated elements of the Evangelicals, of suppressed African traditions, and the radical independence of the American Protestant tradition to form a religiosity that is perhaps the best of American religion—and America, this most religious and powerful of Western nations, is the center of Protestantism in the world today. Because the Black Church has always come from a position on the margins, it has avoided the Protestant individualism and rationalism of the mainline churches, and, for very obvious reasons, the reactionary politics of the Evangelicals. Pastors like Howard Thurman and Dr. Martin Luther King Jr. were both mystics and prophets who saw the pursuit of justice for their people and the pursuit of the divine as one in the same. They recognized that the mythology of the Christian story—particularly the enslavement of the Hebrews and Jesus's opposition to power—was more than history. They saw their people, because of their suffering and collective struggle for Earthly liberation, living these myths out every day.

Whether one discusses its mysticism, theology or cosmology, Christianity, like all great faith traditions, conveys its deepest meanings in its stories. The Christmas story, although largely considered ahistorical, describes the Christian union of opposites as well as any mystical theology. Perhaps *because* it is more myth than history, the story of the divine born in the human—the humblest of humans, born impoverished and at the margins—conveys to the Christian that it is at the darkest and loneliest of times that the divine comes forth. The union of opposites is the birth of the divine in the flesh, reconciling and integrating the dualism of the Western worldview.

KABBALAH

Jesus and the Christian mystics who followed him had their roots in the Jewish traditions such as the apocalyptic and prophetic movements. Particularly important in early Jewish mysticism was the book of *Ezekiel*, upon which *Merkabah* mysticism was based. While Kabbalah is used as a catch-all term for Jewish mysticism today, it is most accurate to ascribe the term to the practices and philosophies which developed in Medieval Spain with the *Zohar* and the various movements and permutations that followed. These traditions, in addition to the classical period in Moorish Spain and Provence—which include the Lurianic system from Safed and the Hasidic movement of the Baal Shem Tov in eastern Europe—are based on a holistic vision of individual and cosmos. Earlier Jewish mysticism was based on a dualistic division of Heaven and Earth.

The basic structure of Kabbalistic cosmos provides the context for Kabbalistic mystical practice. The reader will recall that the Kabbalist conceives of the cosmos in terms of the divine emanations of the *sephirot*. Every aspect of the Universe can be said to fit into the hierarchy—here, I use the term hierarchy in its original sense, meaning a shared, sacred origin—and shares in the divine to some degree. While one can certainly describe certain events and ideas as evil, the cosmos is fundamentally good in this worldview because there is nothing that does not participate in the compassion of God. Jewish mysticism, therefore, in spite of the fact that it shares a common heritage with Christianity, begins with a very different core assumption—at least from Augustinian Christianity—in that there is no Original Sin.

Our inability to perceive the compassion of the cosmos is due to our capacity for distinction. By putting people or events in categories of 'good' or 'evil,' we fail to recognize that the divine is present in all. Kabbalah teaches that the *yetsir ha-ra*, the evil inclination we all possess, is not to be extinguished but properly channeled. Satan is not understood dualistically, but as an emissary God. In *Gematria*—the Kabbalistic practice of numerology based on the Hebrew alphabet—the word for serpent has the same numerical value as the word messiah. We bring the messiah not by destroying the serpent but by transforming it. That which appears evil is only so because of our own minds' need to distinguish. This process lies at the heart of the Kabbalistic understanding of human beings. Our ability to consciously recognize our place in creation allows us to give profound expression to the divine. But it also presents a challenge. We, more than any other aspect of creation, are capable of believing in the illusion of our separateness.

Jewish mysticism understands this separation through the story in Genesis of Adam and Eve. The word "Adam" comes from the Hebrew *adama*, meaning Earth. He is an Earth-being, derivative of the Earth, not placed here from beyond. The primordial humans live in PRDS, the Garden of Eden, the state of non-differentiation and embeddedness. Kabbalists refer to this state of being as "*Adam ha-Rishon*," primeval, non-dual consciousness.[30] The goal of the mystic is to return to this primordial state of wholeness.

Adam and Eve are banished from the garden for eating fruit from the Tree of the Knowledge of Good and Evil. This was the birth of human consciousness. Rabbi David Cooper writes: "This was the 'punishment' of discriminating thought. Things became separate; they saw themselves as separate beings. Prior to the serpent, the sense of nakedness did not exist. It comes only when one has an identity, a sense of individuality."[31] Human consciousness comes to us as a blessing and a curse. We possess an amazing ability to deconstruct, to see and understand fragments of the whole; without this ability, civilizations and technology and culture would be impossible. But this ability of the mind to discriminate makes perceiving the whole extremely difficult. A mysticism based on a functional cosmology reintegrates the individual back into the whole, returning us to PRDS. In Kabbalistic terms, this return is called *teshuvah*. On Yom Kippur, Jews perform *zichronot*—remembrances of the divine. Humanity is called upon to remember its common source.

Isaac Luria describes Adam and Eve as "back-to-back Siamese twins," an idea supported by the Talmud.[32] Luria's evolutionary theory is that the separation of male and female allows for face-to-face relationship to develop. The distinction of male and female is not to be permanent; it allows for a deeper, more loving relationship to develop.

The Fall represents our transition from primordial to individual consciousness. God warns Adam and Eve not to eat from the Tree, for they will die.[33] But the serpent says, "Ye shall not surely die; for God doth know that in the day ye eat thereof, then your eyes shall be opened, and ye shall be as God, knowing good and evil."[34] The serpent correctly points out that the fruit of the tree will not *kill* Eve. One mystical understanding is that it will instead give her individual consciousness. She will perceive her personal death as a total death, rather than a part of a holistic, cosmic process. In opening her eyes—to use the serpent's words—to good and evil, Eve's eyes and ours become closed to the whole.

The Tree of the Knowledge of Good and Evil is sometimes understood as the *klippah*, or bark, of the Tree of Life. *Klippah* is a word used to denote any kind of husk or covering, the particular aspect or the exterior form on which one can be too focused. Too much emphasis on the *Gevurah*, the *sephirah* of judgment, can lead to an overemphasis on the particular—on the *klippah*. The first act of Adam and Eve after eating from the tree is to cover themselves, because they are aware of their own nakedness. Their nakedness is only a problem when they understand themselves as autonomous. They have begun to focus on their external and individual selves, rather than the cosmic whole.

In addition to a map of the divine and the cosmos, the Tree of Life can also be understood as a map of the human. The Talmud says that Adam originally extended from one end of the Universe to the other.[35] Jewish mysticism understands the process of cosmic evolution as a particularization of the cosmic whole. *Adam Kadmon*, the *proto-anthropos*, was present at the very beginning of creation, *Hokhmah*. And, at the point of initial singularity, Adam encompassed the entire Universe, because the Universe was infinitely small. As the cosmos complexifies, each individual human becomes a micro-cosmos. The divine can therefore be found by looking within. To understand this process of *pinimiyut*, or interiority, one must understand the Kabbalistic conception of the soul.

"Search and discover the root of your soul," writes a commentator on the *Zohar*, "so that you can fulfill it and restore it to its source, its essence. The more you fulfill yourself, the closer you approach your authentic self."[36] The Hasidic movement of the Baal Shem Tov (1698-1760) took the Kabbalistic map of cosmic and divine evolution and interiorized it. To know the divine, the Kabbalist recognizes that one must not merely look beyond—although it should be remembered that the Kabbalah does not advocate asceticism and, in fact, requires active engagement in the world—but within. As beings who have left PRDS and evolved past an embedded consciousness, we can only see exteriors in our selves and in others. This curse also brings with it the blessing of the ability to find the divine in the depths of one's own soul.

Gershom Scholem writes:

> But God, in His supreme manifestation, where the fullness of His Being finds its final expression in the last and all-embracing of His attributes, is called "I." This is the stage of true individuation in which God as a person says "I" to Himself. This divine Self, this "I," according to the theosophical Kabbalists—and this is one of their most profound and important doctrines—is the Shekinah, the presence and immanence of God in the whole of creation. It is the point where man [sic], in attaining the deepest understanding of his own self, becomes aware of the presence of God.[37]

Kabbalah describes "five worlds," embedded in the Tree of Life [see Figure 3, page 125], corresponding to five dimensions of the soul. While the worlds represent the various stages of cosmic evolution and divine manifestation, the souls represent the process of deepening interiority and union. The journey to our deepest and most authentic self represents the journey toward union with the divine.

The phenomenal world, the world of the *Shekhinah*, is called *Asiyah*. It corresponds to our animal soul, the *nefesh*, the soul of our external, individual identity. *Ruach*, which also means breath, is the emotional soul, corresponding to the *yetsirah*, the world of formation, of the *sephirot* of the six days of creation in the Bible. The *neshama* is the intellectual soul, corresponding to the world of *beriyah*, or creation, and the *sephirah* of *Binah*. In mainstream Judaism these three—the *nefesh*, the *ruach*, and the *neshama*—are the only souls mentioned. They represent the worlds of multiplicity.

Kabbalists recognize two other souls: the *chaya*, or "living soul" and the *yechidah*. The *chaya* is connected to the world of *atzilut*, or emanation, and the *sephirah* of *Binah*. In some systems, this soul and world is combined with the last, the world of *Adam Kadmon* and the soul of *Yechidah*. While *Adam Kadmon* is the pinnacle of universality, the divine unity of *Keter*, the *yechidah* is our deepest self.

The union of opposites of individuation and universality emerges here. Our deepest connections are with those who are the most authentic, who reveal their inner depth and authentic selves, not with those who attempt to connect through broad generalities and represent all perspectives. Similarly, most mystical traditions—Kabbalah is no exception—advocate a deeper approach to one's own tradition, not the invention of a universal religion. It is in discovering the deepest self that we recognize that we all share the same universal soul.

The ability to realize the wholeness and holiness of the cosmos, to become a *baal teshuvah*, or "master of return," is the aim of the Jewish mystic. In this way, God can know itself, and love is created through a dynamic relationship. "[T]he shattering of the vessels was not so much an 'accident' but part of God's creative process," writes Estelle Frankel. "The broken shards were the necessary raw materials from which this world of multiplicity was fashioned."[38]

Union takes place in several other ways. First, the interior and cosmic must integrate through the recognition that the soul and the divine are one. This is the world of *Adam Kadmon*, wherein we can recognize that there is but one universal soul. But the plurality of the cosmos is not to be rejected. The second union is of plurality and unity. While we are fundamentally one—*echad*—we are also unique expressions of that wholeness. Our diversity is an important part of this process, for it allows one to become a *baal teshuvah*. The individuals that make up the whole allow for God to know itself—and this knowing is compassion and love. The active principle of the divine, what Rabbi David Cooper calls "God-ing," is present in this relationship.[39] While patriarchal theology has generally described the active divine principle as masculine, it must be recognized that the *Shekhinah* is present in the relationships of the phenomenal world. Finally, there is the union of good and evil. The mystic comes to recognize that all is God, not merely that which we find unobjectionable. True evil, for the Kabbalist, is an imbalance—too much *din* and *gevurah*, for example—not an autonomous force. Again, the *yetsir ha-ra*, the evil inclination, is considered something to be properly channeled, not repressed.

For any cosmology or any mystical practice to be of value, it must have an ethical component. For the Luraniac Kabbalist, the internal transformation—the healing of the soul or *tikkun nefesh*—is paralleled by the work of *tikkun olam*, the healing of the world. A functional cosmology serves the ultimate purpose of connecting these healings, to recognize that to heal within is to heal the world, and acts of lovingkindness, *Chesed*, are acts that heal the soul.

SUFISM

All the Abrahamic faiths—Christianity, Judaism, and Islam—have seen a backlash against mysticism in the wake of the modern worldview. Whereas the Jewish backlash occurred in a European context and mirrored the Christian one in its adherence to Enlightenment principles, Islamic civilization's encounter with modernity has been fraught with power relationships of Euro-American colonialism that placed traditional Islamic values on the defensive to an even greater degree. As a result, orthodox Islam has become increasingly likely to adopt fundamentalism in a misguided effort to return to the traditional values of Islamic culture. Both Judaism and Christianity do have modern fundamentalist branches that are no less pervasive than in Islam. But whereas Christianity and Judaism rejected—not entirely, of course—their mystical traditions centuries ago because they were not rational enough, Islam's rejection of Sufism has come relatively recently as a result of the fundamentalist adherence to a presumed orthodoxy.

As Islamic cosmology demonstrates, the Islamic civilization need not turn to the moralistic rigidity and superficial piety of fundamentalism in order to distinguish itself from modernity. Islam begins with a notion of what it means to be a human that differs markedly from the modern world. The reader will recall that the human is poised, in Islamic thought, between the worldly and the divine. Each individual possesses a corporeal body and a divine intellect. Each being, in its most authentic and deepest self, is capable of realizing its divinity. The human is the end of the cosmic journey that began with the divine breath of compassion. Each of us is a unique reflection of the *al-insan al-kamil*, the cosmic person who, at the moment of creation, encompasses the entire Universe. It is our task to realize that we share in this cosmic, divine identity, that we are particular representations of the Being of *Allah*. Sufism, the Islamic mystical tradition, is the practice of remembering our true, divine nature.

The locus of remembrance and transformation is the inner chamber, the heart, our deepest interiority and truest self. The heart is the center of the Universe, the interiorization of the *axis mundi*. Sufi practice is the process of unveiling the soul—known as the *nafs*, or lower soul, and the *ruh*, or higher soul. Related to the Hebrew *nefesh* and *ruach*, these correspond to the individual identity and the shared, divine identity. Only *ishq*, or divine love, is eternal at the core of one's being.

The inner struggle to examine, understand, and unveil one's soul can be described as one's *jihad*. While the term *jihad* garners a great deal of attention in the Western media today as 'holy war,' it is more precisely translated as exertion or struggle. Muhammad famously said that the greater *jihad* is *within*.

The Sufi path, like the Kabbalist one, is a mirror interior image of the cosmos. The seven cosmic spheres of traditional cosmologies are, for the Sufi, transmuted into the seven stages of interior transformation.* For the Sufi, the process of unveiling the soul, into the interior of the true self, can be envisioned as a circle. The exterior of the circle is referred to as the *shariah*, or "road." Again, the Western media—and unfortunately, some Muslims—have made much of the superficial rules of *shariah* as the defining characteristic of Islam. Observance of such laws is important for the Sufi, and is not rejected. But this is only the beginning of the path, the external form. Imagine, if you will, a circle, the outside of which represents many disparate perspectives. This is *shariah*, the surface of the sea into which one must dive to find a pearl; or, to use another metaphor, it is the thick, dry skin of the pomegranate. From there, there are seven stages of interiority. This journey within begins with one's desire, or *himmah*. The Sufi does not think in terms of good or bad desires. Any desire is ultimately, at its root, the desire for the beloved, the divine. When one finally reaches the center, or *haquiqah*, one is an *ashiq*, a "lover." Imagine the circle again. From the center, there is no distinction between paths. They all meet at the center. All perspectives now are the same as well. As in many other mystical

---

* The 16ᵗʰ century Spanish mystic Teresa of Avila describes a similar map of the soul in her *Interior Castle*. Teresa, a Christian who had a Jewish background and was undoubtedly affected by the Near Eastern influences on Spanish culture, describes a spiritual journey through seven "mansions."

traditions, Sufism allows one to arrive at a non-dual perspective. From the center, no distinctions can be made.

At this point, considering the extent to which Sufism relates to Islamic cosmology, it is useful to consider the centrality of the concept of *Tawhid* in Islamic thought. If the attribute of *al-Haqq*—"the real"—is only an attribute of *Allah*, and the Islamic worldview is panentheistic, then each of us participates in the reality of the divine. The Sufi doctrine, like that of panentheistic Christianity and Kabbalah, is fundamentally about realizing our participation in the divine unity. Moreover, Sufi practice is a process whereby, when we reach the center of our selves, we only see others from their centers—that is, we see everything and everyone in the cosmos as fundamentally a spark of the divine. The ethical consequences of this are tremendous.

It is important not to take such a map as anything other than a symbolic representation of the path. It always varies and is different for everyone. Sufis also picture this journey in terms of an ascent and a descent, much like the shamanic journey. The first three stages represent an ecstatic journey. The Sufi is drunk with love for the beloved, yearns for this union. The second three stages are the descent or the path of sobriety. The Sufi is now sober in realizing that the divine loves and yearns for the seeker too. The final stage, the stage of the *ashiq*, is a return to the first stage. The "lover" at the center does not only find union with others who have reached this stage, but also with everyone and everything in the cosmos. The Sufi does not leave the cosmos, but loves it more; the Sufi does not merely change the self, but the world.

The beauty and appeal of Sufism lies in its ability to engage deep philosophical concepts without losing touch with the heart. Sufis repeatedly return to the love that lies at the core of their practice and belief. *Ishq* is the center of the human soul and the force that moves the cosmos; it is the goal of the Sufi path. Ibn Arabi writes:

> My heart can take any appearance. The heart varies in accordance with variations of the innermost conscious- ness. It may appear in form as a gazelle meadow, a monkish cloister, an idol temple, a pilgrim Kaaba, the tablets of the Torah for certain sciences, the bequest of the leaves of the Qur'an. My duty is the debt of Love. I accept freely and willingly whatever burden is placed upon me. Love is as the Love of lovers, except that instead of loving the phenomenon, I love the Essential. That religion, that duty, is mine, and is my faith. The purpose of human love is to demonstrate ultimate, real love. This is the love which is conscious. The other is that which makes man unconscious of himself.[40]

The point here is to recognize that erotic love is ultimately no different from divine love.

The love of the Sufi makes one not only yearn for wine like the drunk, but live one's life in a state of drunkenness in relation to the sobriety of conventional society. Mullah Nasruddin tales, for example, are Sufi stories of the wisdom of backward, absurd behavior.[41] Rumi describes this wisdom:

> Conventional knowledge is death to our souls,
> And it is not really ours. It is laid on.
> Yet we keep saying we find "rest" in these "beliefs."
>
> We must become ignorant of what we have been taught
> And instead be bewildered.[42]

185

Ishq, therefore is subversive: Drunkenness helps us to see conventional assumptions inverted. Mysticism teaches us not that everything is unreal, but that the way our conventions have twisted things can be deceptive. The path of mystical bewilderment is not an easy one. Love is not always bright and joyful; there is a sort of death that one undergoes in this process. Like Christians, Sufis enter into a cycle of death—to the conventional way of perceiving the world—and rebirth.

Returning again to Islamic cosmology, it is apparent that, particularly in relation to love and compassion, the human is a microcosm. Just as love drives Sufi metaphysics, love is also the yearning in the heart of each of us for connection. Moreover, the "breath of compassion" that marks creation—and the re-creation of each moment—is interiorized in each of us. At the same time, because the cosmos as a whole is recognized as a single organism, the ethical imperative of the Sufi is to have compassion. Sa'di writes:

> The children of Adam are members of a single body,
> For from the moment of creation they were made of one
> substance.
> When fate causes pain in any member,
> The other members cannot remain still.
> O thou who hath no sorrow in seeing the sorrow of others,
> Thou art not worthy of being called a human being.[43]

We shall see later how the New Cosmology can—if we can re-discover a new union of opposites like that of Sufis—help us to experience the Universe as something like Sa'di's "single body" or an organism.

Ibn 'Arabi's mysticism, like his cosmology, centers on the Imagination. Just as the cosmos as a whole is an intermediate between the divine reality and non-existence which he calls "unbounded imagination," the human soul, or simply the "Imagination", links body and spirit.[44] The human being, as a microcosm, experiences the divine unity that permeates the cosmos through the Imagination. For Ibn 'Arabi, the Imagination is two-fold. First, it enables the divine, the locus of meaning, to become flesh in the human. We are the product of the divine Imagination. Second, it is how the flesh is made into spirit. The human, through the individual Imagination, which is a microcosm of the divine Imagination, has the capacity to create meaning, to transform our corporeal bodies into spirit through our creative energies.[45]

With the perspective of the depths of the soul, the *ashiq* no longer sees the exterior forms, but the inner love of the seeker. Indeed, even if there are those who behave in ways contrary to the theological perspective of the *ashiq*, there is still nothing but love for them. Moreover, at the center all paths have merged. Rumi writes:

> Cross and Christians, end to end, I examined. He was not on the Cross. I went to the Hindu temple, the ancient pagoda. In none of them was there any sign. To the uplands of Herat I went, and to Kandahar. I looked. He was not on the heights or in the lowlands. Resolutely, I went to the summit of the mountain of Kaf. There only was the dwelling of the Anqa bird. I went to the Kaaba of Mecca. He was not there. I asked about him from Avicenna the philosopher. He was beyond the range of Avicenna... I looked into my own heart. In that, his place, I saw him. He was in no other place.[46]

This does not mean that the Sufi wants to create a new religion that includes all the others. On the contrary, the diversity of forms is still appreciated by the Sufi, because each form is a unique expression of the same universal truth. Furthermore, the Islamic cosmology does not advocate a dualism of the interiority and the cosmic. When Rumi says "he was in no other place" than his "own heart," this means not an isolated interiority in the Cartesian sense, but a self that is coextensive with the divine reality shared with the entire Universe.

In addition to the unity of religions, the Sufi perceives two other "unities": the unity of humanity and the unity of creation itself. The entire Universe is *Allah*. The Sufi continues to pray five times a day, continues to live and work as before—this is not a path of asceticism or a rejection of the world. For when the Sufi perceives the unity of all through *Allah*, there is no need to depart from the world.

HINDUISM

The mystical traditions of Hinduism draw on the foundations laid out by the traditional South Asian cosmology and the Vedic religious practices. As described in the section on South Asian cosmology in chapter 6, the primacy of 'consciousness' and the doctrine of karma are central themes throughout the vast and diverse Hindu traditions. With the onset of the period of classical Hindu thought (ca. 200 BCE), the emphasis on cosmic harmony and fire sacrifice in the *Vedas* began to be understood in terms of the interior life of the individual. Ultimately, the consciousness of the Universe is not different from the consciousness of the individual—it may be helpful to read 'wisdom' instead of consciousness here—in Hindu thought. It is in the depths of one's true Self, therefore, that one can connect to the cosmos as a whole. This connection is referred to as Yoga in the Hindu traditions. Although many in the West "do yoga," seldom is there an awareness of the depth and breadth of the yoga traditions in Hinduism. Related to the English word for "yolk"—and similar to the root meaning of the English word "religion"—yoga means to connect, to bind. This can refer to the individual connecting to the divine, or to the cosmos as an organic whole—it refers to whatever one's cosmology considers the ultimate reality.

The yogic traditions involve both philosophy and practice, and there are many different branches. *Karma* yoga refers to the yoga of action. Gandhi was famously referred to as a Karma yogi because his action in the world was his spiritual practice. *Jnana* yoga refers to the yoga of knowledge. Like the Greek philosopher, this type of yogi gains knowledge not only of the world, but also of the self. This is considered an extremely difficult form of yoga. *Bhakti* is the yoga of devotion in which everything one does and says is done with love and devotion to the divine. *Raja* yoga involves varying yoga practices. For example, Patanjali's *Yoga Sutras* describe "Eight Limbs," some of which involve behavior and others having to do with meditative states. The fourth limb, *asana* practice, refers to the postures which later became *hatha* yoga, the type of yoga practice one could find at a New Age center or health club today.

The period of classical Hinduism is called the Upanishadic or Vedantic period. In addition to the *Upanishads* and the *Yoga Sutras*, the *Bhagavad Gita* is the most important text of Hindu mystical practice. It is in the *Gita* that the union of the Self and the cosmos is articulated most concisely and the integration of the non-dual traditions and the dualistic *Samhkya* philosophy occurs.

A proper understanding of the relationship of the Self and the whole—the cosmic Self—in Hinduism requires an understanding of the concepts of *Purusha*, *Atman* and *Brahman*. While these terms each refer to a different vantage point through which to comprehend the divine reality, they are ultimately not different. It is important, however, to distinguish them in order to fully comprehend the subtlety of Hindu thought. Furthermore, as I write from a Western viewpoint, it would be delusory to think that I could simply shift directly from the Cartesian ego to the Hindu Godhead. This would lead to the conflation of my ego with God—the Hindu seeks oneness with God, not equality. Hinduism provides us with a way to avoid this trap by re-imagining the self first.

According to *Samkhya* philosophy, the ego arises through natural evolutionary processes. This is entirely consistent with modern evolutionary theory, which understands evolution as a process of complexification and differentiation. The egoic mind—*manas*—works through the process of differentiation, of distinguishing dualistically. It is the higher mind, the mind of divine wisdom—*bodhi*—that helps us to realize that we all come from *Brahman*, the Godhead.

But before we can contact *Brahman*, we must transform our sense of self. This means a shift from the individual soul to the holistic Self, the *Atman*. The *Atman* is our deepest interiority, and our most authentic identity, beneath our superficial ego. Paradoxically, it is through the depth of interiority, *Atman*, that we find our connection to the whole, *Brahman*, because each of us is a microcosm. As individuals we participate in the cosmic Self through the *Atman*. We each experience the divine not through looking beyond ourselves, but by looking within. The union of opposites, the *Atman-Brahman*, is the paradigmatic experience of the divine in Hindu mysticism. We experience the totality of *Brahman's* Being (*sat*) through the *Atman*.

Mediating these two somewhat abstract concepts is the *Purusha*, commonly translated as the "cosmic person." An alternative understanding of the *Purusha* is that it is the soul or consciousness of *Brahman*; and our soul can be the *Purusha* as well if we are connecting to the *Brahman* through the *Atman*. The entire Universe is the body of the *Purusha*, and we, as aspects of that same body, share in that consciousness.

The *Purusha* provides a foundation for any understanding of compassion in Hindu mysticism, because it through the *Purusha* that we participate in the cosmic whole, and recognize others as expressions of that same whole. While *Samkhya* philosophy emphasizes the dualism of *Prakriti* ("nature") and the disembodied and eternal *Purusha*, the *Prakriti* and *Purusha* are united in yoga. It is through this unity that the *Purusha* can provide a paradigm for experiencing the Self not only as an abstract divinity, but as a part of the cosmic whole, wherein everything and everyone is part of the same body.

The *Upanisads* provide us with the mystical philosophy upon which yoga practice is based. They are typical of many of the other great texts of the Axial Age (approximately 800 BCE to 200 BCE) in that they took a cosmic worldview wherein the consciousness of individuals was embedded in the world, and applied it to the interior of the human—a concept not unlike the teaching of Jesus Christ which says, "The Kingdom of God is within you."[47] It is helpful here to recall that the type of mysticism we are emphasizing is *cosmic*, not ecstatic or ascetic. The *Upanisads* illustrate this type of mysticism perfectly because of their historical position, linking the Vedic and indigenous sense of embeddedness in creation with the Axial notion of individual interiority. I have argued here that mysticism is required, in part, because of the loss of this sense of embeddedness and connection.

And it is in the *Upanisads* that the *Atman-Brahman-Purusha* is articulated. While they speak little of specific techniques to realize this divine unity or of the ethical consequences of it, the *Upanisads* provide a poetic and philosophical foundation for their application. Fundamental to the Vedantic teaching is the unity of our identity and the reality that constitutes the divine spirit of the Universe. The *Chandogya Upanisad* describes this unity: "[A]n invisible and subtle essence is the Spirit of the whole universe. That is Reality. That is Atman. **Thou art that.**"[48] In this analysis, I will place a special emphasis on the *Purusha*, as it provides the link between the divine unity and creation itself.

The *Upanisads* establish the notion of divine unity as present both in creation and in the individual. *Mundaka Upanisad* describes the divine:

> He is beyond thought and invisible, beyond family and colour. He has neither eyes nor ears; he has neither hands nor feet. He is everlasting and omnipresent, infinite in the great and infinite in the small. He is the Eternal whom the sages see as the source of all creation.[49]

The divine, the source of creation, is both infinitely small and infinitely great. And God is not only the source of creation, but as *Svetasvara Upanisad* explains, remains "hidden" *in* creation.[50]

The connection to the ground of being, *Brahman*, is found through the interiority of the *Atman*. And through the *Atman*, the *Upanisads* teach, one finds unity with the entire world: "He who in the mystery of life has found the Atman, the Spirit, and has awakened to his light, to him as creator belongs the world of the Spirit, for he is this world."[51] The divine is therefore understood as both immanent and transcendent, 'Becoming' and 'Being.' *Isa Upanisad* teaches that we require knowledge of both the immanent and the transcendent, and must embrace both *jnana* and *karma*, knowledge and action.[52] It is in *Isa Upanisad* that we find the genesis of the ethical teachings one could derive from this philosophy: "He who sees all beings in his own Self, and his Self in all being, loses all fear."[53]

The author of *Katha Upanisad* writes: "Beyond the Spirit in man [sic] is the Spirit of the universe, and beyond is *Purusha*, the Spirit Supreme. Nothing is beyond Purusha: He is the end of the path."[54] In this text, emphasis is placed on the *Purusha* as the *anima mundi*, or world soul. From the Hindu perspective, it is important to recognize that it is not merely our individual soul—*jiva*—that is the true reality of the Self. The *Atman* is how we as individuals are actually not separate (*advaita*: "not two") from the divine unity of *Brahman*. Thus, the way we relate to the world is defined by our connection to the *Purusha*.

The role of the *Purusha* in the *Upanisads* is fully articulated in the "Castle of Brahman" from *Chandogya Upanisad*.[55] In this brief piece, the "castle" or body is described as having a tiny "shrine" in the center, within the heart, in the shape of a lotus flower. Therein is the *Purusha*, the entire Universe in microcosm:

> The little space within the heart is as great as this vast universe. The heavens and earth are there, and the sun, and the moon, and the stars; the fire and lightning and winds are there; and that now is and all that is not: for the whole universe is Him and He dwells within our heart... This is the real castle of Brahman wherein dwells all the love of the universe. It is Atman, pure spirit, beyond sorrow, old age, and death; beyond evil and hunger and thirst. It is Atman whose love is Truth, whose thoughts are Truth.[56]

The non-dual "Truth" (*Satyam*) that in the Vedic periods was understood in terms of the edge of the cosmic spheres is now found in the interior of the human. The union of opposites, the conjunction of the individual and the whole, occurs in each of us if we realize our true identity. But the *Upanisads* give us little practical help as to how to come to this recognition. For that, we turn to Patanjali's *Yoga Sutras*.

Patanjali's (2ⁿᵈ c. BCE) *Yoga Sutras* provide a practical guide to yoga practice. In my own practice of *hatha* yoga, I have often used Patanjali's eight limbs (*ashtanga*) as a framework. The limbs describe various methods to quiet the mind, beginning with changing our behavior.

For Patanjali, the first two limbs, the ethical and external concepts of *yama* and *niyama* are employed for their utility; that is, they are a means to an end, a way of moving toward the ultimate goal of yoga practice. His emphasis is on the individual practitioner, not collective transformation. I would argue, however, that by employing the eight limbs in a more circular manner the ethical precepts become both a means and an end: when we reach the state of *Samadhi*, we cannot help but be non-violent and truthful (*yama*), self-surrendering and pure (*niyama*). And this behavior will help others come to a realization of God as well.

Like the *Upanisads*, the *Yoga Sutras* emphasize the internalization of Vedic sacrifice. The *tapas* that once referred to the physical fires of the sacrifice are now generated internally, in the body. Although most people think of yoga as a physical process involving movement, according to Patanjali its essence is in stillness of both mind and body. "The restraint of the modifications of the mind-stuff is yoga," he writes.[57]

The practice described by Patanjali can be described as a concentration on the specific and partial to know the whole, a process of movement to know stillness. "Gradually one's mastery in concentration extends from the primal atom to the greatest magnitude."[58] For example, in my own form of *hatha* practice, *vinyasa*, the intention is to reach a state of stillness through constant movement. Similarly, Patanjali emphasizes the body in large part to let go of an attachment to it: "By purification arises disgust for one's own body and for contact with other bodies."[59]

In spite of the occasional tendency toward the rejection of the body in the *Yoga Sutras*, part of the appeal of *hatha* yoga is that it is *embodied*. There is a yearning, particularly in the West, for a more embodied form of spirituality. The significance of the body in yoga is best understood by putting the practice in a cosmic perspective. Yoga is a process of recognizing that our truest self is the *Atman*, which is at one with *Brahman*. And these two are connected through the cosmic soul of the *Purusha*, defined by Patanjali as the "true Self."[60] While we should not be attached to our physical bodies, it would be an error to dualistically reject the body, because the body is a part of the cosmic whole. We know the whole through the part, because each part, when we recognize it for its most authentic identity—the *Purusha*—is a microcosm, an individual expression of the whole. Central to Patanjali's yoga is the notion that one's perception of the Universe is not the Cartesian, subject-object dualism we often mistake it to be. The true perceiver, the consciousness through which we perceive anything, is the *Purusha*. The dualism of knower and known is eliminated.

The modern, Western application of yoga, just like other forms of New Ageism, comes from a place of genuine yearning for connection—recall that yoga, in fact, means connection. But it can easily be reduced to an egoic practice, whether it becomes a competitive physical exercise to make the body look better or an individualistic pursuit of personal salvation. To unify yogic praxis and the cosmic philosophical perspective, we must return to the *Bhagavad Gita*.

In the concept of the *Purusha*, the *Gita* details the cosmic nature of the mystical experience. At the same time, much more than the *Yoga Sutras* or the *Upanisads*, the *Gita* is, on the surface, a theistic text. Krishna represents a personalized figure of divinity, separate from but intervening in creation. A closer reading, however, demonstrates that the *Gita* is actually panentheistic—as in the *Upanisads*, the divine is both immanent and transcendent. Krishna, as the *Purusha*—and like the Christ in Trinitarian theology—connects the two:

> In these two aspects of my nature [*Purusha, Prakriti*] is
>   the womb of all creation.
> The birth and dissolution of the entire universe take
>   place within Me.
> There is nothing which exists separate from Me, Arjuna.
> The entire universe is suspended from Me as my necklace
>   of jewels. (7:6-7)[61]

Krishna is establishing his identity not only as the *Purusha* in contrast to the *Prakriti*, but as the *Purushottoma*, encompassing both *Purusha* and *Prakriti*.[62] Eknath Easwaran explains:

> Everything in the cosmos, he tells Arjuna, takes its rise
> from him, and one day it will be dissolved back into him
> again. This is not a matter of the Lord standing *here* and
> creating something *over there*; Sri Krishna is trying to

explain in these verses that the ever-changing world of time and space, matter and energy called prakriti, and the changeless reality that underlies that world, are simply two aspects of his divine nature."[63]

While it is not stated explicitly in the text, the mention of the womb cannot but conjure up notions of maternal compassion. We become compassionate not by being told how to act, but through recognizing our inherent divinity, that our consciousness is one with the *Purusha*. Later, when the cosmic vision has been revealed to Arjuna, he tells Krishna, "You are the knower and the thing which is known. You are the home of all; with your infinite form you pervade the cosmos."[64] As in the *Yoga Sutras*, the dualism of knower and known is eradicated through the *Purusha*. We who perceive the cosmos are not separate from the cosmos; and our true, non-dual identity is the *Purusha*. Krishna goes on to say:

> Arjuna, I am the taste of pure water and the radiance of
>   the sun and moon.
> I am the sacred word and the sound heard in the air, and
>   the courage of human beings. (7:8)[65]

Krishna is not only infinitely vast, but he permeates each individual thing. He calls upon the seeker to become conscious of him "ruling the cosmos"[66] in the *adhibhuta* ("the perishable body"), the *adhidaiva* ("the Purusha, the eternal spirit") and the *adhiyajna* ("the supreme sacrifice" made to Krishna as the Lord within us).[67] And because each of us is an aspect of the cosmic whole, we are inseparable from the divine. Along with this comes the realization that each and every being or action we encounter is also divine: "Brahman is attained by he who sees Brahman in every action."[68]

This raises the question of yogic practice in the *Gita*. As stated above, Krishna does not teach absolute morality to Arjuna; rather, Arjuna is bound by the duty of his specific *varna*.* The essence of the practical teachings of the *Gita* is that one cannot renounce action altogether. The simple fact of our presence in the world means we are acting. What we must do, however, is let go of the fruits of our actions:

> You are obliged to act, Arjuna, even to maintain your body.
> Fulfill your duties; action is better than inaction.
> The world is imprisoned in selfish action, Kauteya;
> act selflessly, without any thought of personal profit. (3:8-9)[69]

Krishna does not teach Arjuna to renounce the world, but to let go of any egoic attachment to gain in this world. The true Self, unlike the ego, is that which transcends the world.

An often criticized aspect of the *Gita* in terms of its ethics is its insistence that Arjuna must fight. Over and over again, Krishna tells Arjuna to "engage in this great war" (2:38) or something to that effect.[70] However, as Easwaran explains, the external battle should be understood as symbolic of a deeper, internal one:

> We are all born to fight the ego, to do battle against the three phalanxes of the ego's formidable army: fear, which is the infantry; anger, which is the cavalry; and lust, the most powerful of all, which is the elephantry. . . [I]f we talk in terms of a million lives, against the background of evolution, this war is going on all the time.

---

* The *varnas* are the particular roles that a person must have in Hindu society based upon one's Karma from previous lives.

The war is between what is selfish in me and what is
selfless in me."[71]

Like Muhammad when he said that the greater *jihad* is within,
Easwaran is suggesting that it is the internal battle between the
ego and the true Self in which we must be engaged. For this
reason, the ethical imperative of the *Gita* is not to conform to a
prescribed set of rules or guidelines; it does not even attempt to
dictate how one must feel toward another. The *Gita* focuses on a
higher ethics, that of transcending duality altogether.

The *Purusha*, the true, cosmic Self is the key to this realization, for it is the *Purusha*—or the *Purushotomma*—that transcends
the dualities we project upon the world with our reptilian brains
(*manas*). The Purusha can only be contacted through the higher
mind (*bodhi*). In chapter fifteen, "The Supreme Self," Krishna
describes this transcendent Self:

> In this world there are two orders of being, the perishable,
>   separate creature and the changeless spirit.
> But beyond these there is another, the supreme Self, the
>   eternal Lord, who enters into the entire cosmos and
>   supports it from within.
> I am that supreme Self, praised in the scriptures as beyond
>   the changing and the changless.
> Those who see in Me that supreme Self see truly.
> They have found the source of all wisdom, Arjuna, and
>   they
>   worship me with all their heart. (15:16-19)[72]

Krishna is suggesting that one must not reject the world, or
action in the world, but integrate the eternal and the transient.
Somewhat paradoxically, the *Gita* wavers between the theistic

notions of the above passage and the more prevalent notion of the divine within, found in the *Yoga Sutras* and the *Upanisads*. For example, while the above passage suggests that the source of wisdom is Krishna, in Chapter Four, verse 38, it states that yoga "leads to the path within."[73] While these verses may appear to be contradictory, they actually demonstrate the notion that the external, theistic divine is inseparable from the internal divine. Ultimately, any understanding of such concepts through discursive reason (*manas*) fails. "But what use is it to you to know all this, Arjuna?" asks Krishna after detailing some of the ways He is manifested in creation. "Just remember that I am, and that I support the entire cosmos with only a fragment of my being." (10:42)[74]

Theistic theology is employed not to give one a sense of the divine being separate, but to convey a sense of grace. Our egos are not in control; our minds cannot grasp the true nature of the cosmos or the divine. However, it is possible through yoga to unite our small selves with the cosmic Self of the *Purusha*. And, according to Krishna, this unity is best found neither through *karma* nor *jnana*, but through *bhakti*. We must let go of what we can know or do and simply love. This is how the *Purusha* connects us to the divine and the whole of the cosmos through the path of yoga; and this is the foundation for compassion.

BUDDHISM

The application of Western categories to Buddhism presents certain difficulties. Mysticism, in the sense that traditional Western scholarship understands it, is particularly difficult to apply because the Buddhist cosmology lacks fixed categories. Without a concrete self or a transcendent divinity, Buddhism would seem to lack the basic constituents of mystical union. However, the more fluid and flexible notions of union in cosmosophy fit quite well with the uniqueness of the Buddhist worldview.

Buddhist cosmology, as described in chapter 6, describes a Universe in constant flux and in which nothing, even the soul, can be considered to have any independent reality. This does not mean that it is not real, but that it is impossible to separate it from everyone and everything else. As a result, the union sought by the Buddhist is not to a fixed entity but to a never ceasing flow about which nothing definitive or absolute can be asserted.

The historical Buddha (born Siddhartha Gautama during the 6th century BCE in what is now Nepal) developed his teaching in the same cultural context as Hinduism in which he would have been expected to adhere to the Dharma of his particular social standing. However, he moved past his personal Dharma, or even the Dharma of his *yuga* (or "age"), to a *Moksha* Dharma, beyond any norm understood up to that point in his culture. Like all mystics, Siddhartha Gautama broke through a boundary. His was not a Dharma that could be reached by an intermediary. Realizing that he possessed in his own heart something Universal, a truth that could not be separated from the rest of the cosmos, the Buddha looked *within*. So, although any notion of a god in Buddhism is not explicitly rejected, the theism of the *Gita*—or of Christianity—is not embraced. In addition, the Buddha rejected altogether the notion of a Self, replacing the Hindu *atman*, with the Buddhist *anatman*—"no self." For the Buddha, the fixed self was something illusory; the task of the Buddhist is not to recognize the permanent, immutable soul, but to realize the essential emptiness of all.

This emptiness, or *shunyata*, however, is not quite as empty as it may seem. Corresponding to the notion of *shunyata* is the doctrine of *tathagatagarbhah*, the "Womb of Buddhahood."[75] While there is no fixed self, this emptiness is "pregnant" with the

201

potential for enlightenment.[76] That is, emptiness—especially for the Mahayanists who were influenced heavily by Chinese cosmology—means interdependence.[77] For the Buddhist, mysticism has little meaning when it refers to a fixed self and a fixed deity. Everything is in flux; nothing is absolute. This is the principle of *shunyata*. However, Buddhism offers a way to participate with this reality—to "wake up"—by examining one's interiority that is interdependent and interconnected with the entire cosmos.

Fundamental to this process is the concept of *Bodhicitta*, or "awakened mind." Buddhist cosmology holds that the Universe pulses to life from the cosmic processes of *citta*, or mind. Unlike the Cartesian mind, in South Asian cosmology this is the animating principal of the Universe. *Cintamani* is the imagination, enabling us to imagine worlds and experiences beyond our own. Indeed, in the Buddhist worldview, we create our world through our thoughts and intentions. The capacity to wake the mind up—*Bodhicitta*—is to attain the compassionate awareness that everything in the Universe, including the very thoughts that come up with such ideas, is part of the same, holistic process.

Buddhist teaching begins with an acknowledgment that *dukkha*, generally translated as "suffering," is an inherent part of life. More than suffering, however, *dukkha* refers to anything that arises from conditioned experience. We experience *dukkha* not only as pain and suffering, but as the limitation of time and space. Early Buddhism focuses on the teachings of the historical Buddha, Gautama, and the liberation of the individual from this suffering through meditation. To perceive the true nature of things, escaping from the cycle of death and rebirth—*samsara*—allows one to attain liberation.

But as Buddhism spread from the Indian subcontinent to the Far East, (perhaps beginning as early as the first century C.E.) a new form emerged, the Mahayana, or "Great Wheel". "[C] ompassion takes on a particular significance in the *Mahayana*," writes Thupten Jinpa, the Dalai Lama's translator.[78] Central to the Mahayana path is the Bodhisattva, the enlightened one who, out of compassion, returns to the world of suffering in order to help all sentient beings attain enlightenment themselves.

While the Mahayanist does not reject the older Buddhist view of the interdependence and impermanence of all things, the phenomenal world is also embraced, in an unattached way:

> The tendency to regard the phenomenal world as something unreal that doesn't really matter is rejected by Buddhists as nihilism. The tendency to regard it as something permanent, real in itself, that matters utterly and everlastingly is rejected as eternalism. Nihilism and eternalism are known in the Buddha Dharma as the two extremes.[79]

A subtle, dialectical tension between the two extremes remains, never fully resolved. As in the *Gita*, the Buddhist is called upon to act in the world as though it were real, but to remain unattached as though it were not. But the emphasis in Buddhism, unlike in the Hindu tradition, is not on metaphysical or ontological truths, but on what will be the most expedient means for the practitioner.

Ultimately, Buddhist teaching attempts to facilitate compassion in the practitioner. "In the Buddhist context," says the Dalai Lama, "one can refer to the concept of rebirth to assist in the practice of equanimity."[80] Because of the Buddhist principle of *anatman*, rebirth is a part of the interconnectivity of all things, and the ability of the mind to reify. There is no ontologically independent soul that is reborn. But the *concept* of rebirth becomes important to the degree it encourages the individual to embody equanimity—that is, compassion for all.

The Mahayana transformation involved the recognition that if one were truly enlightened, it would be impossible to seek individual liberation without wanting the same for all sentient beings. The reality we create is not done through our isolated, individual consciousness—as the self-help books suggest—but collectively. This is the essence of the Buddhist notion of compassion. Many of these teachings came into being long after Gautama had died through the insight of Buddhists who were able to recognize their own "Buddha Nature"; that is, by looking within, the individual can gain insight into the true nature of things. When this insight involves compassion for all sentient beings, it is *prajna*, or wisdom. The Dalai Lama describes compassion as the "merging of intellect and heart."[81] For Buddhists, *prajna* is the merging of the head and heart, resulting in compassion. This merging involves an inner empiricism, a deep journey of reflection and insight in to one's own Buddha Nature.

The inward journey toward one's Buddha Nature leads one to the realization of an inherent interconnectivity. At this stage, compassion is not emotional, but the result of inquiry. Compassion that is merely emotional is considered "less firm."[82] This wisdom is explained by Gyalwa Gendun Gyatso, the second Dalai Lama: "He who gains this understanding becomes a sage abiding in knowledge of the inseparable nature, the common ground of emptiness and interdependent origination."[83] The interior dimension of Buddhist practice is now reflected in a cosmic dimension. "We are in the center of the world, always, moment after moment," writes the great Zen teacher Shunryu Suzuki. "So we are completely dependent and independent."[84] When we become aware of our true nature, we also become aware of the true nature of the entire cosmos, and the two are inseparable.

Compassion and wisdom are embodied as the feminine in several different Buddhist expressions. *Prajnaparamita*, or the transcendent wisdom that can see emptiness, is described as the mother of all Buddhas and depicted in the female form in *Vajrayana* Buddhism.[85] *Tara* represents compassion in the Tibetan tradition. In Chinese Buddhism, *Kuan Yin* is the Bodhisattva of compassion.

This repeated association of the feminine with both wisdom and compassion in Buddhism seems to have to do the archetypal feminine as the caring mother and the association of the feminine with interiority. It is the union of these two—looking inward to find wisdom and the compassion of the cosmic womb—that leads to enlightenment. The *Metta Sutta* describes the connection between maternal compassion and cosmic compassion:

> As a mother watches over her child, willing to risk her
> own life to protect her only child, so with boundless
> heart should one cherish all living beings, suffusing the
> whole world with unobstructed loving-kindness.[86]

In *Metta* practice, maternal compassion is used to help foster compassion for all sentient beings.

In Buddhism, access to wisdom is an interior process. By looking within, the practitioner must experience that the deepest individuality is actually universal. "The realizational teachings are upheld by cultivating that experience within yourself,"[87] says the Dalai Lama. Indeed, the Buddha admonished his followers not to believe his teachings because he said them, but to participate with the teachings and come to their own realization. It is the interior transformation, the awakening to the realization that our deepest self is inseparable from anyone or anything else, that allows for true compassion.

Taoism

The Chinese worldview combines several different wisdom traditions, including the Buddhism. Taoism could be considered China's oldest wisdom tradition in that its roots clearly lie in Shamanic practices. Among the major traditions native to China, Taoism is probably the most mystical because it deals simultaneously with cosmos and interiority, whereas the Confucian tradition primarily emphasizes a cosmic vision that is mirrored in society. Jeaneane Fowler suggests that Taoism's mysticism lies in Lao Tzu's positing "an inner reality that transcends both the self and the outer world."[88] The Taoist path interiorizes the cosmic vision, uniting multiple polarities through the mysterious Tao. Lao Tzu writes:

> These two come from the same source, but are different
> in name.
> The same source is called Mystery.
> Mystery and more mystery.
> It is the gateway to myriad subtleties.[89]

The term "mystery" (*hsuan*) originally meant black, and is used as a philosophical term to describe the Tao.[90] Rather than mere confusion or lack of clarity, the Tao represents a holistic vision of cosmos and self, and various means of connecting the interior life to harmony of the cosmos. Its mystery lies in our inability to conceptualize it through the conventional means of distinction.

It should be noted that there are several different approaches that are referred to as Taoism: first, there is an organized religion called Taoism; second, there are practices and techniques for meditation and health; and third, there is Taoist philosophy. This work focuses primarily on the latter two. Taoism is not an exception to the general pattern that organized hierarchies tend to stifle the freedom and openness of mystical participation. Religious Taoism, because of its structure, has a concreteness that seems to contradict much of the early Taoist philosophy.

Taoist philosophy and practice is based upon the Chinese cosmology that understands the human as fundamentally a microcosm of an organic whole. The traditional Chinese cosmology understood the human to be positioned between heaven and Earth. Taoist practice, therefore, is a process of taking these polarities and integrating them within the interiority of the human. The mystic's interiority can thereby participate in the processes of cosmic whole—the Tao.

Other than Lao Tzu, the greatest early Taoist philosopher is Chuang Tzu, whose primary emphasis is *Shou Yao* or "freedom."[91] For Chuang Tzu, freedom differs from both the Buddhist and Western concepts. In Buddhism—particularly in the Hinayana traditions—freedom is conceived of psychologically; that is, it is the liberation of the mind. In the West, freedom is largely materialistic and individualistic, based upon the rights of the individual to do and possess certain things. Chuang Tzu's freedom is holistic, limited by neither the body nor the mind. It allows one to let go entirely of all relativism, all ideas about what is 'right' and 'wrong.' According to Chuang Tzu, when this absolute freedom occurs we have no agendas, no desire. In Section I of his collected writings, "Free and Easy Wandering," Chuang Tzu relays a story about a cicada and a little dove who cannot imagine traveling beyond the limitations of their own experience.[92] They are limited by a narrow perspective. There is a fish, however, who comes from "the northern darkness"—that is, beyond our senses—who transforms into a bird who can fly to the Lake of Heaven.[93] The fish and bird unite upper and lower, just as the journey of the bird unite *yin* (northern darkness) and *yang* (Lake of Heaven).

The transformation exemplified in the story of the cicada, the dove, and the fish is another key element for Chuang Tzu. In Section II, he tells the story of Chuang Chou dreaming he is a butterfly—a symbol of transformation—who is unable to determine if "he was Chuang Chou who had dreamt he was a butterfly, or a butterfly dreaming he was Chuang Chou. There must be some distinction! This is called the Transformation of Things."[94] It is precisely from such distinctions between observer and observed that Chuang Tzu is suggesting we would become free if we were to undergo a transformation.

The transformation of the self involves reversal. In Chapter 40, Lao Tzu writes:

> Reversal is the movement of the Way.
> Weakness is the function of the Way.
> All things in the world live in Being,
> And Being lives in Non-being.[95]

Reversal, for the Taoist, is a way of channeling the natural energy flow in the Universe. The way in which the Tao finds expression in nature is called *te*, and Taoist practice requires one to find harmony with this energy. Taoist meditation, like yoga and Buddhist practice, emphasizes the quieting of the mind. Chuang Tzu calls upon us to become free of the complications and distinctions of the world to find this harmony:

> The heart of the wise [person] is tranquil.
> It is the mirror of heaven and earth
> The glass of everything.
> Emptiness, stillness, tranquility, tastelessness,
> Silence, non-action: this is the level of heaven and earth
> This is perfect Tao. Wise [people] find here

Their resting place.

Resting, they are empty.[96]

The quiet within allows one to harmonize with the never ceasing change and flux of the world, which, paradoxically, reflects the unchanging Tao. Reversal occurs because the general pattern of nature, according to the Tao, is not linear. Eventually, if one can harmonize with the Tao, one will return to the original state of undifferentiation. That is, it is not by fighting change but by embracing it that one can recover that which is truly constant. The Universe has evolved, according to Chinese cosmology, from a point of undifferentiation. The union of opposites in Taoist practice occurs when—through harmonizing with the constant transformation of the Tao—the individual can realize this undifferentiated state within. In this way, the Taoist makes no distinctions between any one or any thing. Reversal, therefore, involves a certain counter-cultural aspect. Whereas conventional culture favors power, the Tao advocates "weakness."

Among the most popular influences of Taoist practice and philosophy on the West are the martial arts, particularly the internal arts such as *Tai Chi Chuan* and *Bagua Zhang*. These arts involve both devastating martial aspects as well as healing practices. Rather than relying solely on speed and strength, as Lao Tzu teaches, they favor a balance of *yin* and *yang*, with an emphasis on softness and flexibility:

One who is living is soft and weak.
One who is dead is hard and rigid.
All living things, like grass and trees, are soft and frail.
With death, they become withered and dry.
Therefore, hardness and rigidity are associated with
    death.

> Softness and weakness are associated with life.
> Therefore, powerful weapons will not win;
> Massive trees will be cut down;
> The strong and great will be laid low;
> The soft and weak will be exalted.[97]

One can see clearly the parallels to the subversive mysticism—the inversion of society's norms beyond the barrier—of Jesus. Moreover, the basis for Taoist philosophy lies in the nature of the organic world. Life requires us not to be too hard or too inflexible. Someone who is too hard to change cannot survive—or is already dead.

For the Taoist, the human body—not a soul that is somehow separate from the body—is a microcosm. Like other systems, Taoism holds that there are two levels of souls, the *p'o*, or personal souls, and the *hun*, the inner nature.[98] Quite different from some Western traditions, however, is that the immortality sought by the Taoist is often *bodily*. It is the integration of all levels of soul with the body, not the separation of soul from body, that leads to immortality. The body itself is understood in terms of the Three Treasures: *ching*, or vital essence which generates all life; *shen*, the spirit or soul of the individual; and *ch'i*, the energy of the Tao, expressed in nature as *te* or *yin* and *yang* energy. These three aspects are the functioning energies of the Tao in the cosmos as well as the "life-giving essences of the body."[99] Among them, *ch'i* is particularly important both for the role it plays in the cosmos as a whole and in the individual. *Ch'i* links spirit and matter and is therefore the key energy in both traditional healing arts and martial arts.

The Taoist alchemists sought to develop a "Spirit Embryo" that was both physical and spiritual, the cultivation of one's physical capacities and the potentiality of the essential emptiness of one's being.[100] By balancing one's internal energy, through the cultivation of *ch'i*, the interior transformation could be manifested externally. This transformation leads to an entirely new approach to life, best conveyed through the concept of *wu wei*. Literally— and somewhat misleadingly in English translation—meaning "non-action," it refers to the letting go of one's personal agendas and desires, and of the fruits of one's actions. Rather attempting to assert one's self powerfully over others and over nature, *wu wei* indicates that a better path is to harmonize with nature and redirect the energy that runs counter to the Tao. For example, in my martial arts practice, *bagua zhang*, we learn not to meet hard fist with hard fist, strength with strength. Rather, we must use our opponents' strength against them. Of course, there are still times when we must be hard—it all depends on the energy we encounter. Lao Tzu writes:

> Act through non-action,
> Serve through non-doing,
> Taste through non-tasting,
> Do the great through the small, deal with the myriad things
>   with the few,
> Repay malice with virtue,
> Solve the difficult problem at its easiest,
> Do the great work at is smallest.
> The difficult affairs of the world surely start from the easy,
> The great works of the world surely begin from the small.
> Therefore, the sage, never doing anything for greatness,
> Is able to achieve greatness.
> One who promises lightly surely will not be trustworthy;
> One who thinks everything easy will end in more difficulty.
> Therefore, the sage, taking everything as difficult,
> Will have no difficulty in the end.[101]

For Lao Tzu, the transformation of our way of thinking—that is, a shift in worldview or *metanoia*—comes before any authentic change. In the face of crisis, the Taoist realizes that one cannot force change. Indeed, it is interesting the extent to which activists today attempt to assert themselves quite militantly against the powers that be. George Orwell's warnings in *Animal Farm* have still not been heeded.[*]

Both *wu wei* and the notion of reversal demonstrate the counter-cultural element of Taoism that has often made it so compelling to Westerners. It is important, however, to remember that Lao Tzu and Chuang Tzu's writings were based upon a Chinese cosmology that was far less individualistic than our own. Modern psychology and Taoism can certainly be linked, but a full understanding of Taoist practice is more than psychological. It has to do with our basic assumptions about the cosmos. Most fundamental to each of us is not the psyche, but the cultivation of the spirit embryo, an interiority that is both physical and spiritual. The human body and the psyche make up an organic whole in microcosm of the organic macrocosmos. The union of opposites, for the Taoist mystic, links not only psyche and cosmos, but also the individual body to the cosmic body. In the spirit womb, we connect to the living womb of the cosmos.

Each of the world's wisdom traditions has a mystical path that connects the innermost psyche of the individual with the living

---

[*] George Orwell, *Animal Farm* (New York: Harcourt, Brace, 1954). This novel describes an allegorical revolution on a farm in which the leaders of the rebellion, the pigs, turn into their former oppressors, the farmers, after gaining power.

womb of the cosmos. These mystics live at the edge of their traditions, just as their souls possess an awareness of the edge of the cosmic womb—they are tapping into the Universe's capacity to give birth to novelty. These traditions are based upon the fundamental assumptions laid out in their cosmologies. Without understanding this foundation, one cannot truly grasp the wisdom these mystics embody.

Mysticism is important for us today as much as, or perhaps even more than, it was during the development of classical mystical systems. We are alienated from the cosmos as never before. Humanity and the Earth of which humanity is a part are suffering because of our actions—actions that are based on a dysfunctional cosmology and a failure to participate meaningfully with the world. We lack a framework and practice to unite the opposites of our individual interiority and the cosmic whole.

In today's world, however, we have begun to understand the world in an entirely new way. The New Cosmology will be based on a Universe that is not static, an ultimately reality that is not fixed. We are part of an interconnected, organic whole that is constantly birthing. The mystical systems of the wisdom traditions give us great insight into how one might unite the opposites and participate more meaningfully in our world. But to create a worldview based on the New Cosmology, we must implement a new kind of mysticism. That is, to tell a new myth we require a new set of assumptions about the world (*cosmosophia*) and a new discipline (cosmosophy) if we are to find the wisdom for this moment.

Cosmosophia

All'altra fantasia qui mancò possa;
Ma già volgeva il mio disiro e il velle,
Sì come rota ch'egualmente è mossa,
L'amor che move il sole e l'altre stelle.
—Dante, *Paradiso*, Canto xxxiii, 142-145[1]

C OSMOSOPHIA COMES FROM two Greek words, *cosmos* and *sophia*. It refers to the wisdom (*sophia*) that is inherent to the process of our unfolding Universe. Like ancient philosophy, it recognizes that wisdom comes from remembering our true nature. It is through our interiority, not simply from external information and observation, that we discover wisdom. However, unlike much of the ancient Greek philosophy, it does not hold that our true nature is something apart from the cosmic processes. Wisdom is how the Universe continually remembers its unity—just as the mystic does on an individual basis—even as new subjectivity and perspectives arise. Human wisdom, therefore, must be understood in this cosmic context: philosophy is a subset of cosmosophy.

---

* "Here the power of the high fantasy was lost;/ but already my desire and will were rolled/ like a wheel that moves equally/ by the love that moves the sun and the other stars." [translation mine]

215

In this section, the various elements of the previous sections will be integrated with modern science to present the following: first, the basic components of the discipline of cosmosophy as an approach to arriving at a new cosmology; second, the mythic and symbolic framework of *cosmosophia*, the core values upon which I believe a new cosmology can be based; third, a new vision of what it means to be human in light of modern science, the wisdom traditions, and *cosmosophia*; and, finally, a new myth, a story of the Universe and ourselves.

While each of the mystical traditions described in chapter 9 can be valuable to us today, they have their limitations. We must remember, above all else, that their true meaning and value is found in the embodiment—not only understanding, but also living—of their cosmologies. This means, for example, that the Sufi must inhabit a Sufi Universe, not just accept Sufi ideas on the weekends; an adherent to African spirituality must fully embody that worldview, or risk misappropriating that spirituality. My concern is more than giving offense—although surely Westerners do offend when they appropriate another's spirituality—but also that we delude ourselves in this process. As long as we continue to live in the Newtonian-Cartesian Worldview, mysticism will be reduced to psychology—useful, but hardly transformative on a planetary level.

As beautiful and as functional as the cosmologies of the Wisdom traditions were, none was a cosmo-genesis. Cosmosophy is an approach—one of many possibilities—to engage in a mysticism grounded in modern science in order to give rise to a new myth that has the potential to heal our relationships with the Earth and our fellow beings.

Chapter Ten
Cosmosophy

COSMOSOPHY, LIKE PHILOSOPHY, is a discipline. Like ancient philosophy, it is much more than a mere *academic* discipline—it is an approach to life. In fact, there is little to separate it from the role that religion has played in people's lives, except for the fact that there is nothing to *join*. Like religion, cosmosophy is a way to create a worldview that connects us to one another, to the whole. It is an approach to life based on the wisdom that is an inherent part of the processes of the cosmos and on *cosmosophia*, a symbolic framework to approach wisdom in an evolving Universe.

So far, this study has focused on the cosmologies and mystical philosophies of the world's wisdom traditions. In each example, it has been shown that the way in which one participates deeply and meaningfully with the ultimate reality—mysticism—depends on one's cosmology. While the mystics of the past teach us a great deal about the world today, they also show us that to be a true mystic is to be on the edge, ready to give birth to novelty. The world's wisdom traditions were created around cosmologies to which most of us no longer adhere. This does not mean that we ought to reject them, but that their wisdom is found in adapting them to today's cosmology. In this way, a worldview can be created based on the wisdom of our ancestors—both human and cosmic ancestors.

Birthing a New Worldview

To return to "The Crisis" laid out in the second chapter, the cosmosophical process is a means of telling a new myth, one that functions better than the one that has led to so many problems. While this has involved, in part, philosophical critiques of the current worldview, it is not intended to be mere criticism, but to foster openness to the fact that our world, and the perspective from which we perceive that world, is constantly birthing itself anew. We must be open to these changes in order to tell a story that serves us best, a story that is fundamentally a story of cosmic wisdom.

Humanity's construction of a worldview began with participation, not detached observation. The world we observe is the world in which we are embedded, the world that has birthed us. The early myths and cosmologies were based on the ways in which people connected to their world. Later, as humans began to widen their perspectives, cosmologies were developed that integrated new insights with the intuitions people had about their relationship to their world. Science, however, presents us with a new epistemology based on objective observation, consilience with established principles, and empiricism. Humanity has been able to learn an astounding amount of information about our world, expanding our perspective immeasurably. But we have not yet figured out how to integrate this knowledge into our intuitive sense of connection to this vast whole. We have not learned how to tell a new myth about this Universe.

The cosmosophical process involves four limbs. They should not be approached in a linear way; rather, we are always dealing in one way or another with each. There is no end to the process. The Universe is constantly in flux, always evolving, always birthing. The pursuit of wisdom, therefore, is a never-ending, always changing process.

The first limb of the cosmosophical process is *science and observation*. Paradoxically, it is the last of the limbs to arise among humans. For most of human history, the human participated with the cosmos without the scientific idea of objective observation. Rather than a complete break from the past, however, science can be better viewed as an extension of already-present aspects of this participation. Life always takes in external information toward which it attempts to develop appropriate behaviors. Even the simplest living cells make determinations about the nature of their environment. Behavior, and ultimately, the way an organism evolves, is based on this interaction. Evolution occurs not through individual cognition, but through collective processes. The human extends this capacity by using symbolic systems of communication. Based on the way we believe the Universe to be, we create a worldview. The role of science, however, is not to engage in the meaning-making, worldview-building process.

For this reason, the second limb of cosmosophy is *philosophy*. The task of philosophers is to find meaning in the knowledge our science unveils. Everyone engages in at least a little bit of philosophy, admitted or not. Even when we reduce our discussion to 'scientific cosmology,' philosophy is required to determine what these facts mean. For example, some—most notably Steve Weinberg—have concluded that our world is utterly meaningless based on a lack of empirical evidence for God, a highly simplistic concept of divinity far closer to the fundamentalists' than to the mystics' described in this study.* Others have recently determined that, based on the same empirical process, we must change our way of life to save ourselves from global warming.[1] Each of these involves an implicit philosophical assumption based on scientific information. This is not a critique. To think about how our way of life should correspond to the world before us is profoundly important.

Ideas about the world, however, generally do not change the way we relate to it. The third limb, therefore, is *mystical participation*. This involves practices and ways of life that allow individuals to connect to the cosmos that our science and philosophy attempt to describe and explain. Behind any mysticism are certain assumptions about reality as observed in our science and relayed philosophically. But mysticism can do more than help one connect to the facts and ideas as they are known. The mystic is at the edge, breaking through the cosmic and cultural barriers to know things in an entirely new way. One should tread carefully here, however. Mysticism that is developed from a dualistic framework often runs counter to the observations we make. The mystic should balance unique subjectivity and novelty with an adherence to what the first two limbs suggest about the world, drawing on well developed philosophical foundations and practices that involve the body, compassion for one another, and connections to nature. It is through mystical participation that it becomes apparent that wisdom is not primarily something the human creates, but an attribute of the cosmos to which the human gives particular expression.

---

* Weinberg writes: "The more the universe [sic] seems comprehensible, the more it also seems meaningless." Steven Wienberg, *The First Three Minutes: A Modern View of the Origin of the Universe* (New York: Basic Books, 1993) p.154

This form of expression is the fourth limb, the *imagination and creative expression* through which a new myth is born. Just as the Universe is fundamentally a birther, the human gives birth to poetry, song, and story. Collectively, our mystics, our philosophers, our scientists, and our artists produce the mythology that teaches us how to live our lives, teaches us what has the most value and meaning. This meaning is never fixed. The myths of the middle ages were not wrong, but we cannot live lives in the world based solely on them. The mystics of the past connected to the Universe as they knew it; the artists told stories about that world. We can draw on those myths and mystical philosophies—indeed, it would be a mistake not to draw on them—but a worldview must combine a consistency and connection to the past with novel ideas and observations. Just as biological evolution operates according to an adherence to long established norms—any mutation that is too extreme generally cannot be carried on—and novelty that is consistent with a changing ecosystem, worldviews change based on the wisdom of our traditions and new ideas that allow us to live more sustainable, meaningful, compassionate lives. A trait is never adopted in a vacuum; it always depends on the community of life around it.

THE MYTHIC FRAMEWORK OF *COSMOSOPHIA*

Through the four-fold cosmosophical process, it is possible to give birth to a new myth. But the myth we create depends on our basic assumptions, values and core metaphors about the Universe. There is no such thing as the person or culture that makes choices based on purely rational, objective choices. The core values of a culture always inform those choices, and provide the parameters within which the rational mind can work. This is true in the case of all the wisdom traditions. Drawing from the insights of those traditions and from contemporary science, *cosmosophia* holds the following as the symbolic foundation of a new cosmology:

I. *The cosmos is our womb.* This is the core metaphor of *cosmosophia*. For the human, the experience of the womb is a fundamental symbol of compassion and connection. Just as the embryo is embedded in the womb, everything in the Universe is, from the very beginning, embedded in the cosmic womb. This means that from the moment of its conception, the cosmos itself, as a whole, has *interiority*—a wisdom that allows it to operate as a single whole. As participants in this womb, none of us is separate from one another. When we recognize our true, cosmic identity, we are naturally compassionate to all the cosmos. The felt sense of the womb is that of non-differentiation and seamlessness.

It is particularly important to note that this metaphor is organic. It has become commonplace in modernity to decry anthropomorphism and the implementation of metaphoric language. But Modernity is so awash in *mechanomorphic* metaphors that it is difficult for anyone to even perceive them. That is, there is no trouble with metaphors of the Universe as a *machine*, but there is opposition to metaphors that are *living*. It would be correct to point out, however, that any metaphor is limited. Human language did not develop to convey literally the deepest mysteries of the Universe. Every discussion—scientific, theological, philosophical—uses metaphor. What is important is that our metaphors convey what we value. *Cosmosophia* holds that the Universe as an organic whole is fundamentally sacred.

II. *The cosmos is a birth-giving process.* More than a place, the Universe is a process because it unfolds not *in* space, but through the space-time continuum. Space and time emerge together. The womb in which we are embedded is not static; it continuously gives birth. While this process is seamless, there is also a repeated occurrence of the special time, the *kairos*, in which novelty arises.

This is where the metaphor of mammalian birth breaks down—we are not born *beyond* the cosmic womb, but as new interiors *within* the interior of the previous womb. As a new womb arises, it contains its own wisdom, its own interiority. At the same time, it possesses the wisdom of the whole in its depths.

There is a danger here of believing we have left the womb altogether. The issue of rebirth among Platonists and Christians exemplifies this problem. Their static cosmologies, in which time is seen as moving through space, led them to believe that immortality could be attained only when the soul moved beyond the cosmos. *Cosmosophia* suggests that transcendence is found not only beyond the cosmos, but also in the capacity of a community of individuals to come together to form a whole that is greater than the sum of its parts. The interiority of these new wholes, new wombs, can consequently make connections to other wholes. Rebirth, therefore, is not beyond the cosmic sphere but into a new womb of deeper interiority and vaster communion. This can be seen in the way in which a community of elements comes together to form a star, a community of molecules comes together to form a living being, or the way a community of human beings can come together to form a culture. Recall the apocalyptics who believed their world was ending. The world did not end, but gave birth to a new world. In each case, the wisdom of the new community has a capacity to form new connections.

III. *The interiority of each new womb is cosmic, with the capacity to connect compassionately to the whole.* Each new womb is a microcosm wherein the wisdom of the whole is present. Each womb gives unique expression to the cosmic whole. The Earth, for example, has a particular wisdom, a way in which its processes bring about order and beauty—it is a microcosm. An ecosystem expresses this wisdom in its unique way, enabling it to find harmonious internal balance. It too has a sort of interiority, a unique wisdom. This does not mean, of course, that either the Earth or the ecosystem is isolated or independent. Each remains part of the cosmic whole, part of an interdependent web of relationships.

Drawing from the wisdom of the mystics, the human has the capacity to unite the opposites of the interior and the cosmic. There is an element of rebirth and return here. The birthing process is a sort of death—we have lost the felt sense of the womb whence we have come. But we are reborn in the realization that we have emerged into a new womb. Just as the unfolding Universe gives birth to new wombs, each with a wisdom that is a unique expression of a new perspective, the human, too, has a unique form of wisdom. The Universe, not only the isolated individual, has birthed this wisdom. Interiority, in contrast to the Cartesian mind, is *cosmic*. The authenticity of our unique experience connects us to the universal. According to Matthew Fox, Thomas Aquinas refers to this cosmic interiority as *capax universi*—"the capacity of the Universe".[2] We have within us the wisdom of our ancestors—13.7 billion years of cosmic unfolding.

IV. *Because we are embedded in this birthing process, we are creating our world.* Just as we have the capacity of the Universe from our shared ancestry, we also possess the capacity to create our future through the imagination. The human possesses an interiority that is unique to the human—not better, but different from any other. We use the creation of culture through the imagination to create our world. This does not mean we 'create our own reality' in a psychological way. Rather, we are participants in the unfolding process of the whole. As the stars create new stars that can give birth to living planets, as life continuously gives birth to new forms of life, the human determines the world in which we live through culture. The stories we tell and the songs we sing express what is most meaningful to us, what we value most. These stories, in today's world, determine the fate not only of humanity, but myriad living beings.

Through our creative spark, through the imagination, the human can express the transcendent. Because we live in a living, ensouled cosmos—the womb—we have within us the creative capacities of our history. This is the presence of the immanent divine. We also have the capacity to give birth, to imagine that which is not yet present. This imaginative capacity allows for the human expression of the transcendent divine. *Cosmosophia* is therefore a panentheistic approach, uniting the mystical co-participation of the immanent with the imaginal co-creation of the transcendent.

Through the fourfold process of cosmosophy and the fourfold core assumptions of *cosmosophia*, humanity can engage in a process of creating a new myth. These assumptions are only one approach, one way of looking at the world. They can become concretized and misused like any other set of ideas. Before a possibility for a new myth is offered, *cosmosophia* must be further developed to be sure that the new worldview and the new myth we tell about this vision is one that allows us to create more sustainable communities and more compassionate values. For it is not only *about* the world, but a means of participating in the world. This returns us to the question asked by all the great mystical traditions and cosmological systems: What does it mean to be a human in the world? That is, before one can tell a story about the world, one must have not only some external knowledge, but also some intuition about what it means to be a human being.

Chapter Eleven
Anthropos
Cosmosophos

I T IS EASY TO GET LOST in our metaphors and abuse them, or to turn a suggested process into a rigid set of guidelines. Just as easy is to focus on the concepts as an intellectual or academic exercise. The concepts outlined in the previous chapter are only as good as the behaviors they engender. That is, the value of *cosmosophia*, or any set of ideas, is the way in which it can affect our lives and encourage a way of life that is more compassionate, more sustainable, and more meaningful.

This study began with the suggestion that we are currently in crisis. It proposed that a good way of addressing this crisis would be to cultivate the creation of a new cosmology and a new myth—a process that is fundamental to what it means to be human. By looking back at traditional cosmologies and mystical philosophies, I have offered an approach to developing such a myth. As different as they are, these cultures shared in common a desire not only to describe and explain the Universe, but also to understand the role of the human in the cosmos.

Before we can begin to propose a possible new myth, we must do more than have ideas about the Universe. We must change our ideas about what it means to be a human. Every myth that humans tell is based not only on the assumptions their culture makes about the Universe; it is based on the assumptions made about what it means to be a human being.

Modern cosmology tells us that we are isolated in our Cartesian egos, that our primary role in the world is that of consumers. In the context of *cosmosophia*, the human, like every other living being, is a cosmic being. Rather than being cut off from the world, each of us possesses an identity that is at once unique and intimately interconnected with the entire Universe. And as human beings, it is our task to give human expression to cosmic wisdom. In recognizing our cosmic nature we have the capacity to give expression to this wisdom. Then, and only then, will we become the *anthropos cosmosophos*—the cosmosophical human, the human as an expression of the wisdom of the cosmos.

The mythmaking process is without beginning or end. We integrate the stories we hear and they become a part of us. The stories we tell are based on the stories we have been told. Just as the mythmaking process is based on the implicit assumptions we hold, the myths we tell determine the people we become. This chapter is an exploration of both the cosmosophical human as a basis for a new myth, and how such a myth can affect a change in human behavior.

A New Mandala for a New Cosmology:
The Past and Future Causal Light Cone

The "South Asian Cosmology" section of chapter 6 explains how the *mandala* depicts the microcosmic/macrocosmic relationship between the human and the cosmos. In those traditions, the human is envisioned less as an isolated, separate ego than as an expression of the whole with which the self is co-extensive. Through the circular pattern of the *mandala*, these traditions represented a vision for the relationship between the human and the cosmos. These representations are still valid, but, like any representation, have their limitations in the context of today's cosmology because they were designed to reflect the cosmology of that culture. Specifically, those *mandalas* do not represent time—or, perhaps more accurately, space-time—as modern science describes it.

In Chinese cosmology, the human is understood in terms of a triad. The human is poised between heaven and Earth, upper and lower. Like the *mandala*, this understanding of the human has a great deal of value for us; it places the individual in relationship to the whole. But, also like the *mandala*, the Confucian triad, based upon the foundation of the cosmology of its culture, does not fully integrate the idea of space-time held by modern science. The challenge, therefore, from a cosmosophical perspective, is to represent the human in terms of the traditional notions of the human as microcosm, as part of the interconnected web of relationships, and as poised between the heaven and Earth energies, while integrating the insight of modern science that space and time are entwined.

One method today's scientists use to represent space-time is the "Past and Future Causal Light Cone." [See Figure 4, overleaf] This diagram demonstrates the capacity for an individual to be affected by light and information from the past and for that individual to have an effect on the future. It draws on one of the key insights of modern science: the linking of space and time and the speed of light. Modern scientists understand that, looking out into the nighttime sky, the light they see from the stars is not only coming from a particular distance, but also from the past. As we look further and further into the distance, we are looking further into our shared past—at our ancestors, to use a human, organic metaphor. Because of the limits of light speed, not all light in the Universe can reach a given individual at a given moment. The cone expands as one looks farther and farther away, because light from a vaster portion of the Universe has had the time to reach us. Strangely—and perhaps this is where the limits of this two dimensional model breaks down—when we look into this expanding past we are also looking into a smaller Universe.[1]

The repeated critique of anthropomorphism against traditional cultures can be addressed in these terms. While it is entirely appropriate to criticize literalistic notions of God that envision "Him" as a man on a throne, traditional cultures often anthropomorphize nature because they understand that we are more than just individuals, but the story of a process that gave rise to each of us. As such, the human is the cosmos in microcosm. *We are nature*.[2] To anthropomorphize—for traditional cultures, not for modern fundamentalists who do so as a way of privileging a narrow definition of divinity—is not so much an expression of human projection onto nature, but a reflection of the intuition that the human is an aspect of nature. The only way we can express this is in our uniquely human way. To look out into the depths of space-time, at our ancestors, is to look at an expansion of the self. The perception that the Universe is a seamless process allows us to see that each of us once encompassed the entire Universe.

In the future, the light emitted from each individual acts according to the same principles. Nearby stars can receive the light from our Solar System relatively soon. Further into the future, our light can affect the entire galaxy. Still further, the light from this moment and this place can affect the surrounding galaxies. As time passes, the light emitted from a particular moment in space-time can be seen by a greater and greater area of the Universe.

230

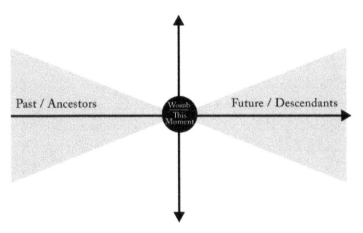

**Figure 4: The New Mandala:
Past and Future Causal Light Cone**

What conclusions can be drawn about this relatively simple depiction of the Universe? While science teachers use this diagram to demonstrate the principle of space-time, I propose that these insights also express a deeper meaning, a new vision of what it means to be a human being. In a traditional view, such as that held in Islamic cosmology, the human being is poised between the spiritual and the worldly, or the heavens and the Earth. This diagram, or "*mandala*," shows how the human is poised between *past* and *future*. Each individual is an expression of our shared past and is giving birth to the future in a unique way. A story about the creation of the Universe—a creation myth—is more than just a story about how things came to be; it is a story of who we are as human beings. Our basic identity is the story of the process that gave birth to us.

The *New Mandala* can be understood as an extension of what genetics teaches us. Humans have long understood that an individual is an expression of a particular lineage. We are made up of those who came before us, our ancestors. Similarly, we can live on in the future through our descendents. Modern genetics has given us the insight that, first, all humans share a common African ancestor; and, second, all life shares a common ancestor. The New Mandala includes and extends the genetic, biological identity of the human to recognize that we are not only individuals, or humans, or living beings, but that we are *energy*. Each being has existed from the moment the Universe was birthed and continues to live on in the future. The causal light cone represents not only that which has affected us; in a sense, it *is* us. Our identity is not only this moment, but the presence of our entire history expressed through us at this moment.

Modern science has changed profoundly the way we conceptualize the basic structure of the Universe. In linking space and time, the notion that heaven is above and Earth below no longer suffices. The Earth energies the Confucians speak of is our past; the spiritual or heavenly energies are the imagination we have for the future. In this way, we are always at the edge of our Universe, giving birth to novelty with every moment. The notion that mystics and shamans once had of reaching the edge of space is thereby radically changed. We cannot reach the spatial edge of the cosmos; for the Universe is expanding faster than we could move. But, in another way, we are always at the edge of the Universe *temporally*. Each moment is the location in the space-time continuum at which the Universe gives birth. As it turns out, the realized eschatology of Jesus was more accurate than we ever knew. As discussed in chapter 9, Jesus adapted the notion of a spatial and temporal edge of the cosmos of the apocalyptic tradition to be something present in each person at each moment. In the New Mandala of the New Cosmology, we are always already at this edge, too.

In this vision, the imaginative capacity we each possess to see that which is not yet present is what defines our humanity. As the Sufis suggest, we are 'in-between'—not spatially, but temporally.

The past is present in us at each moment. The imagination of our ancestors—this can go back to the spark of pure Being at the beginning of time—gave birth to us. And our imaginative capacities at this moment give birth to the future. In terms of the womb, this moment is the place where the womb of each individual occurs. Each perspective, each womb, is at least somewhat different. In the womb of our unique perspective, made up of billions of years of cosmic birthing, we give birth to new possibilities with the uniqueness of our imagination.

COMPASSION & ETHICS

The cosmosophical human emerges as an individual womb in the greater cosmic womb, a microcosm of the Universe in which the wisdom of the whole is present. The capacity to recognize our identity as cosmic lies at the core of the cosmosophical approach to ethics. One approach to ethics is to call on people to follow certain rules to improve the way they treat the other. This would be described as "altruism," a word that is related to the word "other."[3] This requires one to act primarily as an individual in opposition to one's own self interest and natural inclination.

Cosmosophical ethics, however, are based on *compassion*. Instead of requiring an individual to act against self interest, compassion is the radical re-visioning of the self. It does not require the elimination of the individual—indeed, the uniqueness of individual perspectives is extremely important in cosmosophy—but the expansion of one's identity to the point that one sees another's joy and pain as one's own. This means that one is required not to act against self interest, but to equate one's own interests with the interests of the whole of which one is a part.

In terms of the New Mandala, this expansion of the self involves the perception that in each moment the entire process of the Universe is present. Paradoxically, I am both my own unique perspective *and* the processes that birthed me. This means that, as one expands one's sense of self back in time, an individual begins to perceive how deeply connected one is to others. For example, genetics teaches us that we are all related as human beings. In this way, just as I can feel the pain of my crying mother, or the laughter of my daughter, I can also have compassion for all humans. We can extend this genetically to include all life, or cosmically to include the entire Universe.

The South Asian traditions teach that karmic processes give rise to phenomena. Rather than a concrete, unchanging soul, the Buddhists emphasize how we co-arise with an interconnected web of being. They demonstrate this through *mandala* practice, just as the New Mandala shows how various factors have come together at this moment to give rise to each individual. At each moment, the individual changes as new information and new karmic forces are integrated. The individual then has the opportunity to make choices about what course of action to take. The New Mandala represents the way in which one's actions have an immeasurable affect. As time goes on, our karma can affect more and more of the Universe, giving rise to other beings whose actions, like ours, is based on the actions of others.

Compassion, in both the Buddhist and the cosmosophical sense, is cultivated through the expansion of what it means to be a human. Ethics, because it is based on this compassion, is how we live this expansion. That is, when we begin to see our selves not as limited individuals but as cosmic beings, expressions of cosmic wisdom, we can then act with an appreciation for the consequences of our actions. The fullness of our past is what gives rise to the potential we possess to create the future. As we expand our awareness of the New Mandala into the past, we naturally expand our awareness into the future, recognizing the consequences of our actions.

CHAOLOGY

The science that has emerged in the last century reveals an evolving, living Universe. Evolution teaches us that our world is created not by an external, transcendent artificer or planner, but through the relationships within the Universe. Creation occurs not once, but constantly, and the cosmos itself participates in this creation. These relationships are not ordered in the sense that patriarchal hierarchies generally suppose. Moreover, when applied to theology, evolution speaks as much to the notion of the divine as immanent Becoming as static Being.

Although our culture has yet to realize the philosophical implications of these discoveries, the door has at least been opened for the return of the generative feminine principle. The discovery of dark matter could be seen as the recognition of dark *mater*, the Dark Mother Goddess, an immanent principle compassionately holding the Universe together. Of course, knowledge alone will not give us the meaning we so desperately need. Perhaps most problematic with the current Western worldview is that it leads us to repress—or oppress—that which we cannot understand. The Dark Mother is the goddess of the unknown, and our fear of her is a fear of the chaos that is central to the cosmic process of unfolding and evolution.

With this in mind, a healthy cosmo-logy—the study of the meaning (*logos*) of the beautiful order of the universe (*cosmos*)— is balanced by *chaology*: the study of the meaning of chaos and uncertainty. What a boring world it would be without surprise. Indeed, we have paved over much of our world in the pursuit of order and evading surprise. Part of this evasion comes out of a desire to avoid suffering. At times, however, it is through an active engagement with suffering and chaos that we are able to be reborn. The birthing process is often painful.

The future causal cone of the New Mandala demonstrates the expansiveness of the effect of our actions and the increasing possibilities in the future. This expansiveness cannot be reduced to a line. I once knew someone who planned his life out for thirty years. He had a timeline, a list of goals for each year, even each month. Not only is this a bit boring and compulsive—it limits possibility. The future, according to the vision of the New Mandala, is an expanding cone, not a line. Our future is not a single path, but an expansion into multiple possibilities. We cannot know with certitude what will happen, nor would we want to. The surprises that our world holds—the chaos—is part of what makes it beautiful. In spite of what patriarchal cultures have held for centuries, it is not only order that makes the Universe beautiful, but the dance of *chaos* and *cosmos*.

I would suggest that much of the repression of the feminine and the marginalization of non-Western perspectives has been due to the fear of chaos. A cosmology tells us what we value; Western cosmology, to a large extent, values order, an order that requires the suppression of diverse perspectives. To counter this suppression requires a sensibility that embraces the chaos of diversity. There seems to be a parallel between the destruction of the biosphere, which limits biological diversity, and social oppression through globalization and imperialism, which leads to the limitation of cultural diversity. Just as biological diversity is required for a healthy ecosystem, the health of humanity requires cultural diversity.

Because the future and past are both present in each moment, the integration that occurs in the individual is also chaotic. Each womb is a chaotic matrix of past and future. To borrow a term from the alchemists, each moment is the *alembic*, integrating the story of our creation and giving birth to the future. This womb of potentiality is common to many of the wisdom traditions. In

Taoism, for example, the *tai chi* is the integration of *yin* and *yang* at the birth of creation and in the individual mystic. The New Mandala adds the temporal dimension to this insight: the womb of the present moment is the integration of past and future.

CREATIVITY & IMAGINATION

The role of creativity and imagination has been addressed thoroughly in this work. The human being, like all beings, participates in the creativity of the Universe in its unique way. For the human, this happens less through biological transformation than through culture: we use symbolic language to give meaning—uniquely human meaning—to our world. In this way, we create the world just as the ecological world is created through evolutionary processes. In the womb of the ecosystem, relationships are cultivated that give rise to novelty. Human beings enter into this process, too, but add a unique approach: *we have the capacity, through the imagination, to give birth in the present to that which does not yet exist.* In terms of the New Mandala, the imagination is the presence of future possibilities in each moment. Ibn 'Arabi saw the human as arising due to the divine imagination and attaining transcendence, spiritualizing, through human imagination. Imagination is not merely ideas about the future; it is the birthing of possibility in the present moment, the womb of creative potential. For example, irrational and imaginary numbers were once thought to be purely academic and not found in nature. However, quantum theory has revealed that the waves represented by these numbers are actually fundamental to the workings of our Universe.[4]

In the cosmosophical process (see chapter 10) the role of creativity and the imagination is central. The language of the mystics—those who participate deeply with the cosmos—is metaphor and poetry. It is this language that touches us in ways that truly affect our basic assumptions about the world. To give birth to a new worldview requires more than ideas, but their creative expression. The way we connect to the world is not generally through discursive reason, but through the connections we feel, connections that are evoked through participation in the creative process of the mythmaker. The artist has overtaken the role of the mythmaker in the modern world, but unfortunately has been marginalized.

In the West, Dante is perhaps the last example of the poet who defined the world for an entire culture. His was a holistic vision of politics and ethics, cosmology and philosophy, theology and mysticism. Dante intended to offer a basis for a more peaceful society, but he recognized that his philosophical ideas could not touch people until he employed the imagination.[5] He was more than a philosopher or a poet. He was the philosopher-poet, connecting his ideals to images in the imagination of the reader—"*imagine*"[6]—that would move people to live in ways that allowed for a more peaceful society.

The United States of America, the country in which I write, has the benefit of the incredible diversity empire brings, but also lacks cohesiveness. An imaginal, mythic vision of the human often gives way to the jingoism and patriotism of a people without the security that comes from a sense of people-hood. In American culture, Walt Whitman is the first great poet to attempt to define America holistically. His vision, like Dante's, celebrates the unity and interconnection of creation while also affirming its diversity. The tradition of the Black Church, due in no small part to its position at the margins of American society, also connects to this mythic sensibility in a way that American Protestantism has generally failed. Prophetic leaders such as Dr. Martin Luther King have seen how their people lived out Biblical myths. His speeches are mythic participation at its best, in which he sees himself both participating in the past ("I have been to the mountaintop") and giving voice to an as yet unrealized hope for the future ("I have a dream").

Modern astronomical cosmology gives us a stunning vision of the vastness of the cosmos, spatially and temporally. At the same time, the Western worldview that gives rise to this vision has posited a dramatically reduced conceptualization of the human. Every traditional cosmology had an integrated vision of cosmos and psyche. The diversity of the world's cosmologies shows how one can find, even with the knowledge brought forth in modern science, commonality. While it requires a great deal of imaginative work, a vision of the human that parallels the wisdom traditions and is consilient with science can be born. This does not mean that it will hold an identical vision, but that it will share common principles while changing appropriately in a changing Universe.

The individual is not only the psyche, but also the body, because the body arises in the context of billions of years of cosmic unfolding. The body-soul dualism is eliminated in this vision—they co-arise. The cosmic processes that birthed the human body are seen as sacred; any mysticism in this understanding of the human must come from a deeper communion with, not escape from, the material world. This deep connection allows for the imaginative, the transcendent to come forth. A rejection of the body and the material world gives rise to the failure of the imagination and exploitation of the material world we call consumerism.

The cosmosophical human is a return to the vision of the human as cosmic within the context of the New Cosmology. Just as the individual is a microcosm of the whole spatially, each is also an integration of past and future. Each of us carries a trinity of time—past, present, and future—which encompasses the entire cosmos. This is a radically pluralistic vision, in which each unique viewpoint is central in space and at the temporal edge giving birth to a microcosmos of novelty. Our cosmology and mythology, the story we tell about how we have come to be, is our past; the mystical participation of each of us from our unique perspective in the matrix of potentiality, is the present; and the imagination, our capacity to create that which is not yet present, is the future. The New Mandala is far more than the "past and future causal light cone"; for it is far more than a way to understand space-time—it a new vision of the human in which past and future are present with each of us at this moment. In the womb of the moment, we can realize our cosmic identity.

With this vision of the *anthropos cosmosophos*, the full significance of the story of the Universe becomes apparent. It is the story of each of us. To know who we are, and how to live in concert with the wisdom of the cosmos, we must know the story of our becoming—to create, as humans always have, a new myth.

Chapter Twelve
A New Myth

I F WE ARE TO EXPERIENCE the Universe as our womb, if we are to truly regain a felt sense of the cosmic *uroboros*—the connection of our individual interiority and the cosmic whole—then these truths must be reflected in the myth we tell ourselves about the Universe. As the previous chapter explains, a myth of the Universe is not about something other than us, not something we look at from the outside; it is the story of who we are. The myths of human cultures throughout the world are at once strikingly similar and incredibly diverse. Because a myth of the Universe is the story of each of us, there are as many such stories as there are unique perspectives in the Universe.

The myth making process is therefore *participatory*. The myth is told in the symbolic language of the mystic who engages in a deep participation with the cosmos. This is not a rejection of the scientific method. Indeed, most of the content of this chapter is derived from the insights of science. While science generally seeks to tell us only about the Universe as an object of our observations, the deepest insights of today's science suggest that Universe is a seamless process—a *cosmo-genesis* in which each aspect, including humans, is created by and creates the world. We who observe this process are part of it, too. The cosmosophical mystic engages the insights of science and interiorizes them in order to participate more meaningfully and compassionately in the world.

The "New Myth" put forth here is not intended to be definitive. The myth making process is *collective* and *pluralistic*; that is, each of us contributes to perceptions about our world that are held in common, but this commonality does not diminish the value of the uniqueness of individual perspectives. As tempting as it is to suggest that humanity needs a single myth to guide us in our shared planet, I would suggest that holding commonality and diversity is one of the core cosmosophical values, a value that should be a part of any new *mythos*.

In addition to the principle of cosmo-genesis, this chapter attempts to describe our story in a way that is consistent with core assumptions of *cosmosophia* (see chapter 10). These concepts are derived from the wisdom of humanity's philosophical, mystical, and cosmological traditions as well as modern science. The reader also will recall that the mythmaking, creative, imaginative phase is one of the stages of the cosmosophical process. This myth understands the insights of modern science in terms of the philosophical and mystical "core assumptions" of *cosmosophia*. It begins with the metaphor that the cosmos is our womb. I have replaced the seven cosmic spheres with seven cosmic wombs. Any number of phases could have been used to describe this process—from "one," because the Universe is a seamless process, to a number beyond recognition, because the Universe is in constant change. I have chosen the number seven for its historical connection to traditional cosmologies.

In each *kairos*, the Universe gives birth to a new womb, a new whole, in which a trinity of factors is present. First, the Universe (1) differentiates. But instead of becoming lost in a cold Universe, the Universe forms new wombs which possess a (2) subjectivity or interiority. Finally, because these new wombs remain a part of the same whole, the new subjectivity allows for new connections or (3) communion.[1] This communion is the "Great Work" of each phase. Simply put, the communion of the interiority of the new womb with the whole or with others is cosmic wisdom. I have avoided the controversial subject of consciousness, because I believe too much focus on whether the Universe is conscious from the beginning or if consciousness is an emergent phenomenon in the human gets us bogged down in semantics. Instead, I prefer the term wisdom; that is, whether we call it "conscious" or not, the Universe possesses a capacity—wisdom—to self-organize and to foster meaningful relationships at each level, each womb.

I. Singularity:
The Womb of Potentiality

While scientists, like those in any other discipline, can rightly be said to have certain prejudices and shortcomings, science is singular in its adaptability. That is, although scientists can get attached to certain assumptions, as we all do, the rigor of science allows for information to come to light that old cosmologies can obscure. Today's science arose in the context of a scientific community that had previously assumed nearly the opposite of what it revealed. Einstein, as stated previously, was so deeply invested in the Newtonian Universe he simply could not perceive the expanding Universe his equations revealed. But scientists, like mystics (and unlike religious authorities) are dedicated to honoring what they can see, experience, or perceive, not what they assume. When the observations revealed an expanding Universe,

Einstein had no choice but to acknowledge its veracity and all of its implications.

From every perspective in the Universe one would observe galaxies moving away at greater and greater velocities. This insight alone is extremely difficult to comprehend. At first, the fact that the galaxies are moving away from the Earth might lead one to assume that we are the center of the Universe. This is not entirely untrue. However, it fails to account for the fact that the Universe is expanding not in space but in space-time. The "center" or source of the explosion that is the Big Bang exists not in a place but at a time.[2] Every location in the cosmos participated in this event. As the Universe expands—not because we are moving through space, but because space itself is stretching—everything grows farther apart. When we rewind the cosmic clock to t=0, we find that everything in space comes from the same point—*singularity*.

As the previous chapter describes in its discussion of the "Causal Light Cone," scientists understand that as one looks deeper into space one is also looking into the past. Our observations tell us that the Universe becomes increasingly homogeneous in the past. This is because the past—that is, greater and greater distances from this location—is closer to the birth of the Universe. Strangely, we are looking out at the Universe *in every direction*, into the depths of time, toward the center, toward the moment of the birth of the Universe. The edge of the Universe is not beyond, but everywhere, in the present moment. The center is present everywhere, too, in that each location is the product of the unfolding of that initial birth. Just as we, looking deep into space, see the young Universe, there could be conscious beings looking back at us from that same location. But instead of us, they too would see the young Universe. Like Dante's cosmos, when we reach the edge of the cosmos, everything is inverted. The center—for Dante, the Earth—becomes the margin; the edge—the divine point of light from beyond the stars—is the center.

The notion of singularity is beyond anyone's capacity to truly comprehend. It is perhaps the most profound scientific equivalent to the mystical notion of the non-dual. The reader will recall that for the Kabbalists, the infinite of *Ein Sof* and the emptiness of *Ayin* come together at the birth of the cosmos; for the Chinese, *yin* and *yang* are integrated through the *tai chi*. This "pregnant void" is an aspect of quantum physics as well, one that continues to be present. Paul Dirac, one of the founders of quantum physics, explains: "All matter is created out of some imperceptible substratum and… the creation of matter leaves behind a 'hole' in this substratum which appears as antimatter. …[I]t is a peculiarly material form of nothingness, out of which matter is created."[3] In the singularity before the differentiation of space-time, pure energy—everything that will exist in the Universe—is present; at the same time, within this and every subsequent moment in the cosmos, there is the presence of pure potentiality, an emptiness pregnant with possibility.

This duality of plentitude and emptiness will remain a common feature throughout this new myth. As we shall see, the Universe possesses a capacity to unfold in such a way that new interiors are formed. Each interior, each individual self, each womb is empty—that is, like the Buddhist concept of *shunyata* and the womb of potentiality, it cannot be said to have any independent identity in itself and it is filled with limitless potentiality. Many of the wisdom traditions refer to this womb of potentiality. At the same time, each interior is unbounded, a microcosm filled with the wisdom of the entire cosmos. Part of the wisdom of this duality is the recognition that it represents a paradox, a dance, not a dual*ism*. Their contrast belies their fundamental unity, a unity exemplified in the initial point of singularity.

According to one modern theory, nothing exists at t=0 but this single point. This does not mean that empty space exists into which the Big Bang occurs. Rather, there is absolutely nothing. One cannot envision the Big Bang from the outside, because there is no outside, no transcendent perspective. Paradoxically, although science was originally based on the objective perspective, the scientific view is helpful in that it grounds us in our position within cosmic processes. The limitations of the scientific method have been revealed to us most clearly through the scientific method itself. The scientific revolution came about in part due to centuries of the privileging of transcendence in Western culture. Science has turned this view upside down, and rejects the very notion.

At the same time, there is a danger in a reductionism that sees each of us only for the parts that have come together to make each of us whole. While the cells that make up the human body are a useful way of understanding us, it would be insufficient to limit our understanding of the human to the cells of the body. We are not only that which birthed us, but also that which we can express as whole beings. Singularity, therefore, is far more than a mere "point." Islamic cosmology might recognize the presence of "Unbounded Imagination" in that "point," the pure potentiality of the divine. Many early cultures would conceive of this tiny Universe as the primordial human—*Adam Kadmon* or the *Purusha*—the wisdom present at the moment of creation which would later become individualized in each of us. This is not to anthropomorphize the Universe, but to acknowledge that our bodies and our minds *are* the Universe, not limited to what the Anglo-American writer Alan Watts called the "skin-encapsulated ego".[4]

Modern science says little to nothing of how, why or by whom the Universe was created, or why the safety and connectivity of

singularity was lost. In part this is because there is no definitive evidence for these events. Moreover, such questions often
presume that we are living in a *finished* Universe. Cosmo-genesis
teaches us that the Universe is still being created. Perhaps only
in the depths of the human imagination is any *telos* present. I, for
one, am at least partially happy with this agnosticism. A bit of
not knowing seems alright to me, and even healthy. The problem
arises when we fall into the despair of meaninglessness. It is *our*
job to make meaning out of this process.

Singularity surely does mean that every aspect of the Universe is part of the same seamless process. Nothing is outside of
the process, nothing is static. The names we give to the different
phases of cosmic unfolding can be misleading. For the Universe
is a single event.

Singularity is important to understand for another reason. As
the Universe unfolds, we can identify, perhaps, the way in which
singularity—that is, pure potentiality and wholeness—is repli-
cated. In each of the "wombs" there is an element of singularity.
For each is a new microcosm of creativity. Scientists have even
observed a replication of singularity in the phenomena known as
black holes. A black hole is an event in which the force of gravity
is so strong that the escape velocity—that is, the speed required
to leave the gravitational pull of that object—exceeds the speed
of light. The black hole is a singularity. While it is extraordinarily
rare for any information to leave it, it has been speculated that
on the "other side" of a black hole is a big bang giving birth to a
new Universe.[5] In this way, a black hole is something like a black
whole.

II. The Primordial Flaring Forth:
The Chaotic Womb

About 13.7 billion years ago, an event began for reasons we do not know.[6] This event, now called "the Universe" by some of its participants, began in conditions of unimaginable heat and density. The Universe was birthed in fire. While a few minutes may seem insignificant compared to the immensity of cosmic time, the dynamics of the first moments of the early Universe have affected everything that has happened since. Like the Buddhist cosmology suggests, actions never truly end, but continue to have karmic affects for eternity. Swimme and Berry explain:

> The original body of the Universe maintained itself in a delicate balance. If either the rate of spatiation or the power of gravitation had wavered too far one way or the other, the adventure of the universe would have ceased. For instance, the universe would never have reached the moment when living cells sprouted forth. The vitality of the dolphin as it squiggles high in the summer sun, then, is directly dependent upon the elegance of the dynamics at the beginning of time. We cannot regard the dolphin and the first Flaring Forth as entirely separate events. The universe is a coherent whole, a seamless multileveled creative event. The graceful expansion of the original body is the life blood of all future bodies in the universe.[7]

The "original body" to which is Swimme and Berry refer is the womb of chaos, what they call the All Nourishing Abyss, the womb that will give birth to the multiplicity of new wombs in the Universe, and, at the same time, will continue to contain all that ever will be.

Scientists do not ascribe to the Primordial Flaring Forth any outside forces because there is no outside. Within this process—and *everything* is within—creativity is embedded, not imposed. The Universe is a process of co-arising, as the Buddhists would say, of the mysterious relationships within this interconnected womb. This does not deny the possibility of a creator. It does, however, imply that a transcendent creator does not need to deposit novelty into a static Universe. The Universe was created in such a way that, from the very beginning, it was endowed with the potentiality for creative transformation. This potentiality arises in many different forms, depending on the conditions of the Universe at a particular moment. Ibn 'Arabi's cosmology describes it as "Imagination." For the young Universe, possibilities were limitless and determining factors were minimal. This was the world of the fecund quantum vacuum.

As one approaches the moment of creation, it becomes increasingly clear that there is no such moment, for space-time as we know it did not yet exist. The original cosmic womb was small enough that the laws of quantum physics best describe it. There exists in such a state only space and energy, subject to the probabilistic laws of quantum physics, and no time.[8] That is, as one approaches singularity, one approaches the infinite, the absence of time. The early Universe, therefore, could be described as "imaginary."[9] This does not mean that it did not exist, but that the conditions were such that nothing definite or absolute could be stated about either time or space. The early Universe was *empty*—empty of the absolute distinction of space and time one finds in classical physics. Scientists have sometimes referred to this as a "fuzzy" Universe.[10] While such a designation connotes what is lacking, it fails to capture the awesome potentiality.

Indeed, this quantum Universe is imaginary not only because of what it lacks, but also because of the capacity for novelty it possesses. Today's world is far more predictable.

The description of such a small Universe is not only "fuzzy" due to the difficulty of seeing that far back in time, but because a quantum Universe would have been fuzzy by nature.[11] It was more chaos than cosmos, more potentiality than actuality. The early, tiny, quantum Universe has been compared to the chaos of mythology, both due to our inability to understand it and the inherent disorder of a quantum Universe.[12]

The quantum Universe is *probabilistic*, meaning no definite location can be pinned down of anything. We can only ascribe a range of probability to it. The *wave*, not the point, best describes the most fundamental constituents of the Universe. Waves are represented mathematically by the imaginary number, which, as it turns out, really describe nature at its most fundamental level. Many have speculated that the most fundamental unit in nature is not the particle, but the vibration. Like Pythagoras, modern science seems to suggest that the Universe is vibrating, pulsating to life. Finally, the quantum Universe is inherently uncertain. Again, no specific location can be ascribed to anything, but, as Werner Heisenberg's "Uncertainty Principle" explains, motion is not deterministic.[13] The exact location we ascribe to something is affected by our observation of it.

To some degree, we impose order on a fundamentally chaotic world in an attempt to make sense of it. In an evolutionary sense, we recognize certain things because our survival depends on it. If we could perceive the quantum fuzziness of the Universe that remains even today, we would not have survived because we could not have distinguished predator from prey, food from family member. Our brains have evolved in ways to help us perceive what is most useful to our survival. Culture then adds another level to these primal notions. A cosmology allows people to find order in the world, to makes sense of what might otherwise be too confusing. However, a cosmology often makes it difficult to see alternatives.

From the insights of quantum physics, we can say that the early Universe had a complete unity of the fundamental forces (gravity, strong and weak nuclear forces, and electromagnetism). It was not until the Universe began to expand into larger scales that these forces differentiated. All that had been determined initially was the rate of expansion. Elegantly, beautifully, perfectly, the Universe expanded at the precise rate to allow for the emergence of life, of humans who can look at the stars in amazement and write and read books. Had the expansion been slower, the Universe would have collapsed back on itself; had it been any faster, it would have been too spread out for any of the dynamic relationships of life to form.

In the fecundity of the quantum vacuum, particles pulsated into life. Each particle had an accompanying antiparticle, and, when the two encountered one another, they disappeared into energy. Before a second had even elapsed—a second in which millions of transformations had already occurred—the Universe had expanded enough so that new particles could be brought forth. While the number of particles dropped steadily, there was a slight imbalance of particles and antiparticles. A fraction—one in three billion— of the original particles endured.[14] Instead of pulsating in and out of existence, matter could now exist in ways to cultivate new relationships.[15]

In several ways, the Universe grows due to a delicate balance of balance and imbalance. Indeed, life could not exist without some asymmetry.[16] The slight imbalance of particles and antiparticles allowed for matter to endure. The imbalance of dark matter and dark energy—forces of gravity and expansion—allows for just the right rate of expansion. The asymmetry of the "tangled network" of the primordial cosmic strings allows for the eventual large scale structure of the galaxies.[17] Because of entropy—the tendency of things to lose energy—the Universe would indeed be a cold and lonely place without some asymmetry. For asymmetry allows for new "wombs" to form. Eric Chaisson explains:

> So, even as the average cosmic density and temperature continue to decline with the expansion of the Universe on the largest scales, small, localized "islands" called stars arise wherein their densities and temperatures increase. Stars buck the cosmic trend of decreasing temperature and density; they also go against the tendency of the Universe to become more disordered, for stars are clearly sites of rising complexity and greater order, especially as their thermal and elemental gradients steepen with time from core to surface. These, in turn, accompany increased energy flows, but again, only locally where stars reside. Such energy flows are likely key to the emergence of order and structure in the Universe.[18]

Even as the Universe as a whole becomes disordered and loses energy, the way in which energy comes together allows for order and energy to increase in some places. This requires the formation of meaningful relationships.

The quantum Universe gave rise to particles, which made the first element, hydrogen. From this matter, the stars were created, which came together to form galaxies. Each spiral galaxy is a birther of new stars, which, in turn, is a potential birther of living planets. At the core of these galaxies, of which ours is only one of billions, is a black hole.

Understanding the dynamics of the early Universe is important not only because they affect the Universe today, but also because these conditions continue to exist. The quantum world did not disappear with the expansion of the Universe and the birth of the stars, but continues to exist in the tiniest microcosms within the new worlds the Universe has birthed. Quantum entanglement suggests that, in spite of the degree to which the Universe has expanded and differentiated, we remain interconnected. Like Indra's Net, entanglement implies an intimacy with ethical connotations. With the expansion of the Universe, the cosmic womb as a single whole would have been lost if not for the amazing capacity for new wholes to form in which the same ability to form connections was fostered. Even in the context of the immensity of today's Universe, even in the ordered cosmos that science has sought to understand and observe with such clarity, the chaos and potentiality of the early cosmos endures.

III. Sacrificial Star: The Stellar Womb

The chaos of the early cosmic womb birthed matter, fundamental forces and particles that would be the basis for further relationships in the Universe. From these conditions, there was little to indicate how the Universe would organize itself. Even if, as theist or deist theologies would suggest, external forces chose to impose on the Universe the conditions to allow for the formation of stars, it appears as though we live in a Universe in which communion and interconnection is always sought. In the chaotic womb, the differentiation of forces and of matter allowed for a new form of communion, matter, to arise. The individuality of the particle could have been a lonely existence, but instead, due to fundamental forces such as gravity and the rate of expansion—forces so fundamental that science cannot explain *why* they are as they are—the Universe gave birth to a new form of organization, of interiority, the star.

The star, like other forms of interiority in our Universe, is birthed in fragmentation, in isolation. The interconnected womb of the early Universe was no more; for the rate of expansion was such that the Universe became so vast that some parts of it could never be reached by the light from other parts. But suffering, as the cycles of birth, death and rebirth indicate in our wisdom traditions, allows for new forms of being, of communion. The Christian story is particularly poignant in this regard. Jesus is born in darkness, in the humblest of circumstances, but he brings the light of God to humanity; and Jesus dies painfully, horrifically, but is reborn. Without the space provided by this expansion, without this fragmentation of the Universe, the star could not exist. The star is born in suffering, and, as Swimme and Berry put it, dies in a great sacrificial act, the supernova.[19] As we have seen, early forms of sacrifice, such as in the Vedic tradition, were a form of re-membering the Universe, of reconstituting the initial harmony of creation. The sacrifice of the star births the Universe anew.

The star is a process in which the particles of the early Universe come together to release tremendous energy. Our understanding of a star, if we remain caught in the old worldview, can be reduced to the gases within and the processes of fusion occurring at this moment. But a star can neither be separated from the quantum processes of the primordial flaring forth nor from the living processes on Earth today. We are the stars. Furthermore, even without knowledge of the history of cosmic processes giving rise to the star, the human has always participated meaningfully in communion with the stars. How often our quest for meaning has turned to the Sun's great gifts of light and heat; how often has our imagining been influenced by dark nights gazing up at the stars. While modern life has given us a greater understanding of stars, and a new appreciation for just how we are connected them, we have strangely lost some of our gratitude to, our awe of, the stars.

Star formation begins with an implosion caused by gravity. Spiral galaxies contain more than just stars; they also consist of great gravitational arms, bending space-time. When a very specific density of hydrogen and helium atoms is present, an implosion occurs, bringing these atoms into close contact. In the accelerated movement and increased heat, the process of nuclear fusion commences. That is, if it is hot enough to overcome the electromagnetism holding together the nucleus and electrons, the electrons are stripped off; matter is then converted back into energy.

Long ago, the Universe had cooled enough for energy to transform into matter, a process that also required space and for the interiority of atomic nuclei to be created. The element is an individual, unlike the pulsating quanta. The star, however, is a coming together of a collection of individuals in which a new form of creativity occurs. The individual interiority of the atom is sacrificed for the new interiority of the star. The womb of the star possesses the wisdom to maintain its individual, interior processes, as well as the wisdom to make connections beyond itself. While the star's formation requires a certain amount of imbalance, the already formed star remains in dynamic equilibrium, transforming itself into energy, energy that, in the case of our Sun, gives energy to living beings.

But the primordial stars had no such beings to whom they could give their energy; for the early Universe lacked the elements of which life would be made. However, when one of these stars runs out of hydrogen, the process of nuclear fusion ends. If the star is of sufficient size to create enough heat in its core, that star will begin to produce increasingly heavier elements, including carbon. At the synthesis of iron, the heaviest element that a star can synthesize, the star implodes and rebounds, dispersing particles into space which recombine as elements.

The West was slow to recognize the existence of the supernova. While Asian and Arab manuscripts recorded a supernova in 1054 AD, it is unmentioned in Europe, perhaps due to the fact that it would have threatened the Aristotelian cosmology that dictated the permanence of celestial objects like stars.[20] When Tycho Brahe finally did observe and record a supernova in 1572, Western science was changed forever, forced to recognize that the stars, like the Earth, were in constant flux. We have not, however, learned to fully integrate this insight into our worldview. We still look at the star as an object in the sky rather than a process in which we are intimately involved.

Eventually, the star birthing process occurs again with the new elements formed in the star and dispersed in the supernova. About four and a half billion years ago, our grandmother star sacrificed herself. The elements that this star—or, likely, combination of stars—birthed what would become the body of the Earth and the body of each of us.

From our vantage point, we can see clearly that, at least in our Solar System, the formation of a star also involves planets. While 99% of the mass of the Solar System is contained within the Sun, there were also elements that would become the planets. The Sun was formed out of a cloud of dust, spinning in space. A disc of elements swirled around the Sun, eventually condensing, like the Sun condensed, into planets. These planets were not nearly large enough to become stars—Jupiter comes the closest—so, unlike some stellar systems, ours remained with only a single star— probably a good thing for life. The denser elements are found in the interior planets, like Earth.

The Solar System dances through space, the planets rotating

around the Sun. The Sun is not static either. It moves around the center of the Milky Way Galaxy, through the band of stars that we see in the night sky and have called "Milky Way." Our Sun rotates up and down through this band, like the dolphin diving in and out of the water.[21] And even within our Solar System the Sun is not static, for the planets' gravitational force causes the Sun to wobble slightly as the planets revolve. All centers, in this Universe, are relative to one's perspective.

And from one of those planets, the Earth, we pause to reflect on the gifts of the Sun and the majesty of the stars. Planets, too, were considered to be simply "wandering stars" until fairly recently. Humanity, in its imagining, has so often looked to the Sun, the planets, and the stars for inspiration. There is, I believe, an intuition at work in recognizing that those stars are our ancestors. The stellar womb has birthed us. From our grandmother stars' supernovae, from the same elements from which our Sun was made, our home, the Earth was born.

IV. Earth and Evolution:
The Gaian Womb

In many mythological traditions, the Earth is recognized as the mother. These cultures intuited that the human was birthed from the Earth, and that the human remains within the womb of the Earth. According to modern science, the human is not merely living on the exterior of the Earth but is actually an Earth-being, like Adam, a part of the Earth, inseparable not only from biological processes, but from geological processes as well. If we could only live long enough, we could see the continents moving, the mountains and rivers being birthed and growing old, mammals and birds arising from these mountains and from the forests and deserts.[22]

Science fiction stories about space travel have often ignored

257

this simple reality—that the human is a part of the Earth and our survival in space or on another planet would require taking part of the Earth with us. Humans can survive permanently no more in space—even with a space craft—than fish could survive on land. We would require not only air to breath, but a variety of other living beings on whom we depend for our survival.

The speculation about whether or not there is life on other planets—the emerging field of astrobiology—begins with studying the uniqueness of the Earth. While, at first glance, it seems unlikely that among the billions of stars there are no other living systems, the incredibly complex and apparently unlikely conditions for life on the Earth give us pause. The Earth is not only at the exact location in our galaxy to avoid excessive strikes from space that would destroy life before it really got started; it is also located at the exact location in our Solar System making its temperature hospitable. Furthermore, it has the right elements, particularly carbon, to sustain life. Perhaps less well known is the Earth's dynamic, fluid quality. It is a planet in constant motion. Plate tectonics allows for the Earth's convection cycles to continuously bring energy from the Earth's core into the atmosphere.[23]

About four billion years ago the first life forms emerged in the Earth's oceans, single-celled beings that reproduced through the process of bacterial reproduction. Our microbial roots, hard as they are to believe, are consistent with the pattern of the other processes of the Universe. We have no trouble believing that the individual begins in the womb as a microscopic being. The individual, the Universe as a whole, and life on Earth all emerge from a form of singularity, and grow in complexity and diversity. And just as the star is composed of a community of individual particles coming together to form a new whole, larger life forms are similarly composed of these smaller cells. Each individual is a community of beings.

What exactly is life? What makes up a living individual? In both cases, at least on Earth, the answer has to do with the formation of a membrane, a means of self-containment. The membrane is the new womb that allows for an individual's interiority to emerge. Evolution reveals that interiority does not begin with an individual, but arises out of the relationships of a community. Lynn Margulis describes life as "a series of selves... chemically connected to its past."[24] That is, life *remembers*. This capacity to remember occurs chemically through the DNA. Human beings later introduce a new form of memory through symbolic language. In each case, without some form of containment, some way of distinguishing one's individuality, life would not be possible.

At the same time, life cannot be cut off and isolated. Each living being is part of a community. Margulis argues that evolution often occurs through the process of *symbiogenesis*; that is, a long-term symbiotic relationship can lead to the evolution of new traits or organisms as the relationship of two separate species becomes a single species.[25] "All organisms large enough for us to see are composed of once-independent microbes, teamed up to become larger wholes. As they merged, many lost what we in retrospect recognize as their former individuality."[26] Evolution therefore operates according to mutation, the spontaneous creativity of the individual; through selection, in which life differentiates; and through the communion of symbiosis. This process parallels the three-fold process of cosmogenesis: subjectivity, differentiation, and communion.

Even as life differentiates and diversifies, the Earth remains a living whole. Margulis and James Lovelock's "Gaia Theory," which holds that the Earth is like a living organism, has been met with a great deal of skepticism in the scientific community. Some of this had to do with a fear, with some justification, that this theory would be taken up by those with a non-scientific agenda to promote the notion that the Earth was actually a conscious being. Gaia Theory actually suggests no such thing. Instead, it offers a way of looking at the Earth in the same way one might view an individual organism: as a collection of living beings that make up an organic whole. That is, it is a self-regulating or *autopoietic* system. The Earth, of course, contains a great deal of non-living matter, just as all life does. The point is that, if one looks at its capacity to self-organize as a whole, one can say it is living. Moreover, the Universe as a whole, although largely non-living, can also be said to be living as a whole, because it is the context for life. Although this is a semantic argument, there is more at stake than semantics here. This is a question of our basic values. Is the Earth, or the Universe valuable other than as a resource for human exploitation? Whether we call it living, or divine, or sacred, human culture must create language that describes how the Earth as a whole is valuable. A functional cosmology will be non-dual and non-hierarchical. In such a world, everything is sacred or nothing is.

One of the great misperceptions about evolution is the tendency to project onto it the notion of hierarchy and progress. Evolution, in the biological sense, does not mean improvement. Paleontologist Richard Fortey explains the scientific view on this issue:

[I]t is difficult to avoid the language of improvement, of adaptations getting better and better still, to describe the changes that happened in the ecosystem through time; but the use of such language is misleading. The fairly obvious improvements in the musculature of the jaw, or in po ture, among the reptiles are not a matter for the ecology, which works rather as a system. If one of the early reptilian predators had suddenly acquired the speed and efficiency of a tiger, the whole Pangaean system might have collapsed immediately. Changes in the ecology happen by animals interacting with one another.[27]

Life does not get better over time, but adapts and transforms to satisfy changing conditions. Moreover, one cannot say that anything is more evolved at a given moment than anything else. Evolution occurs as a single process. The human is no more evolved than the monkey, or the rose, or the fly. In each case, the Earth is the primary context for evolution. Just as the large organism, made up of many smaller microbial organisms, evolves together as a single whole, the Earth evolves as a single whole.

Today, in an interconnected planet in which humanity, for the first time since we left Africa, is now able to communicate with every other human group with relative ease, we perceive for the first time that we are living on a single, spherical planet. It is possible—as I did a few years ago—to circumnavigate our planet, to finish a journey where we started by simply moving in the same direction. We also have the ability, unique among species, to destroy the living systems of the planet. Human culture and the human mind were not shaped, however, by a planetary sensibility. We learned to live, as all species, in very specific ecological contexts, in the womb of the ecosystem.

V. THE COMMUNITY OF LIFE:
THE ECOLOGICAL WOMB

Around one billion years ago, sexual reproduction, death and multicellularity emerged. Heterotrophy—eating other living

beings—came forth around 600 million years ago. These factors increased the Earth's capacity to complexify and diversify
immensely. Evolution would henceforth occur through an
increasingly complex set of relationships. The context for these
relationships is the ecosystem.

Sexuality led to a more complex way of mixing genes, allowing for greater diversity. Furthermore, it ultimately led to a greater
capacity on the part of the individual to choose, and thus to play
a conscious role in the evolutionary process. This was combined
with a deeper intimacy between beings. The beauty and pain of
humanity's erotic love, the inspiration for so much of our art and
music and central to so many lives, begins with microbial sexuality. Death was introduced along with sexual reproduction and
multicellularity. As Stanislav Grof has pointed out, there seems
to be a psychological connection between birth, death and sex.[28]
In fact, this connection is not merely psychological, but evolutionary. This triad of phenomena involves an end of the previous
order—this is a return to the chaotic matrix of creation—and
re-creation of the cosmic order anew. For the first several billion
years of life on Earth, death could only occur by accident; that is,
there was no such thing as dying of old age as plants and animals
do. With sexuality and death, however, each new generation is
genetically different from the previous. The cycle of death and
rebirth had begun.

At the same time, eating other beings brought forth a very
different form of intimacy. Predator and prey determine how
one another survives, the shape of one another's body and brain.
Human beings have turned the predator into something 'evil'
because we have become alienated from the ecosystem. In an
ecosystem, there exists a dynamic equilibrium in which species
co-evolve. Like the Buddhist concept of co-arising, co-evolution
describes the way in which species evolve together in community.

The context for this process is the ecosystem. Within the ecosystem, a species is adapted not only to the climate and topography, but also according to the behaviors of other species. The speed of the lion dictates the very structure of the body of the gazelle, and vice versa. In the context of the womb of the ecosystem, the predator is not evil, but co-creates the world along with the prey. In our fear of the harsh realities of nature, we have turned such intimacy into evil. As a result, we have grown increasingly alienated from ecology, and have sought to destroy the great predators upon whom every ecosystem depends.

In the dance of predator and prey, as with natural selection, there is also an element of choice. Swimme and Berry describe the evolutionary paths of the bison and horse as one affected by choice. The two species share a common ancestor. When faced with a predator, the ancestor of the horse chose to flee, whereas the bison's ancestor stayed to fight. From the time thereafter as the speciation occurred between the two, horses selected for speed, whereas bison selected for strength.[29]

Perhaps nothing demonstrates chaos better than evolution. Mutations occur randomly. Catastrophes occur that cause mass extinctions. None of this is deterministic or predictable, nor is it something that anyone can control. A major reason, I would argue, for the resistance to evolution from religious fundamentalists is not scriptural, but from an unconscious adherence to a cosmology that favors order over wildness.

Just as our cosmologies teach us what we can perceive, the niche we inhabit in the ecosystem determines our perceptive capacities. The frog, for example, can only see a fly that is moving. It would starve even with an edible, but unmoving, fly in front of its face. Its eyes have been shaped by the need to catch flies. The human eye, like the eyes of all living beings, just happens to be able to see the very wavelengths of the light from stars.[30] Some would see this as evidence of a wise creator. However, evolution suggests that it is through the inherent wisdom of the cosmos, embedded in the process, that the human eye has evolved in concert with the stars. We see those wavelengths because the light in our presence is the light of the Sun.

In each ecosystem, a particular wisdom arises from each niche. As humans spread across the globe, we developed cosmologies that were strikingly similar, but also based upon the specific ecosystem we inhabited. The ecosystem, while not independent of the Earth, just as the Earth is not independent of the Sun and the Sun not independent of the Milky Way Galaxy, forms a womb in which predators and prey find another form of dynamic equilibrium. The womb of the ecosystem is the original context for the human.

Humanity was birthed in the wake of destruction. The age of the dinosaurs ended 65 million years ago when the Earth was struck with a meteorite, allowing for mammals to occupy vacant niches. As always, death and destruction opened the door for novelty and creativity. The mammal introduced to the Earth community a new form of compassion, the capacity to continue to nurture even after birth, through lactation. While other forms of life also possessed a certain capacity to care for their young, the mammal embodies this compassion in a uniquely personal way. Surely, the ecosystem as a whole cares for the sustenance of life as a whole. But the mammalian mother loves her young as individuals; and mammalian social structure introduces an enhanced level of cooperation. Fortey explains that cats and dogs "established social systems" to assist with hunting to nourish their young. "Social communication demanded mutual understanding, and that in turn probably placed a premium on greater intelligence."[31] This capacity for care and cooperation would play a central role among a group of primates who arose in Africa.

VI. Humanity:
The Cultural Womb

Every living being on Earth has been shaped by the specific characteristics of its ecosystem. For the human, this embeddedness
can be understood both biologically and culturally. Biologically,
the human emerged on the African savannah. Our long limbs
grew so we could walk the long distances required to find food.
Our minds were shaped by these circumstances. The tall grass
and the predatory cats sculpted us. We learned cooperation and
care in the context of the familial and tribal groups we formed.
Human culture co-arose with the human body. As the mind and
body were shaped by the warm African sun and the vast African
plain, the way we relate to our world symbolically, then and now,
was established. Added to the capacity of living systems to self-
make, *autopoiesis*, was the capacity of cultural systems to create
meaning, called *mythopoiesis* by Joseph Campbell.[32] Humans create a culture through the imaginative capacity to tell stories, and
a culture regulates and sustains itself through its mythology. Just
as the eyes are shaped by the wavelength of the Sun's rays, that
which we consider to be meaningful is determined by the myths
we inherit. This is the cultural womb.

A great deal is often made of what makes the human unique,
of how we stand apart. Studies of our genes, however, reveal that
we share so much in common with the rest of the living world,
especially the other primates. Indeed, there is no precise moment
of speciation, of separation between humans and primates. The
age of humanity depends largely on when we decide to start
calling a particular group of apes "human." We could argue, as I
have somewhat provocatively suggested, that we still have not yet
become *Homo sapiens*; at the same time, we could argue, as some
of the wisdom traditions suggest, that the Universe is basically a

human body from its beginnings; or, we could argue that there is no way to separate the human from any other life forms, because life is a seamless process. "In spite of the wealth of life-forms," writes Mario Livio, "there is only *one life on Earth*."[33]

The human was the ape who made the choice to leave the forest. Between five and seven million years ago, a group of apes lived in Africa with a trait called neotony, the retention of child-like qualities, particularly *curiosity*. The human, from its very beginnings, was defined, separated from others in its childlike curiosity. This is the same trait we have selected for in our domesticated dogs and cats. When the Hindus refer to the cosmos as *lila*, or "divine play," they have indeed tapped into something primordial in the creation of the human world.

In leaving the forest, our bodies and minds and social structure were reconfigured in concert with our new ecosystem. Most obvious was bipedalism, a far more effective way of moving about across long distances in search of food in the African savannah. As always, this was not an immediate shift, but one of gradual searching and experimentation. There were many human or hominid groups before *Homo sapiens*. Particularly noteworthy is the speciation that occurred around three million years ago. One of those lines would become the now extinct Woodland Ape; the other would become us. In our line, there was a huge jump in brain capacity 2.5 million years ago with *Homo habilis*, the human who used tools. *Homo erectus* followed, a taller, a more upright walker and an efficient hunter who may have used fire to cook what it caught. As the protein they got from meat became an essential part of these humans' diet, the hunt and their relationship to it would become a central theme in human mythology. As the occasional meat we got from hunting and later from domesticated animals became the gluttony of the factory farm culture, our relationship to meat is in flux. We have not figured out how to reconcile the yearning for meat of our wandering ancestors to the modern lifestyle in which our meat consumption is a major factor in ecological destruction.

Homo sapiens emerged around 200,000 years ago. Modern genetics has been able to conclude that every human being on the planet is related through "Mitochodrial Eve", our common genetic female ancestor who lived in Africa around 170,000 years ago.[34] Our common male ancestor, "Adam," is now traced to around 70,000 years ago.[35] Both of these figures represent less than a blink of an eye in terms of geologic time. This means that human beings are extremely closely related. The diversity of our cultures and appearances is deceptive. It seems that the human's uniqueness—our ability to create meaning through culture—has meant that we diversify now not genetically, but culturally, a far faster process than biological evolution. Humans are too dynamic to be cut off in ways that would have allowed us to be separated in order for another speciation to occur. Genetics also shows us that the modern concept of race—the product of the Enlightenment's obsession with fragmentation—is completely false. This pseudoscientific concept, introduced in an effort to justify slavery, has absolutely no genetic validity.[36] The human population in Africa, in fact, is more genetically diverse than humans in the rest of the planet combined.[37]

This was a small group of people with a unique capacity represent the world symbolically through language—so small, in fact, that the modern human nearly did not make it. Around 70,000 years ago, due to ecological shifts—climate change was causing Africa to become drier—*Homo sapiens* was reduced to around 2,000 people. But the human possessed a capacity to work together cooperatively with one another and in communion with the ecosystem. Humanity's incredible adaptability was made possible through our ability to make meaning through symbols. Our innate mammalian compassion was intensified by the way we created a culture in which we cared deeply for one another. We could sacrifice ourselves not only for our young, but for our *friends*. Moreover, humans began to express the wisdom of the cosmos through cultural symbols. We told stories and sang songs. We painted images of our prey—the animals with whom we co-evolved and on whom we depended for survival in times of scarcity—on the walls of caves.

Just as the fire at the beginning of the Universe, the "Primordial Flaring Forth," was the center of the early chaotic womb, and of the cosmic womb as a whole, and the Sun's fire is the center of our Solar System, so too was the fire the center of the cultural womb. We formed circles around those early campfires, under the stars—fireballs each of them—and created anew our world. This creative act of the Universe was no less profound, and no less filled with a fire-like energy than our ancestors, the stars, who birthed us. It would have been there, at the campfire, that we would have told the stories that defined us, and would have collectively, cooperatively, and hopefully, compassionately, made decisions in times of crisis.

Humanity's response to an ecological crisis was the first great migration. This small and relatively homogenous group of people eventually spread throughout the globe, filling nearly every biome. We were fundamentally wanderers, moving constantly. The author of Deuteronomy touches on a universal truth of the human experience when he or she writes, "My father was a wandering Aramean,"[38]—for most of our history, humans were nomads and hunter-gatherers. This lifestyle was, in many ways, far easier than the agricultural and industrial civilizations that followed.[39] We worked less, and probably had far fewer stresses. But we simply ran out of room.

When human beings began to live a more settled lifestyle,

particularly due to the development of horticulture and the domestication of animals, the Neolithic village came into being. Rather than an 'invention' in the sense that modern humans think of it, the domestication of plants and animals arises naturally in the relationship between humans and their ecosystem.[40] In this context, humans—who had been relatively homogeneous when they left Africa—diversified into the multitude of indigenous languages and cultures. What these cultures seem to have had in common, however, was their matriarchal structure, and the fact that they were deeply in touch with the rhythm of the natural world.

As we filled every ecological niche on the planet, human cultural diversity flowered. Each region and sub-region produced a unique culture with its own symbols and language. This diversity, birthed in the ecological diversity of the Earth, is threatened today by the global monoculture. This is a threat not only to the wealth of creativity brought forth by this diversity, but to our capacity to live harmoniously with the living systems in which we are embedded.

The power of the human is in our capacity to tell stories, to make meaning out of our world, to pass down memories not merely through our DNA but through language. Culture and language is our niche. Just as the frog's perception is based on its niche—remember, the frog cannot see the fly unless it is moving because its ecological niche involves catching the moving fly— the human world, what is real and of value to us, is defined by culture. For most of human history, culture was transmitted orally and collectively, through the poet and the storyteller, the musician and the artist. We were able to live in the compassionate womb of our culture and our ecosystem based upon the meaning we gave it, expressed through our symbolic systems of meaning. For millennia, the creative expression of the relationship between human and cosmos was the wisdom of the cultural womb.

VII. This Moment:
The Womb of the Soul

The meaning a culture gives to the world, although it shares a great deal in common with other cultures due to our inherent commonalities, is usually specific to that culture. Each ethnic group gives meaning to its world in ways that generally exclude other groups. Jared Diamond has pointed out that, while indigenous groups are generally peaceful internally compared to a modern American city, interactions between members of different groups have often been violent.[41] Humans have succeeded in persecuting one another and wars have always been fought through the capacity of one group to 'other,' to de-humanize, another group. As Howard Thurman put it, "During times of war we teach men to hate the enemy because if we do not do this, it would be impossible for self-respecting persons to do the things to the enemy that the exigencies of war require."[42]

Ironically, this problem has been exacerbated by the very phenomenon that may be the answer to this problem. The reader will recall that during the Axial Age a new way of looking at the individual emerged. Instead of seeing the human as fundamentally a part of a community, many cultures began to see the individual as primary. There was a recognition in many of the wisdom traditions that the individual was a microcosm, that each of us carries the wisdom of the whole of the Universe within. Wisdom, particularly for the Greek philosophers, came to refer to something that existed in the soul of the individual human.

At its best, the womb of the soul can allow humanity to avoid the tribalism that has often plagued us. The wisdom of the cultural womb can be applied not only to one's specific ecosystem, but also to the Earth as a whole. This allows us to think in terms of planetary sustainability, making us less likely to exploit foreign lands. It also allows us to see in others the divine spark of which we have become aware in ourselves. Our compassion, therefore, would be based not on cultural ties but on a universal vision of what it means to be human.

Rather than a story of the divine soul being placed in the human, the story of the Universe is the story of the soul of the cosmos itself, beginning at singularity, diversifying into the various forms we see around us. Each phase of the Universe is not only a womb, but a soul, an interiority from which infinite possibilities can be imagined. The human soul is no different. We each have the capacity to create a new world from our souls. This divine capacity is indeed transcendent, but not because we are separate from the cosmos. It comes from the very fact that we are a part of the Universe. But we are more than a mere part; the soul is a microcosm, a singularity, from which new worlds are being birthed.

The human soul cannot be encapsulated in our skin, as modern secular materialism would suggest; nor is it satisfactory to suggest that the soul is entirely separate from the body, from the world, because we experience the world completely in our bodies. Neither of these modern answers to the question of the soul suffices. While the soul is centered in the body—indeed, we experience many of life's most profoundly mystical experiences through the body—it is not limited to the body. The soul is co-extensive with the whole of the cosmos. Our identity extends from the center of our unique perspective to the whole of the cosmic womb. Drawing from the principles of cosmosophy, from the *anthropos cosmosophos*, and from the New Myth put forth here, a new way to conceive of the soul is possible. Instead of the isolated, dualistic definition so common in the modern West, *the soul can be defined as the interiority of an individual, constituted by the set of relationships that give it existence and meaning. It is an expression of the*

271

entire cosmos from a unique being, in a unique body, at a particular moment in space-time. The human soul is like a black hole: it can become an isolated, island Universe, cut off from the rest of the cosmos; or, it can explode into infinite creativity, becoming a new Big Bang.

At the same time, there came with this new womb a shadow, a risk of alienation, of forgetting the process that gave birth to the individual. Today, the individual is cut off from the cosmic process. The soul is often understood to be separate from the story that gives birth to it. The *anthropos cosmosophos* has been replaced by an individualism that makes authentic compassion difficult. The Great Work, at this moment, is to find and express the wisdom of the cosmos in the individual soul.

RETURN TO SINGULARITY: THE COSMIC *UROBOROS*

The *uroboros* is a symbol of a snake swallowing its tail, meant to demonstrate the union of opposites. The end of each story, in a common mythic pattern, is the beginning. The journey of the shaman, the mystic, or the hero is one that involves a return to the beginning. The story of the Universe, similarly, is one of return. The beginning of our story—the spark of creation of infinite potential—is also present at the end. In each soul, the spark of possibility resides. We are not merely new individuals, but new universes, each of us. The vision of the myth presented here, like many traditional myths, recognizes that the human soul does not stand in isolation, in opposition to the cosmos; the stars reside in the soul, and the soul in the stars. The *anthropos cosmosophos* does not merely know the story of the Universe, but embodies it within.

The human imagination has made it possible to see nearly to

the beginning of the creation of the Universe. Without wonder, without awe, without gazing out into the nighttime sky, scientists never would have bothered to try to figure out the origins of the Universe. However, the precision science seeks at the moment of creation remains elusive. Perhaps, it is the spark of creation in each of us that holds the answer. This is not to say that the imagination should displace science, but that it is required to give one a felt sense of the fecundity of the primordial womb.

A story of the Universe has always given people a sense of who they are. The creation myth is a way for the individual to enter deeply and meaningfully into communion with the Universe. The imagination of the mystic or shaman creates the myth, just as the myth provides context for other mystics. In the case of the myth presented here, the human is revealed to be the *anthropos cosmosophos*. In each of us we carry the wisdom of 13.7 billion years of cosmic unfolding. In each of us is the infinite potential of the singularity.

The rise of the individual is a sort of singularity. Alone in the Universe, the modern human has often given in to despair. However, it is possible that, with a new myth, we can reenter the human soul into communion with the process we call the Universe. The union of the opposites, at this moment, is the human soul and the singularity before creation. Singularity gave birth to the cosmos. The question at this moment is: what will each of us give birth to?

Ricorso

"The *kairos* is fulfilled, and the kingdom
of God is close at hand."
—Jesus of Nazareth[1]

I HAVE BORROWED THE TERM *"ricorso"* from the Neapolitan
philosopher Giambattista Vico (1668-1744), one of the first
exponents of an evolutionary theory of history. Unlike many
evolutionary philosophers who followed him—Marx and Hegel,
for example—he held that, even as history evolved, it also peri-
odically returned to an earlier phase. For Vico, history was both
linear (*corso*) and cyclical (*ricorso*).[2] I have entitled this final section *"Ricorso"* instead of "Conclusion" because I am aware that
coming to conclusions can be a dangerous thing. The notion that
we can know, once and for all, the complete and unchanging
nature of reality is part and parcel of the old worldview. We live
in a Universe in flux, a cosmo-genesis. While time does have a
direction, there is also a way in which we can, each of us, become
the re-creation of the Universe, and in doing so, return to the
beginning. Moreover, my endeavor, like all endeavors in a continuously self-creating cosmos, has no conclusion. Even when I
stop writing, someone else will pick up this work and see it in
fresh and novel ways. To conclude means we have figured it all
out. I certainly do not want to imply that I have.

275

Chapter Thirteen
The Future

T HERE IS NOTHING more boring, more stifling to creativity
and possibility, than certitude about the future. One of the
problems with the Western worldview is that it has for too long
envisioned the arrow of time as a single line—a line that excludes
other perspectives in the present and other possibilities in the
future. By definition, the future is unknown, uncertain. To enter
into the future is to engage the imagination. While the previous
chapter represented the past, the story of how we have arrived at
this moment, it also represents the future. For how we imagine
the story of our becoming determines what we become in the
future.

The capacity of each living womb to "self-make"—*autopoiesis*—
has given rise to another phase change in the cosmic story. This
shift is no less dramatic than the movement from one "womb"
to the next—from the quantum vacuum to the star, for example,
or from the star to the living planet. We now create our world
through *mythopoiesis*, the myth-making process. Both of these

words share a Greek root with the word poet or poetry, meaning "to make or create."* The poet, or any kind of artist—and we are all artists of some kind—is the maker, the creator, the birther of our world, of our future. The world we live in today was a dream in the imagination of a distant star. When we look out at those stars, we look to our past. The future of life on this planet is a dream in the imagination of humanity. When we look at those same stars, we also see the human soul, the creative matrix that will birth this future.

SUMMARY

This work began with a problem, a crisis with which the modern world is confronted. While we require practical solutions to many of our problems, we also face, above all, a crisis of meaning. This cannot be solved through mere political and economic policy changes. Moreover, I have argued that many of our problems, even those requiring very specific and direct action, have a shared root in our mythology, the stories we have told ourselves about who we are and our relationship to our world. I have offered not a goal but a new approach, an invitation to participate deeply and meaningfully in our world.

I have described a four-fold process to enter into this participation. Modern science has revealed a Universe far different from the one on which our industrial civilization is based. Religion, moreover, cannot continue to ignore the cosmos and expect to be taken seriously. Science is simply a way to understand our world, a primary concern of religion until the modern period. We must also employ philosophy, the pursuit of wisdom, to the scientific

---

* From the Greek word *poein* ("make, create") and *poetes* ("maker"). *Dictionary of Word Origins*, ed. John Ayto, p.401

knowledge we have learned. Our industrial society has surely demonstrated that knowledge without wisdom is disastrous. Einstein's insights can be used to live more compassionately, as I have tried to argue here; but they can also be used to create nuclear bombs. Scientific knowledge and philosophical ideas can be further deepened by mystical participation. A new cosmology requires not only information and ideas about the world, but also connection to the world in a new way. This is the work of the mystic. The mystic, being positioned at the edge, can also break through old ways of thinking that hinder us. Mystics, however, will remain at the margins if their insights do not give rise to poetry and art—new myths—that help discover our selves. The creative, mythmaking process is where our deepest assumptions about reality come from. And from these myths, our actions, and the world we make for our children, are determined.

The mythic pattern offered here is admittedly insufficient. Every myth always is. What I have proposed has been an attempt at a never-finished process, but a process that, if we choose to neglect it, makes us less than human. First, this new myth is guided by *cosmosophia*, the principles put forth as a symbolic and metaphoric framework based upon the insights of science and the cosmological and mystic dimensions of the wisdom traditions. The Universe is an organic whole, birthing new wombs that are microcosms of the whole. Second, this vision brings forth a new vision for what it means to be human—the *anthropos cosmosophos*. We are not merely isolated, individual egos, but unique expressions of the sacred process of cosmic unfolding. Third, I have offered a new myth to tell the story of how we have become who we are today. This myth does not merely tell about the past. It allows us to place ourselves in the embrace of the cosmic womb and to realize that all beings also reside there. This deep participation in the cosmic womb will necessarily lead to a comprehensive

279

compassion in which humanity can care for the children of all species and the planet as a whole. Our mythology—whatever myth we live by—is present in all of us at each moment. It defines us now and informs the future we create.

COSMOSOPHY IN SOCIETY

The point is that our myths define us and define our values. The values of modern industrial society are not all bad, but they have led our civilization to the brink of destroying our capacity to live on the planet. This destruction comes in tandem with increased inequities. Only because of the consumerism and wealth of the few and the poverty of so many have we created such an unsustainable civilization. Above all, these values have led us to live increasingly meaningless lives for which we have poorly sought to compensate through fundamentalism and consumerism. *Cosmosophia* is a call to change these values.

The new myth proposed here is one of repeated birthing, of breaking through the cosmic sphere and of the parameters of old cosmologies, and of the *kairos*, the special time in which a shift occurs. The apocalypse, in this understanding, is not an end altogether, but the end of a particular cosmic era, and of a particular way of perceiving the cosmos. Apocalypse means revelation. As the Universe gives birth to new wombs, something new is revealed about reality. Because the values of any age are determined by the wisdom of that cosmic womb, we can change our values by living in harmony with a particular age. At this moment, this apocalyptic moment, we are called to a particular way of relating to our world, which brings with it a particular set of values.

There is no clear list of rules or proscriptions that can teach us the values appropriate for this age. Part of the new worldview we are birthing is a recognition that we cannot live according to a rulebook. This cosmos is also a chaotic system, and we must be comfortable, first and foremost, with the discomfort of not knowing the exact answers. I will however, mention several general areas that can be transformed, or at least approached differently, in concert with cosmosophical values.

The first is politics. Whereas it is common for some in the New Age movement to reject political action altogether, cosmosophy, as a holistic approach to life, suggests that would be unwise to completely ignore an aspect of the world that has a profound affect on the lives of so many others. To ignore politics in favor of the inner spiritual life is to reinforce the dualism of spirit and matter, interior and worldly, that has so corrupted modernity. Indeed, while cosmosophy is not a political movement, it suggests that it would be unethical to ignore politics altogether.

What then would cosmosophy tell us about politics? The cosmosophical approach to politics rejects the parameters of the political debate as defined in contemporary American politics. First, cosmosophy would reject Liberalism for its failure to disrupt the parameters defined by the mainstream of the culture. In its investment in the maintenance of these parameters, Liberalism is essentially a conservative movement. The Conservative movement would also be rejected for its fear of the dynamic, birthing aspect of the Universe. While Conservatives fear change, they propogate the modern myth of progress and unlimited growth. Indeed, cosmosophy is more conservative than the Conservatives regarding ecology. Finally, the label Progressive would be rejected as well because, in its bias toward progress, it implicitly rejects the wisdom of our ancestors, and of our shared past. Cosmosophical approaches to politics are fundamentally *radical*—a word that means "root"—in that any political change must get to the core of our problems—that is, the basic assumptions and values that lead to our behavior—for any real solution.

The core or root of any question of politics or governance lies in the underlying cosmology or worldview that informs it. That is, the assumptions one makes about what is real or valuable will define the course of political action followed. Because Conservatives, Liberals, and even Progressives and Reactionaries all make the same basic assumptions about our world, their solutions to our problems are not much different from one another. The vision for good government—a philosophical question for millennia in the various philosophical traditions of the world—has always been based on the underlying cosmology of a culture. One needs only to compare Dante's *De Monarchia*—in which he advocates a single ruler guided by "rightly ordered love" because the cosmos itself has a single divinity who rules, through the heavens, by this love[1]—to Lao Tzu's vision of the sage-ruler, who is best when appearing to let the people rule themselves. This is not to say that one of these approaches is better than the other. Each man wanted, it appears, a more peaceful and just society for his people. The differences in their approaches are not due to their motives or intellect, but of the core assumptions they made about their world.

Second, cosmosophy strongly suggests a new approach to education. Our educational system is perhaps the best example of what happens when we use industrialism as a model. The public school—and this comes from someone who has taught in one—is more factory than womb, more mechanical than organic. The emphasis of our schools tends to be on tests, which emphasizes concrete, unchanging information. A universe that is in flux, that is birthing novelty, cannot be properly understood through such means. While the factories and the prisons can expect a steady stream of people, if the human is primarily defined as an expression of the cosmos, and the birther, through the imagination, of a new world, then we cannot continue this kind of educational system. It is important to recognize that it is not only our poor schools that are failing us—it is people with doctorates and Ivy League educations who are contributing to the ecological destruction the most because they are the elites in our society who are consuming far more resources than anyone else and are in position to sustain our most destructive myths.

The primary task of education is to awaken in each individual the awareness of one's place in the Universe—this is the true meaning of *university*. It requires both a deep engagement with the diversity of our world and each person's individual perspectives and gifts, as well as a recognition of our interconnection and participation in a single whole. Few will be convinced to participate in the Great Work while remaining embedded in a cosmology that teaches them to feel separate and isolated from one another, from the cosmos. The Great Work is rooted in the creation of a new cosmology. It is not something we can teach our children through rote, because we simply have not created it yet.[2]

Third is the re-visioning of our economic system. Global capitalism is inconsistent with the natural rhythms of the Earth, because it is based not on the processes of nature but on abstract concepts. As I have stated above, the economic system—whatever it is—must not be primary, but a subset of ecology. Human management of resources and wealth can happen only within the Earth's self-organization of resources and wealth. Moreover, our economics are based primarily on false assumptions—unlimited growth and the dualism between human and natural worlds. Too often, the rhetoric of freedom is used to justify the free market. A system that rewards those with more capital is inherently unjust, and distorts the true consequences of our actions.

The fourth, and perhaps most difficult, is lifestyle. By this I mean that we must return to living in ways that reflect the natural cycles and patterns of the Earth. This means living according to the specific climate of one's bioregion and the patterns of the seasons. There is no reason derived from the wisdom of the natural processes of our planet—which the formulas of our abstract economic system are not—for someone to wake up at the same time in the winter, when it is still dark, as one does in the summer. Living in the desert, when midday temperatures are over one-hundred degrees, it makes little sense to work nine-to-five. The notion that we can even live in the desert in such large numbers, with green lawns and swimming pools, serves as a testament to the absurdity of our alienation. A civilization lives out its myths in the daily life of its people. In ours, we live as though the world is not living, but a machine. A greater degree of harmony with the natural cycles of the Earth and the ecosystem will allow us to see more clearly the consequences of our actions as the current economic system does not. Equally important, the return to a lifestyle in harmony with nature will re-awaken the human imagination. A new cosmology requires not only an opposition to the old but the imaginative endeavor of creating a new one.

Finally, and most fundamental to this work, is religion. If we identify religion as being concerned primarily with our relationship to that which is most real, most valuable, then this creation of a new worldview is precisely about religion. This, of course, is a complex subject. For many in the post-modern world, religion is a word that cannot serve them. They live out their myths in their lifestyle, as humanity always has. But for others, religion is a way to find community, and to hear the myths that make life meaningful. Any religion that is appropriate for the cosmosophical worldview we are birthing must have several attributes. It must be interfaith, while not naively thinking we can reduce all the religions to a simplified and sterile sameness. Interfaith spirituality honors the chaotic diversity of our wisdom traditions, and of our world. This religion must be mystical; that is, it must be fundamentally about participating deeply in the cosmos and the divine, not just about ideas and rituals. At the same time, rituals can be a beautiful form of collective creative expression, particularly of a cosmology. Religion must return to its roots as a culture's way of conveying its cosmology. Religion that focuses only on the individual soul and ignores the cosmos understands neither, and is an expression, unwittingly, of a failed dualistic and fragmented cosmology. Our religions must lift humanity up by recognizing the soul as cosmic, not shrink down the human—and devalue the world—by reducing the soul to individual psychology.

Above all, religion must be primarily about love. This means that religion is a collective expression of our passions, our love for one another and the beauty that is our world. Just as the artist and poet express this love individually, a religion is a way for a culture to express love collectively, in mythic terms, and through ritual practices that embody the cycles of nature and of life. If a religion is indeed about love, then it will convey values of compassion, not consumerism.

There is no end to the process of making life meaningful. We are always called upon to live our lives in communion with other beings, to participate in this world, to experience and create beauty, to love deeply and to feel compassion. This is the pursuit of wisdom, the Great Work of humanity. It is not really too different from the work of the quantum vacuum pulsing matter into being; or of matter coalescing into the star; or of the star giving birth to the elements of the living Earth; or of the Earth churning the elements into life; or of life co-creating the complex web of relations in the ecosystem; or of the African plain giving birth to the curious ape, who created worlds with the stories told beside the fire under the stars. The legacy of this entire process remains with us, in the depths of the womb of the human soul, pregnant with the mysterious and unknown future.

Epilogue
She is on Her Way

"Another world is not only possible, she is on her way.
On a quiet day, I can hear her breathing."
—Arundhati Roy[1]

W E STAND AT THE EDGE of our world. How many times have humans been at such a place? We stood at the edge of our forest, peering out into the plain, dreaming of its vastness, of the possibilities, and gave birth to humanity. When we nearly perished, due to an ecological crisis, we walked out into the world beyond Africa, and gave birth to the diversity of human culture, language, spirituality, and art. Today, we face crises similar but different. We are, as always, at the edge of our world, birthing.

There are many ways to approach our problems. I have presented ideas here, and there will be other ideas far more insightful than mine. I would hope, however, that whether or not readers find any resonance with my views, they will at least follow one simple suggestion. If we are to once again experience the cosmos as our womb, to participate meaningfully in the awesome event called the Universe, then we must simply walk outside, pause, and look at the shining stars, or see a child being born, or listen to a tree's leaves rustling in the wind, and be amazed. Until we regain this capacity, no set of ideas can save us from ourselves.

287

My own amazement is found in all those things, but most profoundly in my young daughter. In watching her birth, I saw the chaotic moment of the Universe creating itself, of an entire genetic history in one tiny body; later, I saw the future of the world in her little eyelids quivering, dreaming. In her body is a Universe of potential, and a story of cosmic beauty.

Just as I began this work with my own childhood dreams, as I looked out at the stars, I end it with the dreams I live through my own child. This, after all, is how the Universe operates—birthing novelty that remembers the story that birthed it. And my daughter, although she is only a few months old and cannot yet talk, loves to hear stories. She somehow perceives that there is a mysterious power in her books. Indeed, even when she is not being read to, she tries to grab, and sometimes eat, her books. As the author Barry Lopez says, sometimes we need a story more than food.[2]

I began this work with the stars, and, like Dante, I return to them. It is, after all, my hope that we will find poets today, like Dante, who bring alive this new myth. It is my dream that my daughter and I will contribute to this process. It is my task, as her father, to convey to her a sense that the Universe is not only beautiful, but alive and ensouled. At this point she seems to recognize that intuitively as she sticks her tongue out to taste the wind, and as she listens to and watches knowingly the leaves waving in the breeze.

In one of those stories I read to my daughter, Antoine de Saint-Exupery's *The Little Prince*, the protagonist is told the following:

'People have stars, but they aren't the same. For travelers, the stars are guides. For other people, they're nothing but tiny lights. And for still others, for scholars, they're problems. For my businessman, they were gold. But all those stars are silent stars. You, though, you'll have stars like nobody else... When you look up at the stars at night, since I'll be living in one of them, since I'll be laughing on one of them, for you it'll be as if all the stars are laughing. You'll have stars that can laugh!'[3]

It is through our stories, and through the human imagination, so present in a child, that we can indeed make a shift from seeing stars as silent, or nothing but lights, or gold, or problems, to feeling the laughter of the stars.

I was thrilled, not long ago, to find a poem by Walt Whitman, one of my favorites, in a collection I read to my daughter each night before bed. It is a testament to the sense of immensity and intimacy with which I would like to leave the reader. And, because I began with a quote from Whitman, it seems appropriate to complete this story like the old stories, told by the fire under the stars, with a return to the beginning:

When I heard the learn'd astronomer,
When the proofs, the figures, were ranged in columns
    before me,
When I was shown the charts and diagrams, to add, to
    divide, and measure them,
When I sitting heard the astronomer where he lectured
    with much applause in the lecture room.
How soon unaccountable I became tired and sick,
Till rising and gliding out I wander'd off by myself,
In the mystical moist night-air, and from time to time,
Look'd up in perfect silence at the stars.

                  —Walt Whitman,
          "When I Heard the Learn'd Astronomer"[4]

Glossary

CHAOLOGY – The study of how chaos can play a meaningful role in our lives.

CHAOS – Mythologically, chaos refers to the state of disorder and undifferentiation before the Universe was created. Today, chaos is the study of the way in which disorder and unpredictability arise even as fundamental principles describe the general patterns of our Universe.

CONSCIOUSNESS – A difficult term to define concisely, it is used in three ways in this study: (1) Awareness or capacity of a being to reflect, frequently used in this sense to refer to "self-reflexive consciousness" of the human; (2) The way the awareness of beings in a particular culture are told to think about their place in the world—e.g. "modern consciousness"; (3) In South Asian thought, this refers to a fundamental ordering principle in the cosmos, similar to the Greek logos or, in this study, "wisdom".

COSMOGONY – pertaining to the origins or creation of the Universe, particularly in mythology.

COSMOLOGY – The basic assumptions about the Universe, how it operates, and the place of the human therein providing the context for meaning and for relationships. When a cosmology is fully integrated, it is synonymous with worldview (see below). However, there is a whole spectrum of ways in which the term cosmology is applied. Often cosmology is used more to refer to the structure and order of the physical Universe with little attention paid to the implications it has for meaning in the culture.

Astronomical Cosmology – A subset of cosmology that deals only with the structure of the Universe.

Scientific Cosmology – A sub-discipline of modern astrophysics concerned with the birth and early development of the Universe. Big Bang theory is an example.

New Cosmology – A cosmology derived from the current scientific knowledge of the Universe. This is still in the process of emerging.

COSMOSOPHIA – A set of core metaphors to help bring about the emergence of a new cosmology/worldview.

COSMOSOPHY – A discipline in the pursuit of creating a new cosmology/worldview.

ESCHATOLOGY – refers to the end of space and time at which a boundary is crossed beyond the cosmos.

EVOLUTION – Most generally, evolution refers to the way in which the Universe unfolds and changes over time. This can refer to cosmic, biological, or cultural changes. However, the term evolution most commonly is used to refer specifically to biological evolution, which refers to the way the life has unfolded and changed over the course of the history of the Earth. Because this is the most common usage of the term, references to evolution in this study generally refer to biological evolution.

MYSTICISM – The union of the individual with the divine, the cosmos—or whatever one's cosmology considers the ultimate reality.

MYTHOLOGY – The story (see below) of a particular cosmology. It brings to life that cosmology for the members of a culture. Through the myth, individuals can integrate and interiorize the cosmology of their culture.

NEW AGE – A diverse set of modern spiritual beliefs generally focused on personal enlightenment and the coming "new age".

ONTOLOGY – pertaining to *being*; i.e. that which is real.

SCIENCE – An organized, systematic enterprise that gathers knowledge about the world and condenses that knowledge into testable laws and principles. [E.O. Wilson]

SOUL – The interiority of an individual, constituted by the set of relationships that give it existence and meaning. It is an expression of the entire cosmos from a unique being, in a unique body, at a particular moment in space-time.

STORY – A coherent narrative that evokes meaning from the listener.

SYNCRETISM – The way in which different religions can be blended to form new religions.

WISDOM – The inherent capacity of the Universe to create meaningful relationships.

WORLDVIEW – See cosmology above. A worldview is the sum total of a culture's cosmology and mythology, fully integrated into its way of life and ethics.

Appendix

La Nuova Commedia[*]

Inferno

Fire
I write these words
With a mind, a hand
A body
On fire
A soul is born
And at its center
Is a cosmos
Of memories
The past
Burning in my depths
A soul
A body
A Universe
Birthed in fire
Dark Matter
Is my Dark Mother,

---

[*] From *Handprints on the Womb*, Theodore Richards (Portland: Inkwater Press, 2009) p.97

I see her in deep in space
Burning
In my heart.
The primordial fireball
The stars,
The fire of
My ancestors
Dance around the fire
Dance around the Sun
Dance around my soul
On fire
My Ancestors,
The stars.

Purgatorio

This dream I have
Standing
In this moment,
At the birth canal,
the alembic,
I realize the eschaton
Today
In this dream
Universe
Giving birth
through
the chaotic matrix
womb of past and future

Heaven and Earth
There is beauty in this bloody moment
In this pregnant moment
Birthing
Birthing
The perfectly fallen flesh
Of humanity
Blood and bone
And stardust and love
Searching for mother's breast
Looking up
At God
At mother
At the stars.

Paradiso

This dream we had
Of a future not built
By engineers
But by poets
Of a journey not on a straight road
Of lines and plans
But of expansion
Into possibility
The vastness of the Imagination
Long ago
We sat around the fires
Under those stars

Burning birthing
Dreams stories
And around those same stars, danced planets
Dreaming of us.
There was fire that burned from the very start
The fire next time will burn on in my heart
Deep in the heavens is the inferno of the past
Deep in the future is the inferno of the past
Deep in my heart is the possibility of paradise
The paradise of possibility
Dreams of the stars born in my heart
Dreams of possibility born in the stars.

Notes

PREFACE

1. Walt Whitman, *Leaves of Grass: The First (1855) Edition* (New York: Penguin Books, 1986) p.54-55

2. Blaise Pascal, *Pensees* (London: Printed for Jacob Towson, 1688), microform, III, 206.

3. "The Divinization of the Cosmos: An Interview with Brian Swimme on Pierre Teilhard de Chardin," *What is Enlightenment*, September-December 2006, p.89

4. See Epigraph for Section III

I. THIS MOMENT

1. Thomas Berry, *The Great Work: Our Way into the Future* (New York: Bell Tower, 1999) p.200

CHAPTER ONE

1. See Ibid.

CHAPTER TWO

1. See Richard Tarnas, *The Passion of the Western Mind: Understanding the Ideas That Have Shaped Our Worldview* (New York: Ballantine Books, 1991)

2. Ibid, p.442

3. See Lucia Chiavola Birnbaum, *Dark Mother: African Origins and Godmothers* (San Jose: Author's Choice Press, 2001) and

Merlin Stone, *When God was a Woman* (New York: Harcourt & Brace, 1976)

4. Thomas Berry in *Teilhard in the 21st Century: The Emerging Spirit of the Earth*, eds. Arthur Fabel & Donald St. John (New York: Orbis Books, 2007) p.78

5. Mark 1:15

CHAPTER THREE

1. *Teilhard in the 21st Century*, eds. Arthur Fabel & Donald St. John, p.77

2. Mircea Eliade, *Myths, Dreams, and Mysteries: The Encounter between Contemporary Faiths and Archaic Realities* (New York: Harper & Brothers, 1960) p.15

3. See Sean Kane, Wisdom of the Mythtellers (Canada: Broadview Press, 2001)

4. Quoted in Edward F. Edinger, *The Christian Archetype: A Jungian Commentary on the Life of Christ* (Toronto: Inner City Books, 1987) p.13

5. Barry Lopez, *Crow and Weasel* (North Point Press, 1990)

6. Berry, *The Dream of the Earth*, p.66

II. COSMOLOGY

1. Dante Alighieri, *The Inferno of Dante Alighieri* (London: J.M. Dent & Sons, 1946) p.390

2. The Gospel According to John, Chapter 1

CHAPTER FOUR

1. Alfred North Whitehead, *Science and the Modern World* (Free Press: New York, 1967) p.48

2. Joanna Macy, *World as Lover, World as Self: Courage for Global Justice and Ecological Renewal* (Berkeley: Parallax Press, 2007) p.156

3. Norris S. Hetherington, ed., *Cosmology: Historical, Literary, Philosophical, Religious,*
and Scientific Perspectives (New York: Garland Publishing, 1993) p.108

4. Quoted in Hetherington, *Cosmology*, p.83

5. John H. Hayes, *Introduction to the Bible* (Philadelphia: The Westminster Press, 1952) p.113

6. Isaiah 1:15-17, *The New Jerusalem Bible*

7. Christopher Rowland, *The Open Heaven: A Study of Apocalyptic in Judaism and Early Christianity* (London: SPCK, 1982) p. 246

8. Bruce Chilton, *Rabbi Jesus: An Intimate Biography* (New York: Image Books, 2000) p.52

9. I.M. Lewis, *Ecstatic Religion: An Anthropological Study of Spirit Possession and Shamanism* (New York: Penguin, 1978) p. 33.

10. Ithamar Gruenwald, *Apocalyptic and Merkabah Mysticism* (Leiden/Koln: E.J. Brill, 1980) p. 12

11. Christopher Rowland, *The Open Heaven*, p.25

12. John H. Hayes, *Introduction to the Bible*, p. 283

13. Ibid.

14. Vincent Harding, forward to *Jesus and the Disinherited* (Boston: Beacon Press, 1996)

15. Mark 16: 5

16. Luke 17:20-21

17. John Haught, *God After Darwin: A Theology of Evolution* (Boulder, CO: Westview Press, 2008) p.41

Chapter Five

1. First Corinthians 13:12

2. Lucia Chiavola Birnbaum, *Dark Mother: African Origins and Godmothers*

3. See Mircea Eliade, The Myth of the Eternal Return: Cosmos and History, trans. Willard R. Trask (Princeton: Princeton Uni-

versity Press, 1991)

4. Mara Freeman, *Kindling the Celtic Spirit* (San Francisco: Harper San Francisco, 2000) p. 41

5. Ibid., p.142

6. Dames, *Mythic Ireland* (London: Thames & Hudson, 1992) p.33

7. Freeman, *Kindling the Celtic Spirit*, p.79

8. Ibid., p.202

9. Fritjof Capra, *The Tao of Physics* (Boulder: Shambhala, 1983) p.20

10. Pierre Hadot, *What is Ancient Philosophy?*, trans. Michael Chase (Cambridge: Belknap Press, 2002) p.9

11. Ibid., p.21

12. Ibid.

13. Mircea Eliade, *Rites and Symbols of Initiation: Mysteries of Birth and Rebirth* (Connecticut: Apring, 2005) p. 131

14. From Hadot, *What is Ancient Philosophy?* p.45

15. Quoted in Matthew Fox, *Sheer Joy: Conversations with Thomas Aquinas on Creation Spirituality* (San Francisco: Tarcher/Putnam, 2003) p.8

16. Ibid., p.4

17. Summa Contra Gentiless, paragraph 126

18. Ibid., p.518

19. William Anderson, *Dante the Maker* (New York: Crossroad, 1982) p.105

20. J.J. Callahan, "The Curvature of Space in a Finite Universe," *Cosmology + 1*, ed. Owen Gingerich (San Francisco: W.H. Freeman and Company, 1977) p.30

21. See Ann Llewellyn Barstow, *Witchcraze: A New History of the European Witch Hunts* (San Francisco, Pandora, 1994)

22. Tarnas, *The Passion of the Western Mind*, p.237

23. See Max Weber, *The Protestant Ethic and the Spirit of Capi-*

talism, trans. Talcott Parsons (New York: Charles Scribner Sons, 1976)

24. Hetherington, *Cosmology*, p.575

25. Tarnas, *Passion of the Western Mind*, p.269

26. Sir Isaac Newton, *Principia* (London: MacMillan, 1883)

27. Charles Darwin, *On the Origin of Species by Means of Natural Selection* (New York: D. Appleton, 1867)

28. A notable exception can be found in John Haught, *God after Darwin: A Theology of Evolution* (Philadelphia: Westview Press, 2008)

29. David Z. Albert and Rivka Galchen, "Was Einstein Wrong?: A Quantum Threat to Special Relativity" *Scientific American*, March 2009

CHAPTER SIX

1. Birnbaum, *Dark Mother: African Origins and Godmothers*

2. See note on page 11

3. See Ngugi Wa Thiongo, *Decolonizing the Mind: The Politics of Language in African Literature* (James Curry Publishers, 1986)

4. Birnbaum, *Dark Mother: African Origins and Godmothers*, p.xxvii

5. See John Dominic Crossan, *In Search of Paul: How Jesus's Apostle Opposed Rome's Empire with God's Kingdom* (San Francisco: Harper, 2004) for an extensive overview of the Roman imperial cult

6. Ogbu U. Kalu, "The Sacred Egg", *Indigenous Traditions and Ecology: The Interbeing of Cosmology and Community*, ed. John Grim (Cambridge: Harvard University Press, 2001) p.226

7. Augustine Shutte, *Philosophy for Africa* (Milwaukee: Marquette University Press, 1995)

8. Thomas Odhiambo, "Essence and Continuity of Life in African Society", ed. Jean Staune, *Science and the Search for Meaning*

(Philadelphia: Templeton Foundation Press) p.68-70

9. Shutte, Philosophy for Africa, p. 26-27

10. John S. Mbiti, *African Religions and Philosophy* (Nigeria: Heinemann, 1969) p.26

11. Ibid.

12. William C. Chittick, *Ibn 'Arabi: Heir to the Prophets* (Oxford: Oneworld, 2007) p.91

13. Jeaneane Fowler, *Pathways to Immortality: An Introduction to the Philosophy and Religion of Taoism* (Portland, Sussex Academic Press, 2005) p.107

14. *The Book of Lao Tzu* (The Tao Te Ching) Yi Wu trans. (San Bruno: Great Learning Publishing, 1989) p.88

15. Tu Weiming, "Confucianism", Arvind Sharma, ed., *Our Religions: The Seven World Religions Introduced by Preeminent Scholars from each Tradition* (San Francisco: Harper San Francisco, 1993) p.168

16. Ibid., p.169

17. Ibid.

18. From Ibid.

19. From Ibid., p.179

20. Fowler, *Pathways to Immortality*, p.44

21. Howard Reid and Michael Croucher, *The Way of the Warrior: The Paradox of Martial Arts* (Woodstock, NY: The Overlook Press, 1995) p.113

22. Fowler, *Pathways to Immortality*, p.179

23. *From Science and Religion in Search of Cosmic Purpose*, John Haught, ed. (Washington: Georgetown University Press, 2000) p.77

24. Joanna Macy, *World as Lover, World as Self*, p.31

25. Ibid., p.71

26. Ibid., p.63

27. Stanislav Grof, *The Cosmic Game: Explorations of the Frontiers*

of Human Consciousness (Albany: SUNY Press, 1998) p.59

28. From Ibid.

29. Akira Sadakata, *Buddhist Cosmology: Philosophy and Origins*, trans. Gaynor Sekimori (Tokyo: Kosei Publishing, 2004) p.19

30. Ibid., p.127

31. Jamgon Kongtrul, *Treasury of Knowledge: Myriad Worlds* (Ithaca, New York: Snow Lion Publications, 2003) p. 60-61

32. From Paul O. Ingram, "The Jeweled Net of Nature", *Buddhism and Ecology: The Interconnection of Dharma and Deeds*, Mary Evelyn Tucker and Duncan Ryuken Williams (Cambridge: Harvard University Press, 1997) p.75

33. Ibid. p.79

34. From Graham Parkes, "Voices of Mountains, Trees, and Rivers: Kukai, Dogen, and a Deeper Ecology", *Buddhism and Ecology: The Interconnection of Dharma and Deeds*, Mary Evelyn Tucker and Duncan Ryuken Williams (Cambridge: Harvard University Press, 1997) p.118

35. el-Sayed el-Aswad, *Religion and Folk Cosmology: Scenarios of the Visible and Invisible in Rural Egypt* (Westport, Praeger Publishers, 2002) p.41

36. Seyyed Hossein Nasr & Muzaffar Iqbal, *Islam, Science, Muslims, and Technology* (Al-Qalam Publishing: Sherwood Park, 2007) p.100

37. William Chittick, *Ibn 'Arabi, Heir to the Prophets* (Oxford, Oneworld, 2005) p.22

38. William Chittick, *Science of the Cosmos, Science of the Soul: The Pertinence of Islamic Cosmology in the Modern World* (Oxford: Oneworld, 2007) p.31

39. Ibid.

40. Ibid., p.70

41. Ibid., p.87

42. Chittick, *Ibn 'Arabi*, p.20

43. Sachiko Murata, *The Tao of Islam: A Sourcebook on Gender Relationships in Islamic Thought* (Albany: SUNY Press, 1992) p.viii

44. Neil Douglas-Klotz, *The Sufi Book of Life: 99 Pathways of the Heart for the Modern Dervish* (New York: Penguin, 2005) p.8

45. Nasr, *Garden of Truth: The Vision and Promise of Sufism, Islam's Mystical Tradition* (New York: HarperOne, 2007) p. 15

46. From Ibid., p.31

47. Murata, *The Tao of Islam*, p.149

48. Sayyed Hossein Nasr, "Islamic Cosmology" *Science and Religion in Search of Cosmic Purpose*, John Haught, ed. (Washington: Georgetown University Press, 2000) p.45

49. Murata, *The Tao of Islam*, p.216

50. Psalm 139: 7-17

51. Eliahu Klein, *Kabbalah of Creation: Isaac Luria's Earlier Mysticism* (New Jersey: Jason Aronsoc, Inc., 2000) p.50

52. Ed. Daniel Matt, *The Essential Kabbalah: The Heart of Jewish Mysticism* (San Francisco: Harper San Francisco, 1996) p.52

53. Will Parfitt, *The Elements of the Qabalah* (New York: Barnes & Noble, 1991) No page number.

54. Gershom Scholem, *Major Trends in Jewish Mysticism* (Jerusalem, Schocken Publishing House, 1941) p.219. Elohim literally means "the gods".

55. Matt, *The Essential Kabbalah*, p.53

56. Klein, *Kabbalah of Creation*, p.52

57. Scholem, *Major Trends in Jewish Mysticism*, p.207

58. Quoted in Daniel Matt, *God & the Big Bang: Discovering Harmony between Science and Spirituality* (Woodstock, Vermont: Jewish Lights, 2002) p.39

59. Klein, *Kabbalah of Creation*, p.116

60. Ibid., p.89

III. Mysticism

1. Dante Alighieri, *The Purgatorio of Dante Alighieri* (New York: J.M. Dent and Sons, 1952) p.428

Chapter Seven

1. Jared Diamond, *Guns, Germs, and Steel: The Fates of Human Societies* (New York: W.W. Norton & Company, 1999) p.105

2. See Riane Eisler, *The Chalice and the Blade: Our History, Our Future* (Cambridge: Harper & Row, 1987)

3. Sean Kane, *Wisdom of the Mythtellers* (Canada: Broadview Press, 1998) p.36 and Walter J. Ong, *Orality and Literacy* (New York: Routledge, 2006) p.73

4. From Joel R. Primack and Nancy Abrams, *The View from the Center of the Universe: Discovering our Extraordinary Place in the Cosmos* (New York: Riverhead Books, 2006) p.34

5. Mircea Eliade, *Shamanism: Archaic Techniques of Ecstasy* (London: Routledge & Kegan Paul, 1964) p.259

6. Ibid., p.274

7. John Grim, "Ojibway Shamanism," *Shamanism: A Reader*, Graham Harvey, ed., p.99

8. Eliade, *Shamanism*, p.266

9. Ibid., p.259

0. Harvey, *Shamanism: A Reader*, p.7-8

1. See Diamong, *Guns, Germs and Steel*

2. Thomas A. Dowson, "Like People in Prehistory", ed. Harvey, *Shamanism: A Reader*, p.160

3. See note on page 49. In the Zimbabwean uprising against the British, for example, female spirit mediums played a central role. See David Lan, *Guns and Rain: Guerillas & Spirit Mediums in Zimbabwe* (Berkeley: University of California Press, 1985)

4. Piers Vitebsky, "From Cosmology to Environmentalism", *Shamanism: A Reader*, Harvey, ed., p.279

5. Ibid., p.8

6. Harvey, *Shamanism*, p. 155

7. Ibid., "From Cosmology to Environmentalism", p.287

Chapter Eight

1. William James, *The Varieties of Religious Experience: A Study in Human Nature* (New York: Longmans, Green and Co., 1928) p.379-380

2. Pierre Hadot, *What is Ancient Philosophy?*

3. Mark 16:5

4. See Walter Burkert, *Ancient Mystery Cults* (Cambridge, MA: Harvard University Press, 1987)

5. 2nd Corinthians 12:2-4

6. Quoted in Matthew Fox, *The Hidden Spirituality of Men: Ten Metaphors to Awaken the Sacred Masculine* (Novato, CA: New World Library, 2008) p.9

7. Evelyn Underhill, *Mysticism: A Study in the Nature and Development of Spiritual Consciousness* (Mineola: Dover Publications, 2002) p.413

8. *Integral Yoga: The Yoga Sutras of Patanjali*, trans. Sri Swami Satchidananda (Yogaville: Integral Yoga Publications, 1985) p.21-22

9. *Breakthrough: Meister Eckhart's Creation Spirituality in New Translation*, ed. & trans. Matthew Fox. (Garden City: Image, 1980) p.142

10. Jorge N. Ferrer, *Revisioning Transpersonal Theory: A Participatory Vision of Human Spirituality* (Albany: SUNY Press, 2002)

11. Hans Jonas, *The Gnostic Religion: The Message of the Alien God and the Beginnings of Christianity* (Boston: Beacon, 2001) p.263

12. Walt Whitman, *Leaves of Grass*, p.54-55

13. See Wayne Teasdale, *The Mystic Heart: Discovering a Universal Spirituality in the World's Religions.* (Novato: New World Library, 1999)

CHAPTER NINE

1. Matthew Fox attributes the term "creation-centered tradition" to M.D. Chenu (Matthew Fox, February 2, 2009, personal communication)

2. Mark 1:15

3. Rowland, *The Open Heaven*, p. 356, 357

4. John Dominic Crossan and Jonathan Reed, *In Search of Paul: How Jesus's Apostle Opposed Rome's Empire with God's Kingdom* (San Francisco: Harper, 2004) p.69

5. Ibid., p.10

6. Chilton, *Rabbi Jesus,* p.79

7. Norman Perrin, *Rediscovering the Teaching of Jesus* (New York, Harper & Row, 1967) p. 90

8. John Dominic Crossan, *The Historical Jesus: The Life of a Mediterranean Jewish Peasant* (New York: Harper Collins, 1991) p.46

9. Ibid., p. 43

10. Perrin, *Rediscovering the Teaching of Jesus*, p. 94

11. Morton Smith, *Clement of Alexandria and the Secret Gospel of Mark* (Cambridge: Harvard University Press, 1973) p. 235

12. Luke 17:20-21. *Enothen*, the word used by the author of this text, can mean either "within" or "among."

13. This is true of the group of scholars known as the Jesus Seminar. See John Dominic Crossan, *The Historical Jesus: The Life of a Jewish Mediterranean Peasant* (New York: Harper Collins, 1991)

14. 2nd Corinthians, chapter 12

15. *Acts*, chapter 2

16. 1st Corinthians 2:16

17. The Wisdom of Solomon, 2:23-3:1

18. Franz Cumont, *Astrology and Religion among the Greeks and Romans* (Montana: Kessinger Publishing, 1912)

19. Mark 12:25

20. First Corinthians 15: 35-44

21. Mircea Iliade, *Rites and Symbols of Initiation: The Mysteries of Birth and Rebirth* (Putnam, Connecticut: Spring Publications, 2005)

22. Matthew Fox, trans. and ed., introduction to *Breakthrough: Meister Eckhart's Creation Spirituality in New Translation* (Garden City: Image, 1980) p.30

23. Ibid., p.178

24. Ibid., 215

25. Ibid., p.423

26. Ibid., p.71

27. Ibid., p.65

28. Ibid., p.312

29. Gabrielle Uhleine, *Meditations with Hildegard of Bingen* (Santa Fe: Bear & Company, 1983) p.54

30. Rabbi David A. Cooper, *God is a Verb: Kabbalah and the Practice of Mystical Judaism* (New York: Riverhead Books, 1998) p.54

31. Ibid.

32. Klein, *Kabbalah of Creation*, p.147

33. Genesis, 3:3

34. Genesis, 3:4-5

35. Matt, *God & the Big Bang*. p.60

36. Matt, *Essential Kabbalah*, p.127

37. Scholem, *Major Trends in Jewish Mysticism*, p.216

38. Frankel, *Sacred Therapy: Jewish Spiritual Teachings on Emotional Healing and Inner Wholeness* (Boston: Shambhala, 2005) p.37

39. Cooper, *God is a Verb*, p.69

40. Quoted in *The Way of the Sufi*, Idries Shah (New York: Arkana, 1968) p.87

41. Idries Shah, *The Pleasantries of the Incredible Mullah Nasrudin* (New York: Penguin Compass, 1968)

42. *A Year with Rumi: Daily Readings*, trans. Coleman Barks (New

York: Harper Collins, 2006) p.127

43. Nasr, *The Garden of Truth*, p.94

44. William C. Chittick, *Self Disclosure of God: Principles of Ibn al-Arabi's Cosmology*, (Albany: SUNY Press, 1998) p.32

45. Ibid., p263

46. Quoted in *The Way of the Sufi*, Idries Shah (New York: Arkana, 1968) p.113

47. Luke 17:21

48. *The Upanishads*, trans. Juan Mascaro (New York: Penguin, 1965) p.117

49. Ibid., p.75

50. Ibid., p.85

51. Ibid., p.141

52. Ibid., p.49

53. Ibid.

54. Ibid., p.61

55. Ibid., p.120

56. Ibid., p.120-121

57. *Integral Yoga: The Yoga Sutras of Patanjali*, trans. Sri Swami Satchidananda, p.3

58. Ibid., p.21

59. Ibid., p.46

60. Ibid., p.7

61. *The Bhagavad Gita for Daily Living: Chapters 7 through 12*, Eknath Easwaran trans. (Berkeley: Nilgiri Press, 1979) p.42

62. Sri Aurobindo, *The Bhagavad Gita and its Message*, (Twin Lakes: Lotus Press, 2001) p.33

63. Easwaran, *The Bhagavad Gita for Daily Living, Chapters 1 through 12*, p.43

64. Ibid., p.302

65. Ibid., p.45

66. Ibid., p.86

67. Ibid., p.89

68. *The Bhagavad Gita for Daily Living: Chapters 1 through 6*, Eknath Easwaran trans. (Berkeley: Nilgiri Press, 1979) p.268

69. Ibid., p. 157-158

70. Ibid., p.85

71. Ibid.

72. *The Bhagavad Gita for Daily Living: Chapters 13 through 18*, Eknath Easwaran trans. (Berkeley: Nilgiri Press, 1979) p.205, 212

73. *The Bhagavad Gita for Daily Living: Chapters 1 through 6*, Eknath Easwaran trans., p.286

74. *The Bhagavad Gita for Daily Living: Chapters 7 through 12*, Eknath Easwaran trans., p.268

75. Francis H. Cook, *Hua-yen Buddhism: The Jewel Net of Indra* (University Park: Pennsylvania State Press, 1977) p.44

76. Macy, p.67

77. Cook, *Hua-yen Buddhism*, p.48

78. The Dalai Lama, *The Good Heart: A Buddhist Perspective on the Teachings of Jesus* (Boston: Wisdom Publications, 1996) p.168

79. *The Buddha and His Teachings*, Bercholz & Kohn, p.144

80. The Dalai Lama, *The Good Heart*, p. 49

81. Ibid., p.47

82. Ibid., p.64

83. *The Buddha and His Teachings*, Bercholz & Kohn, p.164

84. Ibid., p.234

85. Ibid., following p.174

86. Ibid., p.142

87. The Dalai Lama, *The Good Heart*, p.95

88. Jeaneane Fowler, *An Introduction to the Philosophy and Religion of Taoism*, p.98

89. *The Book of Lao Tzu (The Tao Te Ching)*, trans. and commentary Yi Wu, p.2

90. Ibid., p.5
91. Burton Watson, *Chuang Tzu: Basic Writings* (New York: Columbia University Press, 1964) p. 3
92. Ibid., p.24
93. Ibid., p.23
94. Ibid., p.45
95. *The Book of Lao Tzu (The Tao Te Ching)*, trans. Yi Wu, p.147
96. Fowler, p.115-116
97. *The Book of Lao Tzu (The Tao Te Ching)*, trans. Yi Wu, p.271
98. Fowler, p.171
99. Ibid., p.175-176
100. Ibid., p.178
101. *The Book of Lao Tzu (The Tao Te Ching)*, trans. Yi Wu, p.230

IV. Cosmosophia
1. Dante Alighieri, *The Paradiso of Dante Alighieri* (London: J.M. Dent and Sons, 1954) p.408

Chapter Ten
1. Notably James Hansen of NASA
2. Matthew Fox, *Sheer Joy*, p.32

Chapter Eleven
1. For more information on Causal Light Cones, see Joel R. Primack and Nancy Abrams, *The View from the Center of the Universe: Discovering our Extraordinary Place in the Cosmos* (New York: Riverhead Books, 2006)
2. Paul Hawken, *Blessed Unrest: How the Largest Movement in the World Came into Being and Why No One Saw It Coming* (New York: Viking, 2007) p.171
3. "Etymologically as well as semantically, *altruism* contains the

notion of other people"—*Dictionary of Word Origins*, ed. John Ayto (New York: Arcade Publishing, 1990) p.21

4. See Albert A. Martinez, *Negative Math: How Mathematical Rules Can Be Positively Bent* (Princeton: Princeton University Press, 2005)

5. Gregory B. Stone, *Dante's Pluralism and the Islamic Philosophy of Religion* (New York: Palgrave Macmillan, 2006) p. 109

6. Dante, *Purgatorio*, xvii, 31

CHAPTER TWELVE

1. Swimme and Berry, *The Universe Story* (San Francisco: Harper San Francisco, 1992) p.71

2. Eric Chaisson, *Epic of Evolution: Seven Ages of the Cosmos* (New York: Columbia University Press, 2006) p.23

3. Quoted in Grof, *The Cosmic Game*, p.32

4. Alan Watts, *Eastern Wisdom, Modern Life* (Novato, CA: New World Library, 2006) p.67

5. Kip S. Thorne, *Black Holes & Time Warps: Einstein's Outrageous Legacy* (New York: W.W. Norton & Company, 1994) p.456

6. The naming of this event "The Primordial Flaring Forth" comes from Swimme and Berry, *The Universe Story*

7. Swimme and Berry, *The Universe Story*, p.18

8. Thorne, *Black Holes & Time Warps*, p.476

9. Jonathan J. Halliwell, "Quantum Cosmology and the Creation of the Universe", Norris S. Hetherington, ed., *Cosmology*, p. 493

10. Ibid.

11. Ferris, *The Whole Shebang: A State of the Universe(s) Report* (New York: Simon & Schuster, 1997) p.254

12. Chaisson, *Epic of Evolution*, p.49

13. David Lindley, *Uncertainty: Einstein, Bohr, and the Struggle for the Soul of Science* (New York: Doubleday, 2007)

14. Mario Livio, *The Accelerating Universe: Infinite Expansion, the*

Cosmological Constant, and the Beauty of the Cosmos (New York: John Wiley & Sons, Inc., 2000) p.70

15. Swimme and Berry, *The Universe Story*, p. 21

16. Livio, *The Accelerating Universe*, p. 196

17. Vilenkin, Alexander, "Particle Physics and Cosmology" Norris S. Hetherington, ed., *Cosmology*, p.466

18. Chaisson, *Epic of Evolution*, p. 149

19. Swimme and Berry, *The Universe Story*, p.59

20. Cosmology, ed. Norriss Hetherington, p.5.

21. Brian Swimme, lecture on September 28, 2008

22. I am indebted to my teacher, Brian Swimme, for these insights.

23. See Peter D. Ward and Donald Brownlee, *Rare Earth: Why Complex Life is Uncommon in the Universe* (New York: Copernicus Books, 2000)

24. Lynn Margulis, *Symbiotic Planet: A New Look at Evolution* (Amherst: Basic Books, 1998) p. 79

25. Ibid., p.6

26. Ibid., p.33

27. Richard Fortey, *Life: A Natural History of the First Four Billion Years of Life on Earth* (New York: Vintage, 1997) p.203

28. Grof, *The Cosmic Game*, 136

29. Swimme and Berry, *The Universe Story*, p.137

30. It should be noted that there are some stars, brown dwarfs for example, that we cannot see.

31. Richard Fortey, *Life*, p.279

32. Joseph Campbell, *The Hero with a Thousand Faces* (Princeton: Princeton University Press, 1973)

33. Livio, *The Accelerating Universe*, p.213

34. M. Ingman, et al. "Mitochondrial Genome Variation and the Origin of Modern Humans." *Nature*, 408 (December 2000) 708-13

35. Yuahai Ke at al. "African Origin of Modern Humans in East Asia: A Tale of 12,000 Y Chromosomes." *Science*, 2001, 292: 1151-1153

36. See Steve Martinot, *The Rule of Racialization* (Philadelphia: Temple University, 2003)

37. Fortey, *Life*, p.305

38. Deuteronomy 26:5

39. Jared Diamond, *Guns, Germs, and Steel*, p.104

40. See Ibid.

41. Ibid.

42. Walter Fluker and Catherine Tumber eds., *A Strange Freedom: The Best of Howard Thurman on Religious Experience and Public Life* (Boston: Beacon Press, 1998) p. 128

V. Ricorso

1. Adapted from Mark 1:15

2. Giambattista Vico, The Autobiography of Giambattista Vico, Max Harold Fisch and Thomas Goddard Bergin trans. (Ithaca: Cornell, 1944)

Chapter Thirteen

1. William Anderson, *Dante the Maker* (New York: Crossroad, 1980) p.217

2. The Chicago Wisdom Project (www.chicagowisdomproject.org), the organization I founded, is doing this work. You can also see Matthew Fox, *The A.W.E Project: Reinventing Education, Reinventing the Human* (Saskatoon: Copperhouse, 2006).

Epilogue

1. From Macy, p.17

2. See note on page 28

3. Antoine de Saint-Exupery, *The Little Prince*, trans. Richard Howard (New York: Harcourt, Inc., 2000) p.77

4. From *A Family of Poems: My Favorite Poems for Children*, ed. Caroline Kennedy (New York: Hyperion, 2005) p.122

Bibliography

Abram, David. *The Spell of the Sensuous: Perception and Language in a More-Than-Human World*. New York: Vintage Books, 1996.

Albert, David Z. and Rivka Galchen, "Was Einstein Wrong?: A Quantum Threat to Special Relativity", *Scientific American*. (March 2009)

Alighieri, Dante. *The Paradiso of Dante Alighieri*. London: J.M. Dent & Sons, 1954.

_____. *The Purgatorio of Dante Alighieri*. London: J.M. Dent & Sons, 1954.

_____. *The Inferno of Dante Alighieri*. London: J.M. Dent & Sons, 1954.

Anderson, William. *Dante the Maker*. New York: Crossroad, 1982.

Aristotle. *Essential Thinkers: Aristotle*. New York: Barnes & Noble, 2004.

'Arabi, Ibn. *Perfect Harmony*. Boston: Shambhala, 2002.

Armstrong, Karen. *A History of God: The 4,000-year Quest of Judaism, Christianity and Islam*. New York: Ballantine Books, 1994.

_____. *The Battle for God*. New York: Ballantine Books, 2001.

_____. *Buddha*. New York: Viking, 2001.

el-Aswad, el-Sayed. *Religion and Folk Cosmology: Scenarios of the Visible and Invisible in Rural Egypt*. Westport: Praeger, 2002.

Augustine, Saint. *The Confessions of St. Augustine*, trans. Edward B. Pusey New York: The Modern Library, 1949.

Aurobindo, Sri. *Bhagavad Gita and its Message*. Twin Lakes, WI: Lotus Press, 1995.

_____. *The Future Evolution of Man: The Divine Life upon Earth*. Twin Lakes, WI: Lotus Press, 1990.

Ayto, John, ed. *Dictionary of Word Origins*. New York: Arcade, 1990.

Bamford, Christopher. *An Endless Trace: The Passionate Pursuit of Wisdom in the West*. New Paltz, NY: Codhill Press, 2003.

Barstow, Anne Llewellyn. *Witchcraze: A New History of the European Witch Hunts*. San Francisco: Pandora, 1994.

Bercholz, Samuel and Sherab Chodzin Kohn eds. *The Buddha and His Teachings*. Boston: Shambhala, 2003.

Berry, Thomas. *The Dream of the Earth*. San Francisco, Sierra Club Books, 1988.

_____. *The Great Work: Our Way into the Future*. New York: Bell Tower, 1999

Birnbaum, Lucia Chiavola. *Dark Mother: African Origins and Godmothers*. San Jose: Author's Choice, 2001.

Black Elk, Nicholas, and John G. Neihardt. *Black Elk Speaks*. Lincoln: University of Nebraska Press, 2000.

Blofeld, John. *The Bodhisattva of Compassion: The Mystical Tradition of Kuan Yin*. Boston: Shambhala, 1988.

Borg, Marcus. *Meeting Jesus again for the First Time: The Historical Jesus and the Heart of Contemporary Faith*. New York: Harper Collins, 1994.

Borsch, Frederick. *The Son of Man in Myth and History*. Philadelphia: The Westminster Press, 1967.

Bruno, Giordano. *The Expulsion of the Triumphant Beast*, trans. Arthur D. Imerti Lincoln: University of Nebraska Press, 1992.

Buber, Martin. *Good and Evil.* Upper Saddle River, NJ: Simon & Schuster, 1953.

Burckhardt, Titus. *An Introduction to Sufi Doctrine,* trans D.M. Math-eson. Wellingborough: Thorsons Publishers Limited, 1976.

Burkert, Walter. *Ancient Mystery Cults.* Cambridge, MA: Harvard University Press, 1987.

Cahill, Thomas. *How the Irish Saved Civilization: The Untold Story of Ireland's Heroic Role from the Fall of Rome to the Rise of Medieval Europe.* New York: Anchor Books, 1995.

Campbell, Joseph. *The Hero with a Thousand Faces.* Princeton: Princeton University Press, 1973.

_____. *The Power of Myth.* New York: Doubleday, 1998.

Capra, Fritjof. *The Tao of Physics.* Boulder: Shambhala, 1983.

Carrol, Joseph, "Organism, Environment, and Literary Representation", *Interdisciplinary Studies in Literature and the Environment,* 9.2 (Summer 2002)

Chapple, Christopher K., and Mary Evelyn Tucker, eds. *Hinduism and Ecology: The Intersection of Earth, Sky, and Water.* Cambridge: Harvard University Press,2000.

Chaisson, Eric. *Epic of Evolution: Seven Ages of the Cosmos.* New York: Columbia University Press, 2006.

Chilton, Bruce. *Rabbi Jesus: An Intimate Biography.* New York: Image Books, 2000.

_____. *Mary Magdalene: A Biography.* New York: Doubleday, 2005.

Chittick, William C. *The Sufi Path of Love: The Spiritual Teachings of Rumi.* Albany: SUNY Press, 1983.

_____. *The Self Disclosure of God: Principles of Ibn al-Arabi's Cosmology.* Albany: SUNY Press, 1998.

_____. *Ibn 'Arabi: Heir to the Prophets,* Oxford, Oneworld, 2005.

_____. *Science of the Cosmos, Science of the Soul: The Pertinence of Islamic Cosmology in the Modern World.* Oxford: Oneworld, 2007.

Chodron, Pema. *When Things Fall Apart: Heart Advice for Difficult Times*. Boston: Shambhala, 2005.

Chomsky, Noam. *Powers and Prospects: Reflections on Human Nature and the Social Order*. Boston: South End Press, 1996.

Confucius. *The Analects*. New York: Dover Publications, 1995.

Cook, Francis H. *Hua-Yen Buddhism: The Jewel Net of Indra*. University Park: The Pennsylvania State University Press, 1977.

Cooper, Rabbi David A. *God is a Verb: Kabbalah and the Practice of Mystical Judaism*. New York: Riverhead Books, 1998.

Cousins, Ewert H. *Christ of the 21st Century*. Rockport, Mass.: Element, 1992.

Cleary, Thomas, trans. *The Taoist I Ching*. Boston: Shambhala, 1986.

Crossan, John Dominic, *The Historical Jesus: The Life of a Mediterranean Jewish Peasant*, New York: Harper Collins, 1991

Crossan, John Dominic and Jonathan Reed. *In Search of Paul: How Jesus's Apostle Opposed Rome's Empire with God's Kingdom*. San Francisco: Harper San Francisco, 2004.

Cumont, Franz. *Astrology and Religion among the Greeks and Romans*. Montana: Kessinger Publishing Company, 1912.

Dalai Lama. *The Good Heart: A Buddhist Perspective on the Teachings of Jesus*. Boston: Wisdom Publications, 1998.

_____. *Ethics for the New Millenium*. New York: Riverhead Books, 1999.

Dames, Michael. *Mythic Ireland*. London: Thames & Hudson, 1992.

Demaray, John G. *Dante and the Book of the Cosmos*. Philadelphia: The American Philosophical Society, 1987.

Denny, Frederick M. *Islam*. San Francisco: Harper San Francisco, 1987.

Diamond, Jared. *Guns, Germs, and Steel: The Fates of Human Societies*. New York: W.W. Norton & Co., 1999.

Doniger, Wendy. *The Implied Spider: Politics and Theology in Myth*. New York, Columbia University Press, 1998.

Douglas-Klotz, Neil. *The Sufi Book of Life: 99 Pathways of the Heart for the Modern Dervish*. New York: Penguin Compass, 2005.

_____. *Prayers of the Cosmos: Meditations on the Aramaic Words of Jesus*. San Francisco, Harper San Francisco, 1990.

Earhart, H. Byron. *Japanese Religion: Unity and Diversity*. Belmont: Wadsworth Publishing Company, 1982.

Easwaran, Eknath, trans. *The Bhagavad Gita for Daily Living: Chapters 1 through 6*. Berkeley: Nilgiri Press, 1979.

_____. *The Bhagavad Gita for Daily Living: Chapters 7 through 12* Berkeley: Nilgiri Press, 1979.

_____. *The Bhagavad Gita for Daily Living: Chapters 13 through 18*. Berkeley: Nilgiri Press, 1979.

Eckhart, Meister. *Breakthrough: Meister Eckhart's Creation Spirituality in New Translation*, ed. & trans. Matthew Fox. Garden City: Image, 1980.

Edinger, Edward. *The Christian Archetype: A Jungian Commentary on the Life of Christ*. Toronto: Inner City Books, 1987.

Eiseley, Loren. *The Star Thrower*. New York: Harcourt Brace and Co., 1978.

Eliade, Mircea. *Myths, Dreams, and Mysteries: The Encounter Between Contemporary Faiths and Archaic Realities*. New York: Harper & Brothers, 1960.

_____. *Shamanism: Archaic Techniques of Ecstasy*, London: Routledge & Kegan Paul, 1964.

_____. *The Myth of the Eternal Return: Cosmos and History*, trans. Willard R. Trask. Princeton: Princeton University Press, 1991.

_____. *Rites and Symbols of Initiation: The Mysteries of Birth and Rebirth*. Connecticut: Spring, 2005.

Eliade, Mircea ed. *Essential Sacred Writings From Around the World*. San Francisco: Harper San Francisco, 1977.

Emerson, Ralph Waldo. *Selected Essays*, Larzer Ziff ed. New York: Penguin, 1984.

Evans-Wentz, W.Y. *The Tibetan Book of the Dead*. New York: Oxford University Press, 2000.

Fabel, Arthur and Donald St. John eds. *Teilhard in the 21st Century: The Emerging Spirit of Earth*. New York: Orbis Books, 2007.

Fanning, Steven. *Mystics of the Christian Tradition*. New York: Routledge, 2001.

Ferrer, Jorge. *Revisioning Transpersonal Theory: A Participatory Vision of Human Spirituality*. Albany: SUNY Press, 2002.

Ferris, Timothy. *The Whole Shebang: A State-of-the-Universe(s) Report*. New York: Simon & Schuster, 1997.

Fiorenza, Elizabeth Schussler. *In Memory of Her: A Feminist Theological Reconstruction of Christian Origins*. New York: Cross Road, 1994.

Fortey, Richard. *Life: A Natural History of the First Four Billion Years of Life on Earth*. New York: Vintage, 1997.

Fowler, Jeaneane. *Pathways to Immortality: An Introduction to the Philosophy and Religion of Taoism*. Portland: Sussex Academic Press, 2005.

Fox, Matthew. *Original Blessing*. New York: Tarcher/Putnam, 1983.

————. *Wrestling with the Prophets*. New York: Tacher/Putnam, 1995.

————. *Sheer Joy: Conversations with Thomas Aquinas on Creation Spirituality*. San Francisco: Tarcher/Putnam, 2003.

————. *One River, Many Wells*. New York: Tarcher/Penguin, 2004.

————. *The A.W.E. Project: Reinventing Education, Reinventing the Human*. Saskatoon, SK: Copperhouse, 2006.

————. *The Hidden Spirituality of Men: Ten Metaphors to Awaken the Sacred Masculine*. Novato, CA: New World Library, 2008.

Fox, Matthew and Rupert Sheldrake. *Natural Grace*. New York: Doubleday, 1996.

Flannery, Tim. *The Eternal Frontier: An Ecological History of North America and Its Peoples*. New York: Grove Press, 2001.

Fluker, Walter and Catherine Tumber eds. *A Strange Freedom: The Best of Howard Thurman on Religious Experience and Public Life*. Boston: Beacon Press, 1998.

Frankel, Estelle. *Sacred Therapy: Jewish Spiritual Teachings on Emotional Healing and Inner Wholeness*. Boston: Shambhala, 2005.

Freeman, Mara. *Kindling the Celtic Spirit*. San Francisco: Harper San Francisco, 2000.

Freire, Paulo. *Pedagogy of the Oppressed*, trans. Myra Bergman Ramos. New York: Penguin, 1996.

Gallagher, Joseph. *A Modern Reader's Guide to Dante's the Divine Comedy*. Liguori, Missouri: Liguori/Triumph, 1999.

Gardner, Edmund G. *Dante's Ten Heavens: A Study of the Paradiso*. New York: Charles Scribner's Sons, 1900.

_____. *Dante and the Mystics*. New York: Octagon Books, 1968.

Gingerich, Owen ed. *Cosmology + 1*, San Franscisco: W.H. Freeman and Company, 1977.

Goodenough, Ursula. *The Sacred Depths of Nature*, New York: Oxford University Press, 1998.

Gottlieb, Lynn. *She Who Dwells Within: A Feminist Vision of a Renewed Judaism*. NewYork: Harper Collins, 1995.

Greene, Brian. *The Fabric of the Cosmos: Space, Time, and the Texture of Reality*. New York: Vintage, 2004.

Griffin, David Ray, *et al. The American Empire and the Commonwealth of God: A Political, Economic, Religious Statement*. Louisville: Westminster John Knox, 2006.

Griffin, Paul R. *The Seeds of Racism in the Soul of America*. Naperville: Sourcebooks, 2000.

Griffiths, Bede. *The Cosmic Revelation: The Hindu Way to God*. Springfield: Templegate Publishers, 1983.

Grim., John A. ed. *Indigenous Traditions and Ecology: The Interbeing of Cosmology and Community*. Cambridge: Harvard University Press, 2001.

Grof, Stanislav. *The Cosmic Game: Explorations of the Frontiers of Human Consciousness*. Albany: SUNY Press, 1998.

Gruenwald, Ithamar. *Apocalyptic and Merkabah Mysticism*. Leiden/Koln: E.J. Brill, 1980.

Guthrie, W.K.C. *Orpheus and the Greek Religion*. Princeton: Princeton University Press, 1993.

Hadot, Pierre. *What is Ancient Philosophy?*, trans. Michael Chase. Cambridge: Belknap, 2002.

Hanh, Thich Nhat. *The Miracle of Mindfulness: A Manual on Meditation*, trans. Mobi Ho. Boston: Beacon Press, 1987.

_____. *Living Buddha, Living Christ*. New York: Riverhead Books, 1995.

Hayes, John H. *Introduction to the Bible*. Philadelphia: The Westminster Press, 1952.

Harvey, Andrew. *Son of Man: The Mystical Path to Christ*. New York: Jeremy P. Tarcher/Putnam, 1998.

Harvey, Graham ed. *Shamanism: A Reader*. New York: Routledge, 2003.

Haught, John F. *Science & Religion: From Conflict to Conversation*. New York: Paulist Press, 1995.

_____. *God After Darwin: A Theology of Evolution*. Philadelphia: Westview Press, 2008.

Haught, John F. ed., *Science and Religion in Search of Cosmic Purpose*. Washington: Georgetown University Press, 2000.

Hawken, Paul. *Blessed Unrest: How the Largest Movement in the World Came into Being and Why No One Saw It Coming*. New York: Viking, 2007.

Hawking, Stephen. *The Universe in a Nutshell*. New York: Bantam, 2001.

Herzog, William R. II. *Parables as Subversive Speech: Jesus as Pedagogue of the Oppressed*. Louisville: John Knox Press, 1994.

Hetherington, Norriss S. ed. *Cosmology: Historical, Literary, Philosophi-*

cal, Religious, and Scientific Perspectives. New York: Garland Publishing, 1993.

Hirshfield, Jane. *Nine Gates: Entering the Mind of Poetry*. New York: Harper Perennial, 1998.

Iyengar, B.K.S. *Light on Yoga*. New York: Schocken Books, 1979.

James, William. *The Varieties of Religious Experience*. New York: Longmans, Green and Co., 1928.

Jonas, Hans. *The Gnostic Religion: The Message of the Alien God and the Beginnings of Christianity*. Boston: Beacon, 2001.

Kalu, Ogbu U. "The Sacred Egg: Worldview, Ecology, and Development in West Africa", Grim, John A., Ed., *Indigenous Traditions and Ecology: The Interbeing of Cosmology and Community*. Cambridge: Harvard University Press, 2001.

Kane, Sean. *Wisdom of the Mythtellers*. Canada: Broadview Press, 1998.

Keating, Thomas, M. Basil Pennington and Thomas E. Clarke. *Finding Grace at the Center: The Beginning of Centering Prayer*. Woodstock, VT: Skylight Paths Publishing, 2002.

Khan, Hazrat Inayat. *The Heart of Sufism*. Boston: Shambhala, 1999.

Khayam, Omar. *The Sufistic Quatrains of Omar Khayam*, Edward Fitzgerald trans. New York & London: M. Walter Dunne, 1903.

King, Ursula. *Spirit of Fire: The Life and Vision of Teilhard de Chardin*. New York: Orbis Books, 1996.

_____. *Christian Mystics: Their Lives and Legacies throughout the Ages*. Mahwah, NJ: Hidden Spring, 2001.

Kitagawa, Joseph M. *Religion in Japanese History*. New York: Columbia University Press, 1990.

Klein, Eliahu. *Kabbalah of Creation: Isaac Luria's Earlier Mysticism*. New Jersey: Jason Aronsoc, Inc., 2000.

Kohn, Michael H. trans. *The Shambhala Dictionary of Buddhism and Zen*. Boston: Shambhala,1991.

Kondratiev, Alexei. *The Apple Branch: A Path to Celtic Ritual*. New York: Citadel Press, 2003.

Kongtrul, Jamgon. *The Treasury of Knowledge: Myriad Worlds*. Boulder: Snow Lion, 2003

Korten, David C. *The Post-Corporate World: Life after Capitalism*. San Francisco: Berrett-Koehler Publishers, 1999.

Kung, Hans. *The Catholic Church: A Short History*. New York: The Modern Library, 2003.

Lan, David. *Guns & Rain: Guerillas & Spirit Mediums in Zimbabwe*. Berkeley: University of California Press, 1985.

Lehmann, Arthur C. *et al. Magic, Witchcraft, and Religion: An Anthropological Study of the Supernatural*. Boston: McGraw Hill, 2005.

Leslie, John, ed. *Physical Cosmology and Philosophy*. New York: Macmillan, 1990.

Lewis, I.M. *Ecstatic Religion: An Anthropological Study of Spirit Possession and Shamanism*. New York: Penguin, 1978.

Lewis, R.W.B. *Dante*. New York: Viking, 2001.

Liao, Waysun trans. *T'ai Chi Classics*. Boston: Shambhala, 2000.

Lindley, David. *Uncertainty: Einstein, Bohr, and the Struggle for the Soul of* Science.New York: Doubleday, 2007.

Lings, Martin. *Muhammad: His Life Based on the Earliest Sources*. Rochester: Inner Traditions International, 1983.

Littleton, C. Scott. *Shinto*. Oxford: Oxford University Press, 2002.

Livio, Mario. *The Accelerating Universe: Infinite Expansion, the Cosmological Constant, and the Beauty of the Cosmos*. New York: John Wiley & Sons, Inc., 2000.

Macy, Joanna. *World as Lover, World as Self: Courage for Global Justice and Ecological Renewal*. Berkeley: Parallax Press, 2007.

Margulis, Lynn. *Symbiotic Planet: A New Look at Evolution*. Amherst: Basic Books, 1998.

Martinot, Steve. *The Rule of Racialization*. Philadelphia: Temple University, 2003.

Mascaro, Juan, trans. *The Upanishads*. New York: Penguin, 1965.

Matt, Daniel C. *God & the Big Bang: Discovering Harmony between Science & Spirituality*. Woodstock, Vermont: Jewish Lights, 2001.

Matt, Daniel C. ed. *The Essential Kabbalah: The Heart of Jewish Mysticism*. New York: Harper Collins, 1995

Maturana, Humberto R., and Varela, Francisco J. *The Tree of Knowledge: The Biological Roots of Human Understanding*, trans. Robert Paolucci. Boston & London: Shambhala, 1988.

Mbiti, John S. *African Religions and Philosophy*. Nigeria: Heinemann, 1969.

McManners, John, ed. *The Oxford History of Christianity*. New York: Oxford University Press, 1993.

Merton, Thomas. *Contemplative Prayer*. New York: Image Books, 1996.

Meyer, Marvin ed. *The Ancient Mysteries: A Sourcebook*. San Francisco: Harper & Row, 1987.

Meyer, Marvin and Willis Barnstone eds. *The Gnostic Bible*. Boston & London: Shambhala, 2003.

Moody, T.W. and F.X. Martin eds. *The Course of Irish History*. Cork: The Mercier Press, 1976.

Morin, Edgar. *Homeland Earth: A Manifesto for the New Millenium*, trans. Sean M. Kelly and Roger LaPointe. Cresskill, NJ: Hampton Press, 1999.

Morray-Jones, C.R.A. *A Transparent Illusion: The Dangerous Vision of Water in Hekhalot Mysticism*. Boston: Brill, 2002.

Moser, Mary Beth. *Honoring Darkness: Exploring the Power of Black Madonnas in Italy*. Vashon Island, WA: Dea Madre Publishing, 2005.

Murata, Sachiko. *The Tao of Islam: A Sourcebook on Gender Relationships in Islamic Thought*. Albany: SUNY Press, 1992.

Murata, Sachiko and William C. Chittick. *The Vision of Islam*. St. Paul: Paragon House, 1994.

Nasr, Seyyed Hossein, *An Introduction to Islamic Cosmological Doctrines*. Cambridge: Harvard University Press, 1964.

_____. *The Garden of Truth: The Vision and Promise of Sufism, Islam's Mystical Tradition*. New York: HarperOne, 2007

_____. *Islam, Science, Muslims, and Technology*. Sherwood Park: al-Qalam Publishing, 2007.

_____. "The Sacred Foundations of Justice in Islam", *Parabola*, 33.4. (Winter 2008)

Needleman, Jacob. *Lost Christianity: A Journey of Rediscovery*. New York: Penguin, 1980.

Ngugi Wa Thiongo. *Decolonizing the Mind: The Politics of Language in African Literature*. James Curry Publishers, 1986.

Norman Perrin. *Rediscovering the Teaching of Jesus*. New York, Harper & Row, 1967.

O'Donohue, John, *Anam Cara: A Book of Celtic Wisdom*. New York: Harper Perrenial, 2004

Olschki, Leo S. ed. *L'esperienza Mistica di Dante nella Indicazioni dell'Esegesi Trecentesca*, Firenze: 1969.

O'Murchu, Diarmud. *Evolutionary Faith: Rediscovering God in our G reat Story*. Maryknoll: Orbis, 2002.

Ong, Walter J. *Orality and Literacy*. New York: Routledge, 2006.

Overmeyer, Daniel L. *Religions of China*. New York: Harper San Francisco, 1986.

Pagels, Elaine. *The Gnostic Gospels*. New York: Vintage Books, 1989.

_____. *Beyond Belief: The Secret Gospel of Thomas*. New York: Random House, 2003.

Palihawadana, Mahinda, and John Ross Carter trans. *The Dhammapada*. Oxford: Oxford University Press, 2000.

Pappas, Nickolas. *Routledge Philosophy Guidebook to Plato and the Republic*. New York: Routledge, 1995.

Patai, Raphael. *The Hebrew Goddess*. Detroit: Wayne State University Press, 1990.

Plato. *Early Socratic Dialogues*, Waterfield, Robin, et al, trans. New York: Penguin, 1987.

_____. *The Last Days of Socrates*, Tredennick, Hugh, and Tarrant, Harold, trans. New York: Penguin, 1993.

_____. *Essential Thinkers: Plato*, New York: Barnes & Noble, 2004.

Prabhavananda, Swami. *Vedic Religion and Philosophy*. Mylapore, Madras: Sri Ramakrishna Math Printing Press, 1946.

Primack, Joel R. and Nancy Ellen Abrams. *The View from the Center of the Universe: Discovering our Extraordinary Place in the Cosmos*. New York: Riverhead Books, 2006.

Quinn, Daniel. *Ishmael: An Adventure of Mind and Spirit*. New York: Bantam/Turner, 1992.

Ralphs, Sheila. *Dante's Journey to the Center: Some Patterns in his Allegory*. Manchester: The University Press, 1972.

Rauf, Imam Faisal Abdul. *What's Right with Islam: A New Vision for Muslims and the West*. New York: Harper Collins, 2004.

Rees, Alwyn and Brinley. *Celtic Heritage: Ancient Tradition in Ireland and Wales*. New York: Thames & Hudson, 1995.

Reid, Howard and Michael Croucher. *The Way of the Warrior: The Paradox of the Martial Arts*. Woodstock, NY: The Overlook Press, 1995.

Ritchlin, Sheri. "On the Use of Silence: Living in Accord with the Tao", *Parabola*, 33.1 (Spring 2008)

Robinson, James M. ed. *The Nag Hammadi Library*. San Francisco: Harper San Francisco, 1988.

Rosemont, Henry ed. *Explorations in Early Chinese Cosmology*. Chico, Scholars Press, 1976.

Rowland, Christopher. *The Open Heaven: A Study of Apocalyptic in Judaism and Early Christianity*. London: SPCK, 1982.

Roy, Arundhati. *The Cost of Living*. New York: The Modern Library, 1999.

331

Rumi, Jelaluddin. *Delicious Laughter: Rambunctious Teaching Stories from the Mathnawi*, Barks, Coleman, trans. and ed. Athens, GA.: Maypop Books, 1990.

_____. *Rumi: Bridge to the Soul*, Coleman Barks trans. and ed. New York: Harper Collins, 2007.

Sadakata, Akira. *Buddhist Cosmology: Philosophy and Origins*. Tokyo: Kosei Publishing Co., 2004.

Sandars, N.K.trans. *Poems of Heaven and Hell from Ancient Mesopotamia*. New York: Penguin Books, 1971.

Sandars, N.K. trans. *The Epic of Gilgamesh*. New York: Penguin Books, 1972.

Sardar, Ziauddin and Iwona Abrams. *Introducing Chaos*. Thriplow, Royston, UK: Totem Books, 2005.

Satchidananda, Swami Sri. *Integral Yoga: The Yoga Sutras of Patanjali*. Yogaville: Integral Yoga Publications, 1985.

Schenk, Jim ed. *What Does God Look Like in an Expanding Universe?: An Anthology on God, Life and Death*. Cincinnati: ImagoEarth Publishing, 2006.

Schildgen, Brenda Deen. *Dante and the Orient*. Chicago: University of Illinois, 2002.

Scholem, Gershom. *Major Trends in Jewish Mysticism*. Jerusalem: Schocken Publishing House, 1941.

_____. *Jewish Gnosticism, Merkabah Mysticism, and the Talmudic Tradition*. New York: The Jewish Theological Seminary of America, 1960.

Segal, Alan F. *Paul the Convert: The Apostolate and Apostasy of Saul the Pharisee*. New Haven: Yale University Press, 1990.

Sells, Michael trans. *Approaching the Qur'an: The Early Revelations*. Ashland, OR: White Cloud Press, 1999.

Shah, Idries. *The Pleasantries of the Incredible Mullah Nasrudin*. New York: Compass, 1968.

_____. *The Way of the Sufi*. New York: Arkana, 1990.

_____.*The Commanding Self.* London: The Octagon Press, 1994

Sharma, Arvind ed. *Our Religions: The Seven World Religions Introduced by Preeminent Scholars from each Tradition.* San Francisco: Harper San Francisco, 1993.

Sigmund, Paul E. ed and trans. *St. Thomas Aquinas on Politics and Ethics.* New York: W.W. Norton and Co., 1988.

Smith, Huston.*The World's Religions.* New York: Harper San Francisco, 1991.

Smith, Luther E. Jr. *Howard Thurman: The Mystic as Prophet.* Richmond, IN: Friends United Press, 1991.

Smith, Morton.*Clement of Alexandria and the Secret Gospel of Mark.* Cambridge: Harvard University Press, 1973.

Smoley, Richard and Jay Kinney. *Hidden Wisdom: A Guide to the Western Inner Traditions.* New York: Arkana, 1999.

Stone, Gregory B. *Dante's Pluralism and the Islamic Philosophy of Religion.* New York: Palgrave MacMillan, 2006.

Stone, Merlin. *When God was a Woman.* New York: Harcourt Brace and Company, 1976.

Stryz, Jan ed. *The Wisdom of Meister Eckhart.* St. Paul: New Grail, 2003.

Suzuki, D.T. *Zen Buddhism*, William Barrett ed. Garden City: Double Day and Co., 1956.

Swimme, Brian. *The Universe is a Green Dragon: A Cosmic Creation Story.* Rochester: Bear and Co., 2001.

_____. *The Hidden Heart of the Cosmos: Humanity and the New Story.* Maryknoll: Orbis Books, 2006.

_____. "The Divinization of the Cosmos: An Interview with Brian Swimme on Pierre Teilhard de Chardin," *What is Enlightenment*, September-December 2006.

Swimme, Brian and Thomas Berry. *The Universe Story.* San Francisco: Harper San Francisco, 1992.

Talbot, Michael. *Mysticism and the New Physics*. New York: Bantam, 1981.

Tarnas, Richard. *The Passion of the Western Mind: Understanding the Ideas That Have Shaped Our Worldview*. New York: Ballantine Books, 1991.

Teasdale, Wayne. *The Mystic Heart: Discovering a Universal Spirituality in the World's Religions*. Novato: New World Library, 1999.

Teilhard, Pierre de Chardin. *Christianity and Evolution: Reflections on Science and Religion*, Rene Hague trans. New York: Harcourt, 1971.

_____. *The Heart of Matter*, trans. Rene Hague. New York: Harcourt, 1971

_____. *The Human Phenomenon*, Sarah Appleton-Weber trans. Portland: Sussex Academic Press, 2003.

Thompson, Laurence G. *Chinese Religion: An Introduction*. Belmont: Wadsworth Publishing Company, 1996.

Thorne, Kip S. *Black Holes & Time Warps: Einstein's Outrageous Legacy*. New York: W.W. Norton & Company, 1994.

Thorpe, Doug. "A Just Measure" *Parabola*, 33.4 (Winter 2008)

Thurman, Howard. *Jesus and the Disinherited*. Boston: Beacon Press, 1996.

Toynbee, Paget. *A Dictionary of Proper Names and Notable Matters in the Works of Dante*. Oxford: Clarendon Press, 1968.

Trungpa, Chogyam. *Cutting through Spiritual Materialism*. Boston: Shambhala, 1987.

_____. *Shambhala: The Sacred Path of the Warrior*. Boston: Shambhala, 2003.

Tucker, Mary Evelyn and Duncan Ryuken Williams. *Buddhism and Ecology: The Interconnection of Dharma and Deeds*. Cambridge: Harvard University Press, 1997.

Tucker, Mary Evelyn "The Ecological Spirituality of Teilhard", *Teilhard Studies*, 51 (Fall 2005)

Tully, Mark. *Four Faces: A Journey in Search of Jesus the Divine, the Jew, the Rebel, the Sage*. Berkeley: Ulysses Press, 1997.

Underhill, Evelyn. *Mysticism: A Study in the Nature and Development of Spiritual Consciousness*. Mineola: Dover, 2002.

Uhlein, Gabrielle. *Meditations with Hildegard of Bingen*. Santa Fe: Bear and Co.,1983.

Ulansey, David. *The Origins of the Mithraic Mysteries: Cosmology and Salvation in the Ancient World*. New York: Oxford University Press, 1989.

Versluis, Arthur. *Wisdom's Book: The Sophia Anthology*. St. Paul: Paragon House, 2000.

Vico, Giambattista. *The Autobiography of Giambattista Vico*, Max Harold Fisch and Thomas Goddard Bergin trans. Ithaca: Cornell, 1944.

Ward, Peter D. and Donald Brownlee. *Rare Earth: Why Complex Life is Uncommon in the Universe*. New York: Copernicus Books, 2004.

Waters, Frank. *The Book of the Hopi: The First Revelation of the Hopi's Historical and Religious World-view of Life*. New York: Ballantine Books, 1963.

Watson, Burton trans. *Chuang Tzu: Basic Writings*. New York: Columbia University Press, 1964.

Weber, Max. *The Protestant Ethic and the Spirit of Capitalism*, trans. Talcott Parsons. New York: Charles Scribner's Sons, 1976.

Webster, Yehudi O. *The Racialization of America* New York: St. Martin's, 1992.

Weinberg, Steven. *The First Three Minutes: A Modern View of the Origin of the Universe*. New York: Basic Books, 1993.

West, Cornel. *The Cornel West Reader*. New York: Basic *Civitas* Books, 1999.

Whitehead, Alfred North. *Adventures of Ideas*. New York: The Free Press, 1967.

_____. *Science and the Modern World*. New York: The Free Press, 1967.

Whitman, Walt. *Leaves of Grass: The First (1855) Edition*. New York: Penguin Books, 1986.

Wilber, Ken. *Integral Spirituality: A Startling New Role for Religion in the Postmodern World*. Boston: Integral Books, 2006.

Wilson, Peter Lamborn. *Sacred Drift: Essays on the Margins of Islam*. San Francisco: City Lights, 1993.

Yang, Jwing-Ming. *The Root of Chinese Qigong: Secrets for Health, Longevity, and Enlightenment*. Jamaica Plain, MA: YMAA, 1997.

Yi Wu trans. *The Book of Lao Tzu (The Tao Te Ching)*. San Bruno: Great Learning, 1989.

Acknowledgements

Thank you to my wife, Arianne Richards, for reasons too lengthy to relay here; to my parents, for their support, financial and otherwise, throughout this process; to my grandfather, the late Reverend Thomas Richards, who brought both compassion and humor to the religion of my youth; to my editor, Leslie Browning, and everyone at Hiraeth Press, particularly Jason Kirkey, for believing in this project; to Wisdom University and to the PCC department at the California Institute of Integral Studies, where both my teachers and colleagues, particularly Larry Edwards and Linda Gibler, gave me immeasurable intellectual inspiration; to Matthew Fox and YELLAWE, where my students have taught me far more wisdom than I could ever teach them; to the late Sifu Tony Roberts, my Bagua Zhang teacher, for teaching me the mysteries of the Tao; to E.J. Bailey, for his help with the charts and illustrations; to the Tibetan monks who cared for me when I had altitude sickness, the kind strangers who shared fruit with me in Mozambique and Iran, and the people on the margins, everywhere, who have a wisdom toward which I only aspire.

Thank you to the trees, the mountains and the sea; to the stream behind my house in east Oakland; thank you to the stars; and thank you to the Universe, for the 13.7 billion year gestation process which allowed for the birth of this project.

337

About the Author

THEODORE RICHARDS IS A POET, WRITER, AND RELIGIOUS philosopher. He is a long time student of the Taoist martial art of Bagua and hatha yoga and has traveled, worked and studied in 25 different countries, including the South Pacific, the Far East, the Indian subcontinent, the Middle East, Africa, and Latin America. Theodore has received degrees from the University of Chicago, The California Institute of Integral Studies, Wisdom University, and the New Seminary where he was ordained. He has worked with inner city youth on the South Side of Chicago, Harlem, the South Bronx, and Oakland, where he was the director of YELLAWE, an innovative program for teens. He is the author of *Handprints on the Womb*, a collection of poetry. Theodore Richards is the founder and executive director of The Chicago Wisdom Project (www.chicagowisdomproject.org). He currently resides in Chicago with his wife and daughter.

339

HIRAETH
——PRESS——

We are passionate about creativity as a means of transforming consciousness, both individually and socially. We hope to participate in a revolution to return poetry to the public discourse and a place in the world which matters. Of the many important issues of our times we feel that our relationship to the environment is of the most fundamental concern. Our publications reflect the ideal that falling in love with the earth is nothing short of revolutionary and that through our relationship to nature we can birth a more enlightened vision of life for the future. We believe that art and poetry are the universal language of the human experience and are thus most capable of transforming our vision of self and world.

Visit us on the web at: www.hiraethpress.com
info@hiraethpress.com
P.O. Box 416
Danvers, MA 01923

Printed in the USA
CPSIA information can be obtained
at www.ICGtesting.com
JSHW082150140824
68134JS00014B/162